How To Build
Classic Hot Rod
V-8 Engines

George McNicholl

How To Build
Classic Hot Rod
V-8 Engines

George McNicholl

MOTORBOOKS

First published in 2006 by Motorbooks, an imprint of MBI Publishing Company, Galtier Plaza, Suite 200, 380 Jackson Street, St. Paul, MN 55101-3885 USA

MBI Publishing Company titles are also available at discounts in bulk quantity for industrial or sales-promotional use. For details write to Special Sales Manager at MBI Publishing Company, Galtier Plaza, Suite 200, 380 Jackson Street, St. Paul, MN 55101-3885 USA

ISBN-13: 978-0-7603-2777-7
ISBN-10: 0-7603-2777-7

Editor: Lindsay Hitch
Designer: Michael Cawcutt

Printed in China

Library of Congress Cataloging-in-Publication Data

McNicholl, George, 1947-
  How to build classic hot rod v-8 engines / George
  McNicholl.
     p. cm.
  Includes bibliographical references and index.
  ISBN-13: 978-0-7603-2777-7 (pbk. : alk. paper)
  ISBN-10: 0-7603-2777-7 (pbk. : alk. paper)
  1. Hot rods--Motors--Design and construction. I.
  Title.
TL210.M3578 2005
629.25'04--dc22

                              2006010869

About the author
George McNicholl purchased his first automobile engine (a Ford flathead V-8) when he was 12 years old and has had a hand in car and engine building ever since. He is the author of four other Motorbooks titles: *How To Build a Flathead Ford V-8*, *How To Build Vintage Hot Rod V-8 Engines*, *How To Build Ford Flathead V-8 Horsepower*, and *How To Rebuild Corvette Rolling Chassis 1963–1982*. McNicholl lives in North Vancouver, B.C., Canada.

On the cover:
Main: This 1937 Ford V8-60 horsepower engine is installed in a beautiful black 1915 Ford Model T Roadster owned by Ron Ford. The engine is equipped with original Eddie Meyer Engineering polished-aluminum cylinder heads, super dual-carburetor intake manifold, and air cleaner. The car was purchased in 1962 and restored to its present condition by Roy Brizio in 1995.
Inset: The set-square has been placed flush against the cylinder wall, and the straight edge is slightly above the deck. This photograph shows the 16-degree angle that was the result of the deck being machined at a 74-degree angle.

On the title pages:
This is the Chevrolet 348-ci V-8 engine featured in the first section of this book. It is installed in a professionally restored 1958 Chevrolet Bel Air Impala sports coupe two-door hardtop owned by Jerry Olsen.

On the back cover:
The famous Mickey Thompson 409 Power Ram cast-aluminum, dual-quad, ram-log intake manifold for the 409-ci engine.

CONTENTS

PREFACE

I am the author of *How to Build a Flathead Ford V-8*, *How to Build Vintage Hot Rod V-8 Engines*, and *How to Build Ford Flathead V-8 Horsepower*, published and distributed by MBI Publishing Company of St. Paul, Minnesota. I have always been an avid hot rodder and drag racing fan, and I have built many different engines over the years. The engines that are in three of my current vehicles are featured in *How to Build Vintage Hot Rod V-8 Engines*.

Any time off I have, I spend at Luke's Custom Machine & Design (see Resources) assisting Luke Balogh (the owner) with engine building, detailing, and parts ordering. I shall not depress the readers of this book with a lengthy explanation of my background. Kindly purchase my first book and you can read all about it in the foreword. Do not think I shall benefit from any additional sales of my books—whatever I receive is immediately siphoned off by my son, Tyler, and daughter, Kristina, under the pretense of paying for some new university surcharge.

A longtime friend of mine purchased a 1958 Chevrolet Bel Air Impala sports coupe two-door hardtop in Southern California and had it shipped to Vancouver, BC, Canada, in October 2004. The vehicle was originally equipped with a Chevrolet 348-ci V-8 engine, and the new owner intended to restore the complete car. I was not going to miss the opportunity to describe the buildup of a Chevrolet 348-ci V-8 engine.

Dave Child, the owner of High Performance Engines (see Resources), suggested I should also describe the complete buildup of a legendary Chevrolet 409-ci V-8 engine since I was already writing about the Chevrolet 348. High Performance Engines just happened to be starting the buildup of a Chevrolet 409 in February 2005.

The owner of the blown French flathead V-8 engine described in my third book, *How to Build Ford Flathead V-8 Horsepower*, decided to have a Lincoln 337-ci flathead V-8 engine built by Luke's Custom Machine & Design. That project commenced in March 2005. The Lincoln flathead V-8 engine is not very common today, and information about it is extremely difficult to locate. I thought this was a wonderful opportunity to document the buildup of one.

I had only intended to describe the buildup of three different engines in this book, when the Ford V8-60 engine appeared on the scene suddenly. The engine belonged to the owner of the Chevrolet 409-ci V-8 engine described in this book, and he decided to sell the Ford V8-60 engine in April 2005. It was most unfortunate that the Ford V8-60 engine was not assembled and completed the way the other three engines in this book were. However, I was able to take all the necessary measurements and photographs in order to describe the complete buildup of the engine. I did not want to pass up the opportunity, because information about the 1937–1940 Ford V8-60 engines is very scarce.

Charlie Ryan wrote, sang, and recorded "Hot Rod Lincoln" in 1955. The song was released in 1957 by Souvenir Records and was the first car song to become a major hit. The Beach Boys recorded and released the song "409" in 1962, which also became a big hit. As the title suggests, the engines in this book are truly classic.

ACKNOWLEDGMENTS

I would like to thank my lovely wife, Jillian, for her total lack of interest in my automotive hobby, which gave me the opportunity to write this book undisturbed! I also thank her for the use of her camera (once again), which I used to take every picture in this book.

I would sincerely like to thank Lindsay Hitch, an associate editor at MBI Publishing Company, for her continuing support of my projects. Through her superb efforts, my other books were published and are in great demand.

I owe a debt of gratitude to Dave Child, the owner of High Performance Engines, for permitting me unrestricted access to his shop to take photographs of the machining procedures shown in this book. Dave and his staff (which includes his father, Bud; "T-Bone;" "Mario;" and Dave Cummings) provided me with valuable engine building information and part numbers.

I would like to thank Jerry Olsen, the owner of the Chevrolet 348-ci V-8 engine, and John Vicars, the owner of the Lincoln flathead V-8 engine, for allowing me the opportunity to document the buildup of these engines. Tom Lee is the owner of the Chevrolet 409-ci V-8 engine and a fanatical collector of vintage hot rod parts. I really appreciate Tom allowing me access to his garage, better known as the "409 Bar and Grill," in order to take photographs of many of the parts in his collection.

I greatly appreciate the efforts of Bud Bennett (the recently retired owner of a local speed shop) and his assistant, Don Robinson, in arranging for me to take photographs of a Chevrolet 409-ci V-8 engine they were building and for providing me with some previously unpublished 409 data.

INTRODUCTION

Many engine owners make the mistake of not researching the buildup of an engine properly. All of the parts of an engine must fit correctly and work together to obtain the maximum potential from the engine. Some people rush out and buy the first part that comes to mind, ignoring the fact that that part might not be the correct one for that particular engine. They end up spending unbelievable amounts of money and wondering why their engine does not perform as expected. The engines described in this book are proven models that will function superbly. A lot of research went into building each of them, which is why they work.

I have been compiling the complete buildup information of my own engines and vehicles for over 25 years, as well as the engines I have assisted Luke's Custom Machine & Design with assembling. This data is extremely useful when determining the appraised value of a vehicle for insurance purposes and as a quick reference source.

The information I have provided in this book should be of considerable assistance to hot rod and custom car owners wanting to build a decent V-8 street performance engine. Some of the parts used in the engines have become obsolete or difficult to locate, and I have listed alternative parts and suggestions whenever possible. It was not my intention to list every piece of aftermarket speed equipment available for these engines, and the book is not intended to describe how to build "numbers matching" engines, although there are many parts listed that will assist an owner in doing so. There is good information throughout this book applicable to all the engines described—read the entire book.

I appreciate that most automotive publications do not list the prices for the complete buildup of an engine because those prices can change quickly over a very short period of time. However, I have included the current prices as of December 2005 in order for the reader to fully understand what is involved financially when proceeding with the buildup of the engines described. The costs I have indicated clearly show that a quality engine can be built for a reasonable amount of money. It is not cheap to build one of these engines, but it is not out of line either.

The listed prices do not include any shipping or handling charges, based on the assumption that the owner of the engine will purchase his own parts. This avoids the markup (usually about 20 percent) on the parts' prices if an engine builder or machine shop were to purchase the parts for you. This is a legitimate charge due to the fact that these shops must account for the time it takes to order the parts, inspect the parts, and pay for them. Note: These prices are in U.S. dollars. The prices indicated may vary in different parts of North America and are subject to change without notice.

Section I of this book covers the buildup of an almost-stock Chevrolet 348-ci V-8 engine. Section II covers the buildup of a blown (supercharged) Chevrolet 409-ci V-8 engine. Section III covers the buildup of a Lincoln 337-ci flathead V-8 engine. Section IV covers the buildup of a Ford flathead V8-60 engine.

The first section, "A," of each chapter offers an explanation of the parts, clearances, and machining required for the engine buildup in that chapter. In many instances, there is an explanation of where to locate the parts or services. The second section, "B," of each chapter is a summary and will provide the complete buildup information, including part numbers, clearances, and specifications, along with the prices for those parts.

Good luck with your hot rod or custom car project. Remember to drive safely and sanely.

SECTION I: CHEVROLET 348-CI TURBO-THRUST V-8 ENGINE

CHAPTER 1
ENGINE BLOCK

This overhead-valve (OHV) 1958 Chevrolet 348-ci V-8 engine is a stock rebuild that was installed in a restored 1958 Chevrolet Bel Air Impala sports coupe two-door hardtop. (The name "Impala" was not used by itself until 1959.) The engine was built at High Performance Engines (see Resources) and installed in the vehicle in mid-December 2004.

A. ENGINE BLOCK
PURCHASE AND MAGNAFLUX

The 1958 Chevrolet 348-ci Turbo-Thrust V-8, RPO (regular production option) 576, engine specifications are:

- 347.5-ci (5.7-liter) displacement
- Stock bore: 4.125 inches
- Stock stroke: 3.250 inches
- Stock compression ratio: 9.5:1
- One x four-barrel carburetor
- 250 horsepower at 4,400 rpm and 355 ft-lbs torque at 2,800 rpm

The Chevrolet 348-ci V-8 engine is referred to as a "W" design due to the unique shape of the cylinder heads with the valves staggered diagonally. Many people today believe this engine was originally manufactured for use in heavy-duty trucks, even though approximately 95 percent of the 348-ci engines produced were installed in passenger cars. The 348-ci engine was offered as an option for Chevrolet passenger cars starting in 1958 and ending in 1961, and these engines were available in trucks from 1958 until 1965. The 348-ci engine was the forerunner to the famous Chevrolet muscle-car big-block 409-ci V-8 engine, introduced in 1961. Although the 348-ci engines were very popular in the late 1950s, they did not achieve lasting status as hot street engines because performance peaked at 5,000 rpm, or 6,000 rpm for modified versions.

The Chevrolet 348-ci V-8 engine remained unchanged from 1958 to 1961, with the exception of a relief cut in the top of the cylinder walls (explained in the Machining section of this chapter) and the option of high-performance cylinder heads (explained in the Cylinder Heads section of Chapter 5). The engine block casting numbers and casting dates are located at the top left rear of the engine block (where the bell housing bolts on). The casting numbers are:

3732755: 1959–1961
3732811: 1958
3751872: 1958
3755011: 1959–1961
3771705: 1959–1961
3782012: 1958–1961
3798962: 1962–1965
3815707: 1958–1961
3857655: 1962–1965
3860387: 1958

These are the casting numbers I am aware of; there may well be others. The dimensions and displacement of the 348-ci engine are relatively small, similar to a small-block Chevrolet V-8 engine, yet it is still considered a big-block Chevrolet V-8 engine. The 348-ci engine block weighs 175 pounds (bare), which is approximately 25 pounds more than a 1970 Chevrolet small-block 350-ci engine block (bare). The possibility of locating a new old stock (NOS) Chevrolet 348-ci V-8 engine block is slim to none; as a result, a good used engine block will cost approximately $150. This buildup describes an engine block with a casting number of 3751872 and a casting date of L857 (December 8, 1957).

This 1958 Chevrolet 348-ci V-8 engine block has a casting number of 3751872 and a casting date of L857 (December 8, 1957).

The most powerful 348-ci engine Chevrolet ever offered for passenger cars was the 1961 Special Super Turbo-Thrust model, and the ratings for this engine were: 350 horsepower at 6,000 rpm, and 364 ft-lbs torque at 3,600 rpm. To achieve those ratings, the engine required an 11.25:1 compression ratio, three x two-barrel carburetors, better-designed cylinder heads with bigger head diameter valves, and a solid (mechanical) lifter camshaft.

If you do not know what to look for when purchasing an engine block, take a friend along that does. Visually inspect the engine block for any cracks or obvious damage by thoroughly examining the sides of the engine block, the main bearing webs, the oil pan rails, the valve lifter bosses, the cylinder head bolt holes, and the cylinder walls. Have the engine block professionally examined at a local engine building or machine shop. If the engine block is cracked, take a pass on it. There are always other engine blocks; it just might take some time and patience to locate one. Hemmings Motor News (www.hemmings.com), a local buy-and-sell newspaper, eBay (www.ebay.com), and even the word-of-mouth rumor mill are all avenues to pursue. I have purchased many items off of eBay and have never encountered a problem; however, I only purchase from highly rated sellers.

This is another Chevrolet 348-ci V-8 engine block with a casting number of 3755011 and a casting date of J259 (October 2, 1959).

The engine block should have the main bearing caps attached. If it does not, it is not a disaster; it just means that main bearing caps will have to be located and the engine block align honed or possibly align bored. This additional cost should reduce the purchase price of the engine block. Chevrolet 348-ci V-8 engine blocks can be safely bored 0.125 (1/8) inch oversize, provided there has not been any core shift. Make certain the cylinders were not previously bored to this size. It is entirely up to the builder of an engine whether to buy a complete motor or just the engine block. If the builder has a source for low-cost individual parts, it might be more economical to just buy the engine block.

Have the engine block and main bearing caps and bolts Magnafluxed, technically known as "magnet particle testing". This final test will determine if you have located an acceptable engine block. It will cost approximately $50 to Magnaflux an engine block and the main bearing caps and bolts.

CLEANING

Remove any bolts and fittings, the camshaft bearings, oil seals, water jacket drain plugs, frost plugs, rear camshaft boss plug, and all of the oil gallery line plugs from the engine block. After the engine block has been completely stripped down, have it hot tanked. Do this before the engine block is Magnafluxed to ensure there are no hidden cracks covered up with grease and grime. It will cost approximately $50 to hot tank an engine block.

There are two valve-lifter gallery oil line expansion plugs located at the front of the engine block (behind the camshaft gear). After these plugs have been removed, drill and tap the two holes for 1/4-inch-NPT plugs, and install them using pipe thread sealant when it is time to reassemble the engine. There are three oil line plugs on the lower left, outside of the engine block and just above the oil pan rail.

After these plugs have been removed, drill and tap the holes for 1/8-inch-NPT plugs, and install them using pipe thread sealant when the engine is reassembled. In order to provide better lubrication for the camshaft gear and timing gear chain, drill a 0.030-inch hole in the center of the lower face of the front camshaft boss (behind the camshaft gear). Also drill the two front oil gallery line plugs with a 0.030-inch hole if a gear drive will be installed.

It is a common practice with OHV engines to grind the valve lifter gallery smooth in order to assist with oil return to the oil pan and remove any hidden pockets of sand remaining from the casting process. Use a high-speed grinder with carbide bits or small sanding discs to smooth out the surface. The surface does not have to be ground to a mirror-like finish.

DETAILING THE ENGINE BLOCK

Prior to sending the engine block out to be Redi-Stripped, use a high-speed grinder with small sanding discs to remove all of the rough areas on the outside of the engine block. The entire surface should be as smooth as possible when completed. If the engine block will be installed in a stock, numbers-matching vehicle, omit this step in order to keep the original appearance of the engine block.

RETAP AND CHAMFER BOLT HOLES

Run a tap through every bolt hole in the engine block and through the spark plug holes in the cylinder heads. This will ensure each and every thread is in perfect shape and will enable accurate torque readings when it is time to reassemble the engine. After the engine block is parallel decked, use a countersink bit in a drill and lightly chamfer all the cylinder head bolt holes to help prevent the threads from being pulled when the cylinder head bolts, or studs, are torqued.

REDI-STRIP THE ENGINE BLOCK

Redi-Stripping (see Resources) is a nonacidic chemical process that completely removes all foreign matter from an engine block and is necessary for most used engine blocks. A quality machine shop may insist an engine block be Redi-Stripped prior to working on it. The procedure ensures the water passages are absolutely clean, thus preventing overheating. It will cost approximately $150 to Redi-Strip an engine block.

GLYPTAL

Glyptal G-1228A medium-gray gloss enamel is the paint used on electrical motors. This terrific paint withstands very high temperatures and is almost impossible to chip. I prefer to purchase this product in the spray can (rattle can) form for easy application. As soon as the engine block returns from being Redi-Stripped, mask off the outside of the engine block and the underside of the four oval openings in the valve lifter gallery. Insert 16 plastic plugs of the appropriate size in the valve lifter bosses, and then paint the valve lifter gallery and the front of the engine block (behind the camshaft timing gear) with Glyptal. Glass bead the inside of

This is the 1958 Chevrolet 348-ci V-8 engine block, casting number 3751872, described here. The front of the engine block and valve lifter gallery both have been painted with Glyptal G-1228A medium-gray gloss enamel.

the timing gear cover (unless it is aluminum) and the crankshaft oil slinger, and then paint them with Glyptal. This paint is available from electrical repair outlets.

Install a valve lifter gallery screen kit, such as the Moroso 25001 (for the big-block Chevrolet), in order to keep debris from ending up in the oiling system. The Moroso 25001 kit costs about $10 and should be installed with clear Permatex PermaPoxy general-purpose epoxy after the Glyptal is dry.

MACHINING

I have been using the services of High Performance Engines for my engines for over 30 years, and the company performed the machine work for all the engines described in this book. It is a superb machine shop and engine building company where close tolerances, cleanliness, and strict attention to detail are the standard operating procedures. It may not be a practical proposition for an engine owner located in other parts of North America to use that particular company, but it is imperative to locate a machine shop with similar high standards. There is a world of difference between a machine shop that rebuilds average passenger car engines and a machine shop that specializes in building street performance and serious competition engines. Do not try to cut corners when it comes to machining; the end result will be disappointing.

CYLINDER BORING

Purchase the pistons beforehand and deliver them to the machine shop with the engine block. The machine shop will measure each piston with a micrometer and bore the cylinders accordingly to ensure there is adequate piston-to-bore clearance (after cylinder honing), measured below the bottom of the wrist pin perpendicular to the wrist pin. Chevrolet specified the piston-to-cylinder-bore clearance for the 348-ci engines to be 0.0006 to 0.001 inch. Always adhere to the piston manufacturer's specifications for piston-to-cylinder-bore clearance. The engine block is usually bored to within 0.003 to 0.004 inch of the final bore, and then the cylinders are honed and deglazed, resulting in the final bore.

The 348-ci engine blocks can be safely bored 0.125 (1/8) inch oversize. The maximum cylinder bore size for a used 348-ci engine block is 4.165 inches (0.060 inch oversize) in order for the cylinders to be bored to 4.205 inches (0.080 inch oversize) and have enough material left in case the cylinders need to be bored once again as a result of some unfortunate mishap.

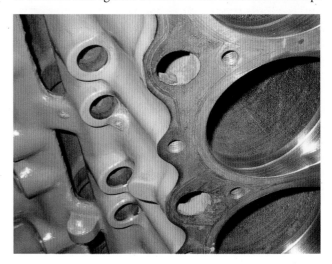

This relief was cut into the cylinder wall of a Chevrolet 348-ci V-8 engine block with a 9.5:1 compression ratio. The relief is for exhaust valve clearance and breathing.

The Chevrolet 348-ci V-8 engines with a 9.5:1 compression ratio have a relief cut into the top of the cylinder walls near the outer edge of the engine block. This relief provides clearance and breathing room for the exhaust valves and is similar to unshrouding, or laying back, the combustion chambers in a typical OHV cylinder head. If larger exhaust valves are installed, the reliefs in the engine block should be enlarged accordingly. The Chevrolet 348-ci V-8 Truck engines with a 7.75:1 compression ratio have two reliefs in each cylinder wall. The Chevrolet 348-ci V-8 engines with an 11.0:1 or 11.25:1 compression ratio have a single, deeper relief in each cylinder wall.

Chevrolet described the pistons in the 348-ci engine with a 9.5:1 compression ratio as being a "gabled roof" shape, and they have also been referred to as a "pent-roof design". The shape of these pistons is similar to the early Chrysler hemispherical pistons. The 9.5:1 compression ratio pistons have a 16-degree angle on each side at the crown. The 16 degrees on the top side of the piston make it flush with the engine block deck when the piston is at top dead center (TDC). The 16 degrees on the lower side of the piston, combined with the 16-degree angle of the

This GM 3751995 cast-aluminum gabled-roof piston, casting number 3747889, has a 9.5:1 compression ratio for a standard bore (4.125 inches) Chevrolet 348-ci V-8 engine. The piston is a slipper-skirt design and weighs 789 grams. The straight-wall wrist pin is 3.265 inches long, its diameter is 0.9896 inch, and its weight is 169 grams.

deck, result in a 32-degree angle in the cylinder. This 32-degree wedge shape is the combustion chamber.

The 11.0:1 or 11.25:1 compression ratio pistons have a 16-degree angle at one side of the crown. The 16 degrees on the top side of the piston make it flush with the engine block deck when the piston is at TDC. The flat top on the lower side of the piston means there is only a 16-degree angle in the cylinder. This 16-degree wedge shape is the combustion chamber.

Boring the cylinders in a 348-ci engine block will not increase the compression ratio because the size of the combustion chambers is enlarged as well. The only way to increase the compression ratio is to install custom pistons.

The combustion chamber area (depth to the bottom of the 32-degree wedge shape) is bored 0.055 inch larger than the

actual cylinder bore in the 348-ci engines with a 9.5:1 compression ratio. This counterbore assists with the installation of piston assemblies. There is no counterbore in the 348-ci engines with 11.0:1 or 11.25:1 compression ratio. In order to compensate for this lost combustion chamber volume, the single relief in each cylinder is enlarged. Due to the lack of a counterbore, installing the piston assemblies is more difficult and time consuming.

Install the main bearing caps and correctly torque them during the boring and honing operation. This procedure places stress on the bottom end of the engine block and prevents the cylinders from distorting after they have been bored and honed, when the crankshaft is installed and torqued in position. It will cost approximately $125 to cylinder bore, hone, and deglaze an eight-cylinder engine block.

The cylinder boring is carried out using a Rottler Boring Bar Company F2B boring bar, or similar machine. Set up the engine block in the boring machine, locate the centerline of the

The cylinders in this Chevrolet 348-ci V-8 engine block are being bored with the use of a Rottler Boring Bar Company F2B boring bar.

The set square has been placed flush against the cylinder wall, and the straight edge is slightly above the deck. This photograph shows the 16-degree angle that was the result of the deck being machined at a 74-degree angle.

The cylinders in this beautiful Brad Anderson Enterprises BAE98 CNC-machined aluminum Chrysler Hemi-style engine block are about to be honed with a Sunnen CK-10 automatic cylinder resizing machine with a torque plate. This 526-ci engine block was going to be installed in a Top Alcohol Funny Car, although it would really wake up a 1958 Chevrolet Bel Air!

crankshaft using a dial indicator, and clamp the engine block in ready position for the actual cylinder boring operation.

OHV engines used for street performance or racing should have the cylinders honed using a torque plate. The torque plate simulates the distortion caused to the engine block when the cylinder heads are torqued in place. With the torque plate, use the same type of fastener used to bolt the cylinder heads in place. Cylinder head studs place a different stress on the engine block than cylinder head bolts, even when these two different types of fasteners are torqued to the same setting.

A special torque plate is required to hone the cylinders in a Chevrolet 348-ci V-8 engine block because the deck surface is at an angle of 74 degrees (toward the centerline of the engine block) and not perpendicular to the cylinder bores. Angling the special torque plate at 16 degrees will compensate for the 74-degree angle. Frank McGurk, the founder of Frank McGurk Engineering in Gardina, California, and a legendary engine builder from the 1950s, used to sell the special torque plate for $45. Good luck trying to find an original one today for that price!

The cylinder boring machines used many years ago were bolted to the deck surface of the engine block, which required a torque plate to prevent distortion to the cylinders and provide a rigid platform for the boring machine. Today, the engine blocks are clamped securely into cylinder boring machines, which means the torque plate is not necessary for the cylinder boring stage of the machining. A torque plate is used when the cylinders are honed and deglazed.

The final stage of the cylinder boring operation is the cylinder honing and deglazing. This important step must be carried out correctly to properly seat the piston rings.

Cylinder honing and deglazing is undertaken using a Sunnen CK-10 automatic cylinder resizing machine or similar equipment. The honing machine removes the last 0.003 to 0.004 inch of material from the cylinder walls using Sunnen 600-series 280-grit stones (for cast-iron rings) or Sunnen 800-series 400-grit stones (for moly piston rings). The final cylinder bore and finish on the cylinder walls will be a crosshatch pattern. The cylinders in the engine block described in this chapter were bored 0.030 inch oversize.

ALIGN HONE AND ALIGN BORE

The centerline of the crankshaft is the point from which all critical measurements are taken. Measuring from the centerline of the crankshaft ensures the engine block main bearing housing bores, with the main bearing caps attached, are exactly parallel to it.

Measure the engine block main bearing housing bores, with the main bearing caps attached, with a dial indicator or inside micrometer to ensure they are in perfect alignment with each other and not tapered. If they are tapered or not aligned perfectly, the engine block will have to be align honed. If the main bearing caps are not the caps originally supplied with the engine block, align honing, and possibly align boring, will be necessary. Each pass with the align honing machine removes approximately 0.0005 inch of material from the main bearing housing bores and caps. This procedure is critical and should only be done at a machine shop specializing in high-performance engine building. It will cost approximately $200 to align hone an engine block.

Use a crankshaft that has been checked for alignment and is guaranteed to be straight to check the main bearing housing bore alignment in the engine block. Install the correct main

This custom aluminum torque plate was fabricated specifically for align honing this small-block Buick V-8 drag racing engine block. The aluminum material was used to simulate the aluminum cylinder heads.

bearings for the crankshaft in the engine block and the main bearing caps, oil the main bearings well, install the crankshaft and the main bearing caps, and correctly torque the main bearing cap bolts (or studs). The crankshaft should turn freely, without any tight spots. If it does, the engine block is acceptable. If it does not, the engine block will have to be align honed. Most engine blocks require align honing, and that was the case for the engine block described in this section. The main bearing housing bores in the Chevrolet 348-ci V-8 engine block are 2.687 to 2.688 inches in diameter.

There is a difference in the distortion created at the bottom end of the engine block when main bearing cap bolts are installed versus main bearing cap studs, even when these two different types of fasteners are torqued to the same setting. If an engine block is align bored or align honed with main bearing cap bolts in place, the bolts cannot be replaced with main bearing cap studs at any time in the future. The reverse situation also applies. You must decide prior to align boring or align honing which type of fastener to use. The GM 3828570 main bearing cap bolts, 1/2 inch NC by 3 1/2 inches long, are of sufficient strength for use in street performance 348-ci engines.

If you intend to equip a Chevrolet 348-ci V-8 engine with a blower (supercharger) for serious street performance use, install main bearing cap studs. Main bearing cap stud kits are not currently available for the 348-ci engine block; however, the main bearing cap stud kits for the big-block Chevrolet V-8 engines are compatible. The Automotive Racing Products (ARP) 135-5402 main bearing cap stud kit for two-bolt main bearing caps without a windage tray retails for $50. The ARP 235-5502 main bearing cap stud kit for two-bolt main bearing caps with a windage tray can be purchased for $60.

Unlike the small-block Chevrolet V-8 engine blocks, the Chevrolet 348-ci V-8 engine blocks cannot be converted to accept splayed four-bolt main bearing caps. There is an oil line inside the 348-ci engine block on the left side above the oil pan rail. Splayed main bearing cap bolts would penetrate this oil line. Main bearing cap support bridges can be fabricated if additional support is required for the bottom end of a 348-ci engine block.

Use a Sunnen CH-100 horizontal hone align boring machine, or similar equipment, to align hone the engine block. Remove approximately 0.005 inch from the mating surface of the main bearing caps by milling prior to align honing.

The engine block must be align bored when custom-made main bearing caps are installed, and possibly when stock main bearing caps are used (if they are not the original main bearing caps). There are a number of align boring machines currently available, including the Sunnen CH-100 horizontal hone with the Sunnen PLB-100 align bore attachment and the Torbin-Arp Manufacturing Company TA15 align boring machine. It will cost approximately $200 to align bore an engine block.

PARALLEL DECK

Parallel deck the engine block to ensure the deck height is the same for all the cylinders and the deck is exactly 90 degrees in relation to the cylinder bores. The Chevrolet 348-ci V-8 engine block is parallel decked at a 74-degree angle, which means the decks are not perpendicular to the cylinder bores. Most engine blocks should be parallel decked, which requires removing approximately 0.005 to 0.012 inch of material from the deck surface. It will cost approximately $120 to parallel deck an engine block.

Use a Repco Automotive Company Type ASG, or similar machine, to parallel deck the engine block. Locate the crankshaft centerline using a dial indicator, clamp the engine block in position, and parallel deck one side of the engine block, followed by the other side. The 348-ci engine block described in this book was parallel decked.

SHOT PEEN

The main bearing caps and main bearing cap bolts can be shot peened while the engine block is at the machine shop being hot tanked and Magnafluxed. Shot peening removes stress from the main bearing caps and bolts. There is a cavity

This is a set of main bearing caps and bolts for a Chevrolet 348-ci V-8 engine block. These items are strong enough for use in street performance engines.

This Chevrolet 348-ci V-8 engine block is being align honed on a Sunnen CH-100 horizontal hone align boring machine.

in the rear main bearing cap where the oil pump is mounted. This cavity should be ground smooth to assist with oil flow.

DEGLAZE

Deglaze the valve lifter bosses with a wheel cylinder or ball hone. Hone the valve lifter bosses just enough to clean them up. Remove only an absolute minimum of material to avoid excess valve lifter clearance, which will result in an oiling problem.

O-RINGS

Fit the engine block with O-rings if it will be equipped with a blower; some engine builders believe this is only necessary if the boost will exceed 5 pounds. Machine a groove in the deck surface around each cylinder, approximately 0.125 inch from the edge. Then, tap a piece of stainless-steel wire, usually 0.035 inch in diameter, into the groove. Machine a receiver groove (the same diameter as the wire) into the cylinder head, directly above the wire in the engine block. The wire in the engine block will press the cylinder head gasket into the receiver groove in the

cylinder head, creating an excellent seal. It will cost approximately $100 to fit an engine block with O-rings and machine a receiver groove in the cylinder heads.

CLEANING AND PAINTING

After completing all of these machining procedures, thoroughly clean the engine block with hot water and soap. Use long, thin engine brushes to reach as far into the oil passages as possible. Spend the time to do this job properly. The term "hospital clean" applies here.

Mask off the engine block with newspaper and use the cylinder head gaskets, timing gear cover gasket, oil pan gaskets, and water pump gaskets as templates. Polyurethane paint is the best paint for an engine block. It is extremely durable and highly resistant to gasoline, lacquer thinner, antifreeze, oil, or brake fluid. Of the numerous manufacturers of polyurethane paint, I have found PPG polyurethane to be an excellent product, and it is available in just about every imaginable color. Polyurethane paint can be purchased at most industrial supply stores, or even from a local body shop.

Polyurethane paint should be sprayed in a temperature-controlled paint booth by an experienced painter. During my early teenage years, I used to spray paint engine blocks and cars in my parent's garage or in the alley behind their house. Aside from being a health hazard and a total environmental disaster, this practice did not endear me to the neighbors. I now have all my engine blocks professionally painted at a local body shop. Even some of us truly obstinate

This early Chrysler Hemi 354-ci V-8 engine block is being parallel decked with a Repco Automotive Company ASG machine.

people have to change with the times!

After the engine block has been painted, install the freeze plugs using Permatex aviation form-a-gasket. Install the oil gallery line plugs and water jacket drain plugs using pipe thread sealant. The most common type of freeze plug is the expansion plug, and it is a very inexpensive item.

No aftermarket manufacturer currently offers a brass freeze plug kit for the Chevrolet 348-ci V-8 engine blocks. The eight freeze plugs are 1 3/4 (1.75) inches outside diameter (o.d.), the same size used in the big-block Chevrolet 454-ci V-8 engine blocks. The camshaft rear boss plug is 2 7/64 (2.109) inches o.d., the same size used in the small-block Chevrolet 350-ci V-8 engine blocks. Most engine building shops have a supply of different-sized freeze plugs on hand, so it should not be a problem to obtain these items.

B. ENGINE BLOCK SUMMARY

- 1958 Chevrolet Bel Air 348-ci Turbo-Thrust V-8 engine block; casting number 3751872; casting date L857 (December 8, 1957); RPO 576. Stock bore, 4.125 inches; stock stroke, 3.250 inches; two-bolt main bearing caps; 9.5:1 compression ratio; one x four-barrel carburetor; 250 horsepower at 4,400 rpm and 355 ft-lbs torque at 2,800 rpm. Engine block weight (bare): 175 pounds **$150**
- Engine block hot tanked and Redi-Stripped; engine block and main bearing caps and bolts Magnafluxed; main bearing caps and bolts shot peened; all threads retapped; cylinder head bolt holes chamfered; valve lifter bosses deglazed, allowing for 0.002-inch valve lifter clearance; and No. 5 main bearing cap oil pump cavity polished. New brass freeze plugs (1.75 inches o.d.) and new camshaft rear boss plug (2.109 inches o.d.) installed using Permatex aviation form-a-gasket. Two front oil gallery line plug holes tapped for 1/4-inch-NPT plugs. New stainless-steel oil gallery line plugs and new stainless-steel water jacket drain plugs installed using pipe thread sealant. A 0.030-inch hole drilled in lower face of front camshaft boss for additional oiling. New Moroso 25001 valve lifter gallery screen kit installed using clear Permatex PermaPoxy general-purpose epoxy. Valve lifter gallery and front of engine block (behind camshaft gear) ground smooth and painted with Glyptal G-1228A medium-gray gloss enamel. Engine block painted with PPG 60914 orange high-gloss polyurethane. **$642.56**
- Engine block bored 0.030 inch oversize, and cylinders honed and deglazed using Sunnen 800-series 400-grit stones with torque plate; final bore of 4.280 inches. Piston-to-bore clearance: 0.0015 inch, measured below bottom of wrist pin perpendicular to the wrist pin. **$125**
- Engine block align honed. **$200**
- Engine block parallel decked to 0.008 inch average, below deck. **$120**

- Engine Block Total: **$1,237.56**

CHAPTER 2
CRANKSHAFT

A. CRANKSHAFT
PURCHASE

High-quality, forged-steel crankshafts were installed in all the Chevrolet 348-ci V-8 engines and are acceptable for use in a blown street performance engine. The GM 3760427 crankshaft, with casting number 3732692, has a stock stroke of 3.250 inches; the main bearing journal diameter is 2.498 to 2.499 inches; the connecting rod journal diameter is 2.199 to 2.200 inches; and the crankshaft weighs 59 pounds. The estimated price for a 348-ci crankshaft in good condition is $150.

The casting numbers for the Chevrolet 348-ci V-8 crankshafts are:

3732692: 1958
3733223
3733226: 1958
3741640: 1959–1961
3741642: 1959–1961
3782692
3795589
3815822: 1959–1961
3824533: 1958–1961
3824553: 1958–1961
3829027
3847466
3838416

These are the casting numbers I am aware of; there may well be others. Purchasing a used crankshaft can be troublesome, as there is a chance the crankshaft is cracked or the journals have been ground to the point that bearings are not available. As a condition of the purchase, have the crankshaft professionally examined by a quality machine shop.

I am not aware of any company today offering a replacement crankshaft for the 348-ci engine. Crankshaft Company (Los Angeles, California), founded by Alex Alexander, produced quality stroker crankshafts for the 348-ci engine in the late 1950s. Strokes of 3.375 inches (1/8 inch longer), 3.500 inches (1/4 inch longer), or 3.625 inches (3/8 inch longer) were offered. A Chevrolet 348-ci V-8 engine with a stroke of 3.625 inches (3/8 inch longer than stock) and a bore of 4.250 inches (1/8 inch larger than stock) will result in an impressive displacement of 411.4 ci (6.7 liters). It might still be possible to locate an original stroker crankshaft. The Chevrolet 409-ci V-8 crankshaft with a 3.50-inch stroke has the same journal sizes as the 348-ci crankshaft; however, the 409's counterweights are thicker. It would be more economical to have the 348-ci crankshaft stroked than to reduce the thickness of the 409-ci crankshaft counterweights.

The GM 3760427 crankshaft snout is not threaded for a harmonic balancer bolt because the GM 3896904 harmonic balancer is a press-fit model (similar to the small-block Chevrolet 283-ci V-8 engines). Thread the crankshaft snout using a 7/16-inch-NF tap, and install a good quality harmonic balancer bolt kit. The current retail price for the ARP 134-2501 harmonic balancer bolt kit is $18.

HOT TANK AND SHOT PEEN

The first thing to do with a crankshaft is to have it hot tanked and shot peened to remove stress within the crankshaft. Prior to hot tanking the crankshaft, remove the crankshaft sprocket, or gear, with a gear puller.

Here is a GM 3760427 forged-steel crankshaft, casting number 3732692, which has been shot peened, aligned, Magnafluxed, and ground 0.010 inch undersize. The oil holes have been chamfered and the journals polished. It is ready for balancing.

MAGNAFLUX

The crankshaft must be Magnafluxed—after the crankshaft has been hot tanked and shot peened—to ensure there are no hidden cracks. It will cost approximately $25 to Magnaflux a crankshaft.

STRAIGHTEN, CHAMFER, AND POLISH

Check the crankshaft for alignment and runout with a dial indicator, and have it straightened if necessary. Chamfer all the oil holes by lightly grinding off the sharp surfaces around the oil holes. Do not create deep oval craters. It will cost approximately $25 to chamfer the oil holes. After the crankshaft has been ground and the oil holes chamfered, polish the journals to ensure an absolutely smooth bearing surface. It will cost approximately $30 to polish the journals.

REGRINDING AND CLEANING

The crankshaft will most likely have to be reground, as was the case of the crankshaft described here, and the estimated cost for this is $110. The main bearing journals were ground 0.010 inch undersize, and the connecting rod journals were ground 0.010 inch undersize.

If the main bearing or connecting rod journals are severely damaged or undersize to the point that bearings are not available, there are two methods to build up the journals. The first method involves wire welding the journal, after which the journal is ground in the usual fashion. Wire welding is a proven method of repair that any high-quality crankshaft grinding company can handle with ease. It will cost approximately $140 to wire weld a crankshaft journal.

The second method of repair consists of spraying molten metal on the journal, after which the journal is ground in the usual manner. The crankshaft journal is then surface nitrided (case hardened) to 60 Rockwell C hardness for an extremely hard bearing surface. It will cost approximately $140 to metal spray a crankshaft journal.

After all these machining procedures have been carried out, thoroughly clean the crankshaft with hot water and soap. The term "surgically clean" applies here.

MAIN BEARINGS

Clevite 77 (Dana Corporation) and Federal-Mogul manufacture high-quality engine bearings for the Chevrolet 348-ci V-8 engine. The Clevite 77 bearings are a tri-metal construction with a soft-alloy outer layer, copper-lead center, and a steel backing. The standard Federal-Mogul bearings are also a tri-metal construction with a steel backing, copper-lead center, thin nickel barrier, and lead-tin-copper outer layer. The current retail price for a set of main bearings is $145.

The Clevite 77 MS-458P main bearings are currently available in 0.010 inch oversize only. The Federal-Mogul 4036M main bearings are presently available in standard size, 0.010 inch oversize, and 0.020 inch oversize. Egge Parts House (see Resources) advertises the availability of main bearings for the Chevrolet 348-ci V-8 engine in these

This set of Clevite 77 MS-458P-10 main bearings, 0.010 inch oversize, was installed in the engine described here.

sizes: standard, 0.001 inch oversize, 0.002 inch oversize, 0.010 inch oversize, 0.020 inch oversize, 0.030 inch oversize, and 0.040 inch oversize. Egge Parts House does not list the manufacturer of these bearings.

Check the main-bearing-to-crankshaft clearance by first inserting the main bearings in the engine block and main bearing caps. Install the main bearing caps and torque them to 100 ft-lbs, then measure the inside diameter of the main bearings with an inside micrometer or dial indicator. Also use the micrometer to measure the diameter of the crankshaft main bearing journals. The difference between these two measurements is the main bearing clearance. Chevrolet specified the main bearing clearance for the 348-ci engine to be 0.0006 to 0.0032 inch.

Check the crankshaft end play by first cleaning the main bearings with wax and grease remover using a clean, lint-free cloth. Then install the main bearings in the engine block and the main bearing caps. Oil the main bearings, install the crankshaft, and install and correctly torque the main bearing caps. Set up a dial indicator at the front of the engine block and attach it to the snout of the crankshaft, or set it up at the rear of the engine block and attach it to the flywheel flange. Insert a pry bar against one of the crankshaft counterweights, and then move the crankshaft forward and backward. The reading on the dial indicator is the crankshaft end play. Chevrolet specified the crankshaft end play for the 348-ci engine to be 0.003 to 0.007 inch. The No. 5 main bearing is the thrust bearing that controls the end play. Always adhere to the engine manufacturer's specifications for clearances and torque settings.

Have the machine shop grind the crankshaft and supply the main and connecting rod bearings. This way you are

This GM 3896904 harmonic balancer, 6 1/4 inches o.d., was used on the Chevrolet 348-ci V-8 engines. Whoever installed it last did not use a harmonic balancer installation tool, because this one has been beaten to death.

certain to have the correct bearings and not something that fits the Red Baron's tri-plane! A reputable machine shop will ensure the crankshaft has the correct main bearing and connecting rod bearing clearance after the crankshaft has been ground and the journals polished. Clevite 77 and Federal-Mogul bearings are available at most automotive parts outlets. The Fel-Pro BS40096 Viton two-piece rear oil seal is similar to the big-block Chevrolet 454-ci V-8 Fel-Pro BS-40096-1 oil seal. The current retail price for the two-piece oil seal is $15.

HARMONIC BALANCER

The GM 3896904 internally balanced, press-fit harmonic balancer (crankshaft damper), 6 1/4 inches o.d., was installed on the Chevrolet 348-ci V-8 engines. This part is no longer available from General Motors. Ensure the crankshaft pulley is located in the stock position for correct V-belt alignment, which means an aftermarket harmonic balancer must be the same width as the stock one. The Pioneer DA3270 nodular-iron, internally balanced harmonic balancer, with a 6 1/4 inches o.d., designed for the small-block Chevrolet 283-ci V-8 engines, will meet this requirement and was used on the engine described in this book. The timing marks on the Pioneer DA-3270 are not in the same position as those on the Chevrolet 348-ci V-8 harmonic balancer. Degreeing the harmonic balancer is an easy, inexpensive job for most automotive machine shops. The current retail price for the Pioneer DA3270 harmonic balancer is $65.

A factory-type harmonic balancer should not be used on a street performance engine. The Fluidampr 620101 internally balanced harmonic balancer is available with a 6 1/4 inches o.d., weighs 7.9 pounds, and meets SFI Specification 18.1. The current retail price for this model is $270. This harmonic balancer will have to be degreed as well.

The Craftsman 947626 harmonic balancer removal tool is on the left, and the Moroso 61744 universal harmonic balancer installation tool is on the right. These tools must be used when removing or installing a harmonic balancer.

Here is a Pioneer DA-3270 nodular-iron internally balanced harmonic balancer, which can be used on 348-ci engines; however, it must be degreed with new timing marks.

This GM 3755820 single-groove crankshaft pulley was used on Chevrolet 348-ci V-8 engines without an air conditioning compressor.

When removing a harmonic balancer, you must use a harmonic balancer puller. When installing a harmonic balancer, you must use a harmonic balancer installation tool to avoid damage. Under no circumstances should a harmonic balancer be installed or removed with a hammer. The Craftsman 947626 harmonic balancer removal tool ($20) is available at most Sears stores, and the Moroso 61744 universal harmonic balancer installation tool ($45) is available at most speed-equipment outlets.

The Chevrolet 348-ci V-8 engines equipped with an air conditioning compressor used the GM 3747479 dual-groove crankshaft pulley with a 6 3/4 inches o.d., while engines without an air conditioning compressor used the GM 3755820 single-groove crankshaft pulley, 6 3/4 inches o.d.

B. CRANKSHAFT SUMMARY

- GM 3760427 forged-steel crankshaft, casting number 3732692, internally balanced. Main bearing journal diameter: 2.4985 inches. Connecting rod journal diameter: 2.200 inches. Crankshaft weight: 59 pounds. **$150**
- Crankshaft shot peened, Magnafluxed, aligned, main bearing journals ground 0.010 inch undersize, connecting rod journals ground 0.010 inch undersize, oil holes chamfered, journals polished, and crankshaft balanced. **$285**
- New Clevite 77 MS-458P-10 main bearings, 0.010 inch oversize, installed allowing for 0.002-inch crankshaft clearance and 0.004-inch end play. GM 3828570 main bearing cap bolts, 1/2 inch NC by 3 1/2 inches long, torqued to 100 ft-lbs using Molykote. **$145**
- New Pioneer DA3270 nodular iron harmonic balancer, 6 1/4 inches o.d., internally balanced, installed with GM 106751 woodruff key. New ARP 134-2501 harmonic balancer bolt kit, 190,000 psi, installed using Loctite and torqued to 85 ft-lbs. Harmonic balancer painted with PPG 60914 orange high-gloss polyurethane. Oil slinger painted with Glyptal G-1228A medium-gray gloss enamel. GM 3755820 single-groove crankshaft pulley, 6 3/4 inches o.d., installed with bolts torqued to 30 ft-lbs using Loctite. Crankshaft pulley painted with PPG DCC 9300 black semi-gloss polyurethane. **$128**

- Crankshaft Total: $708

CHAPTER 3
CONNECTING RODS AND PISTONS

A. CONNECTING RODS AND PISTONS PURCHASE

The GM 3774771 forged-steel I-beam connecting rods were installed in the Chevrolet 348-ci V-8 engines. These are good quality forgings, and they are acceptable for use in street performance engines. The length (from the center of the big end, to the center of the small end) is 6.134 to 6.136 inches, and the diameter of the crankshaft end (the big end) is 2.32470 to 2.32520 inches. They weigh 789 grams and are designed for a pressed-in wrist pin with a diameter of 0.9895 to 0.9898 inch. The connecting rod bolts are 3/8 inch in diameter.

The Chevrolet 348-ci V-8 connecting rods have the same crankshaft end diameter, the same wrist pin end (the small end) diameter, and the same length as the big-block Chevrolet 454-ci V-8 connecting rods. The Chevrolet 454-ci V-8 connecting rods are much stronger, although slightly heavier, and can be used as a substitute for the stock 348-ci connecting rods. Refer to Chapter 13.

The GM 3856240 forged-steel I-beam connecting rods for the Chevrolet 454-ci V-8 engines were heat treated and Magnafluxed at the factory, designed for a pressed-in wrist pin, and came equipped with 3/8-inch-diameter connecting rod bolts. The weight of one of these connecting rods is 845 grams. If a Chevrolet 348-ci V-8 engine is going to be equipped with a blower or used for serious competition, then you should install aftermarket connecting rods. Many companies manufacture I-beam and H-beam connecting rods for the Chevrolet 454-ci V-8 engines.

In the late 1950s, aluminum connecting rods were available for the Chevrolet 348-ci V-8 engines. Mickey Thompson, the famous racer and speed equipment manufacturer, owned one of the companies offering aluminum connecting rods. Aluminum connecting rods are designed for drag racing, and thus should not be used in a street performance engine. Aluminum connecting rods have a tendency to stretch over time and eventually crack, which is why they are inspected after every race. Although lighter, they are also much bulkier than forged-steel connecting rods, meaning the engine block will most likely have to be clearanced to accommodate the aluminum connecting rods.

MAGNAFLUX AND SHOT PEEN

The connecting rods should be shot peened, which will assist in removing stress. Do not shot peen the connecting rod bolts; mask them off with duct tape. After shot peening, the connecting rods should be Magnafluxed to ensure there are no cracks. The estimated cost to Magnaflux eight connecting rods is $30.

This is a set of GM 3774771 forged-steel I-beam connecting rods for Chevrolet 348-ci V-8 engines. The ARP 134-6403 Wave Loc connecting rod bolts have been installed.

A Sunnen TN-111 quick-check rod alignment tool, pictured here, is used to determine if connecting rods are twisted or bent.

This picture shows a connecting rod vise. A connecting rod should never be clamped in anything but a connecting rod vise.

The crankshaft end (the big end) of this GM 3774771 connecting rod is being honed on a Sunnen LLB-1810 Powerstroker heavy-duty precision honing machine.

ALIGN, RESIZE, AND REBUSH

A Sunnen TN-111 quick-check rod alignment tool, or similar instrument, is used to determine if the connecting rods are vertically straight in both the front and side positions—in other words, not twisted or bent. Connecting rods are straightened using a connecting rod vise. Note: A connecting rod should never be clamped in anything other than a connecting rod vise.

Resize the crankshaft end of the connecting rods using a Sunnen LLB-1810 Powerstroker heavy-duty precision honing machine, or similar machine. This procedure will ensure the crankshaft end of the connecting rods is perfectly round and all the connecting rods are the same length. It will cost about $90 to resize eight connecting rods.

The connecting rods for all the early Chevrolet V-8 engines (including the 348-ci engines) were not fitted with wrist pin bushings. The majority of these connecting rods are designed for a pressed-in wrist pin. If the wrist pin end of the connecting rod is excessively worn, hone the connecting rod and install a wrist pin bushing for use with a full-floating wrist pin and piston. The clearance in the wrist pin bushing for the wrist pin should be 0.00015 to 0.002 inch for a street performance engine. Early Chevrolet V-8 connecting rods are still readily available and, in most cases, a connecting rod is replaced if the wrist pin end is excessively worn, rather than installing a wrist pin bushing.

Hone the wrist pin end of the connecting rod with a Sunnen LLB-1499 heavy-duty precision honing machine, or similar equipment. It will cost approximately $120 for rebushing and wrist pin fitting eight connecting rods (this does not include the cost of the wrist pin bushings).

You should upgrade the stock connecting rod bolts in the Chevrolet 348-ci V-8 connecting rods with the ones in the small-block Chevrolet 350-ci V-8 connecting rods, which will fit 348-ci V-8 connecting rods. ARP manufactures some of the finest engine fasteners available today. The ARP 134-6403

This Sunnen LLB-1499 heavy-duty precision honing machine is honing the wrist pin end (the small end) of this early Chrysler 354-ci Hemi 1324222 connecting rod.

Wave Loc connecting rod bolts are manufactured using ARP2000 alloy. They are 3/8 inch in diameter, rated at 220,000 psi, and have 12-point nuts. Torque the connecting rod bolts to 45 ft-lbs to allow for a 0.006-inch stretch. The current retail price for a set of ARP 134-6403 connecting rod bolts is $85. ARP products are available at most speed-equipment outlets.

DEBEAM

Debeaming I-beam connecting rods will remove any hidden imperfections in the sides of the connecting rods, which could lead to cracks and result in connecting rod failure. To debeam connecting rods, use a high-speed grinder with a car-

bide bit and grind the sides to a smooth finish; afterward, sand the sides to a polished finish. Make sure to perform the grinding and sanding in a vertical direction, with the flow of the grain in the connecting rod. Never grind or sand across the grain. Debeam and shot peen the connecting rods prior to having them Magnafluxed.

CONNECTING ROD BEARINGS

The Chevrolet 348-ci V-8 crankshafts use the same size connecting rod bearings as the big-block Chevrolet 454-ci V-8 crankshafts. The Clevite 77 CB-743P connecting rod bearings are available in these sizes: 0.001 inch oversize, 0.002 inch oversize, 0.010 inch oversize, 0.020 inch oversize,

Here is a set of ARP 134-6403 Wave Loc connecting rod bolts (for small-block Chevrolet 350-ci V-8 engines). They are 3/8 inch in diameter, rated at 220,000 psi, and fit Chevrolet 348-ci V-8 connecting rods.

This set of Clevite 77 CB-743P-10 connecting rod bearings (for big-block Chevrolet 454-ci V-8 engines), 0.010 inch oversize, was installed in the Chevrolet 348-ci V-8 engine described here.

0.030 inch oversize, 0.040 inch oversize, and 0.050 inch oversize. The Federal-Mogul 8-3190CP connecting rod bearings are available in the same sizes previously listed, except for 0.050 inch oversize. The current retail price for a set of these connecting rod bearings is $50.

Measure the connecting rod bearing clearance by installing connecting rod bearings in a connecting rod and cap, and clamping the connecting rod in a connecting rod vise. Then correctly torque the connecting rod bolts, and use a dial indicator or an inside micrometer to measure the diameter of the bearings. Measure the diameter of the connecting rod journal for that particular connecting rod with a micrometer. The difference between these two measurements is the connecting rod bearing clearance. Chevrolet specified the connecting rod bearing clearance to be 0.0007 to 0.0027 inch.

To measure the side clearance for a pair of connecting rods (for the same connecting rod journal), install the connecting rod bearings in the two connecting rods and caps, and clamp the connecting rods together in a connecting rod vise. Correctly torque the connecting rod bolts, and then measure the thickness of the crankshaft ends of the two connecting rods with a micrometer. Measure the distance across the connecting rod journal using an inside micrometer. The difference between these two measurements is the connecting rod side clearance for a pair of connecting rods. Check this clearance with a feeler gauge after the connecting rods have been installed in the engine. Chevrolet specified the side clearance for a pair of connecting rods to be 0.008 to 0.014 inch.

PISTONS

The Chevrolet 348-ci V-8 engines with a 9.5:1 compression ratio were equipped with cast-aluminum slipper-skirt pistons, described as having a gabled-roof (pent-roof) design. The GM 3751995 pistons, casting number 3747889, are for a standard-bore (4.125-inch) engine block, and they weigh 789 grams each. These pistons come with a pressed-in wrist pin that is 3.265 inches long, 0.9896 inch in diameter, a straight-wall design, and weighs 169 grams. A picture of this piston and wrist pin is in Chapter 1.

The Chevrolet 348-ci V-8 engines with an 11.0:1 or 11.25:1 compression ratio were fitted with the GM 3781342 and GM 3781344 cast-aluminum pistons (standard bore). A naturally aspirated street performance engine should have a compression ratio not exceeding 10.0:1 for use with today's highest-octane, unleaded gasoline.

The two types of pistons commonly used in the early Chevrolet V-8 engines are pistons designed for a pressed-in wrist pin and pistons designed for a full-floating wrist pin. Chevrolet specified 0.00015- to 0.00025-inch clearance in the piston for a pressed-in wrist pin. The clearance in the piston for a full-floating wrist pin used in a street performance engine is usually 0.0005 to 0.001 inch.

Egge Parts House is one of the few sources for aftermarket, off-the-shelf 348-ci pistons. The 9.5:1 compression ratio pistons are manufactured using cast aluminum and are the

slipper-skirt design, complete with pressed-in wrist pins. The piston rings are cast iron, which is entirely suitable for normal street use. The pistons and rings are available in standard size, 0.020 inch oversize, 0.030 inch oversize, 0.040 inch oversize, 0.060 inch oversize, and 0.080 inch oversize. The pistons currently cost $283 for a set of eight, and a set of the cast-iron piston rings is available for $47. The engine described here had a set of the Egge Parts House L2049.8-030 pistons, 0.030 inch oversize, installed.

Ross Racing Pistons (see Resources) manufactures top-quality forged 2618 T-61 aluminum full-floating pistons for the 348-ci engine. The 17-10 flat-top pistons (11.0:1 com-

This picture shows a set of Egge Parts House L2049.8-030 cast-aluminum pistons with wrist pins. These 0.030-inch-oversize pistons have a gabled-roof design and a 9.5:1 compression ratio.

pression ratio) with straight-wall wrist pins, moly piston rings, and Spirolox retainers are available for the current retail price of $825. If the 17-20 dome-top pistons (9.5:1 compression ratio) are substituted, add $70 to that price. Moly piston rings are much more flexible than cast-iron piston rings. These piston assemblies may seem expensive, but they are necessary for anything other than a stock application of a Chevrolet 348-ci engine.

In the 1950s, the Jahns 1116H cast-aluminum pistons with the gabled-roof design were available with compression ratios 9.5:1, 11.0:1, and 12.0:1 for the Chevrolet 348-ci V-8 engines. The Jahns 1116H-1 models were available in an 11.0:1 or 11.25:1 compression ratio for the optional Police Cruiser engine. The Jahns 1138C Powr-Slot cast-aluminum pistons had a unique oval trough in the piston top. The Jahns pistons were offered for a 4.125-inch bore (standard) and a 4.250-inch bore (1/8 inch larger). The pistons came with a Grant Piston Rings 1871 (standard bore) cast-iron piston ring set.

The piston top of this Jahns 1116H cast-aluminum piston has been milled to reduce the compression ratio from 12.0:1 to 11.0:1. The connecting rod is a GM 3774771 forged-steel I-beam model.

A piston ring installation tool is used to expand a piston ring to install it on a piston without scratching the piston or breaking the piston ring.

To check the end gap of the piston rings, place a piston ring approximately 1 inch from the top of the cylinder in which it is going to be used. The piston ring must be perfectly square in the cylinder bore to obtain an accurate measurement. Use a feeler gauge to determine the end gap of the piston ring. If

This is a Sealed Power MT-135 rotary piston ring filing tool. This type of tool should be used to obtain the correct end gap of piston rings.

this end gap is in accordance with the piston ring manufacturer's end gap specifications, then check all the piston rings for each cylinder. Chevrolet specified the piston ring end gap in the 348-ci engines to be 0.015 inch for the two compression rings and the oil ring. Always adhere to the instructions of the piston ring manufacturer for piston ring end gap.

If the piston ring end gap is not wide enough, file the ends of the piston rings with a rotary piston ring filing tool until you obtain the correct end gap. Use the Sealed Power MT-135 rotary piston ring filing tool, or similar equipment, to ensure the ends of the piston rings remain parallel to each other.

After all the piston rings are correctly gapped, install them on the pistons using a piston ring installation tool. This tool expands the piston rings enough to install them on the pistons without scratching or gouging the aluminum pistons or breaking the piston rings. Prior to installing the piston assemblies in the engine block, individually turn each piston ring on the pistons within the piston ring manufacturer's recommended arc. In other words, position each of the three piston rings on a piston with the end gap of each ring in a different location, known as "preferred ring gap location". Install the piston assemblies in the engine block using a piston ring compressor. This tool evenly compresses the piston rings around the piston, thus permitting the easy installation of the assemblies in the cylinder bores.

Check the valve-to-piston clearance prior to the final assembly of the engine. Install the camshaft bearings and camshaft, the crankshaft main bearings and crankshaft, the piston (without the piston rings) and connecting rod with bearings for the No. 1 cylinder, and the valve lifters for the No. 1 cylinder.

This piston ring compressor is used to compress the piston rings evenly around a piston prior to the installation in the cylinder bore.

Place some putty on the crown of the No. 1 piston, and then install a cylinder head gasket and a cylinder head partially assembled with the No. 1 intake and exhaust valves.

Install four cylinder head bolts (one for each corner) and tighten them snugly. Install the pushrods and rocker arms for the No. 1 cylinder, and adjust the valve lash. Turn the crankshaft in the normal direction of rotation at least two full turns. Remove the cylinder head, and measure the thickness of the valve depressions in the putty. The minimum intake-valve-to-piston clearance should be 0.100 inch, and the minimum exhaust-valve-to-piston clearance should be 0.125 inch, when using forged steel connecting rods.

ENGINE BALANCING

One of the most important steps in building a reliable engine is the balancing of the rotating assembly. Proper engine balancing must be carried out by a high-performance machine shop.

The pistons are weighed on a Toledo digital scale, or similar instrument, to locate the lightest piston. The other seven pistons are lightened to that weight by milling material off the bottom of the wrist pin boss.

The connecting rods are weighed on a Stewart-Warner 329738 connecting rod balancer, or similar instrument, to find the lightest connecting rod. The rest of the connecting rods are lightened to that weight by using a belt sander to remove material from the top of the wrist pin end, the sides of the crankshaft end and connecting rod cap, or the bottom of the connecting rod cap. A connecting rod is balanced by placing the crankshaft end on the balancing machine while the wrist pin end is suspended; this is called a rotating balance. Or a connecting rod can be balanced by placing the wrist pin end on the balancing machine while the crankshaft end is suspended. This is called a reciprocating balance.

The crankshaft is balanced using a Hines Industries digital balancer, or similar machine. The pistons, wrist pins, wrist pin locks, piston rings, connecting rod bearings, connecting rods, connecting rod bolts, and even an estimated amount of lubri-

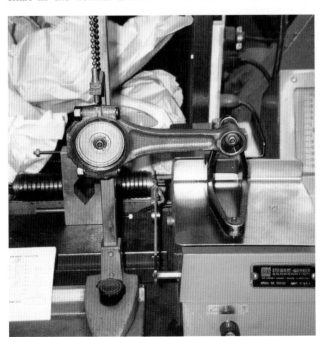

This GM 3774771 connecting rod is undergoing a reciprocating balance on a Stewart-Warner 329738 connecting rod balancer.

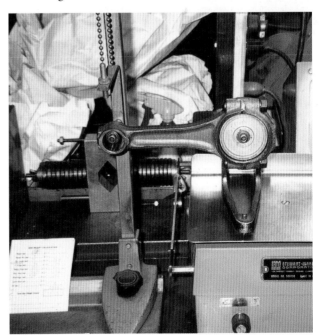

This GM 3774771 connecting rod is undergoing a rotating balance on a Stewart-Warner 329738 rod balancer.

This Eagle Specialty Products 103023400 cast-steel crankshaft (for a small-block Ford 302-ci V-8) is being balanced on a Hines Industries digital balancer. Bob weights are attached to the connecting rod journals.

cating oil is calculated, and a final weight is tallied up. This exact amount of weight, in the form of an attachable bob weight, is bolted to each crankshaft journal. The crankshaft is then spun on the balancing machine. In order to compensate for any imbalance, weight is removed by drilling material from the bottom of the crankshaft counterweights, or weight is added by drilling holes in the sides of the crankshaft counterweights and installing heavy metal (Mallory metal).

The following is how to calculate the bob weight:

Piston weight (each)	x 1 = ___	grams
Wrist pin (each)	x 1 = ___	grams
Wrist pin locks (pair/piston)	x 1 = ___	grams
Piston rings (set/piston)	x 1 = ___	grams
Reciprocating connecting rod (each)	x 1 = ___	grams
Rotating connecting rod (each)	x 2 = ___	grams
Connecting rod bearings (set/rod)	x 2 = ___	grams
Connecting rod bolts (pair)	x 2 = ___	grams
Oil (estimated)	x 1 = ___	grams
	*Total bob weight: ___	grams

A special thank you to Bud Child at High Performance Engines for providing me with this valuable engine balancing information.

If using a manual (standard) transmission, deliver the crankshaft pulley, flywheel, clutch disc, and pressure plate to the machine shop for balancing. If installing an automatic transmission, deliver the crankshaft pulley and flexplate to the machine shop for balancing. A complete V-8 engine balance will eliminate any internal vibration and ensure long bearing life, provided you change the oil and oil filter on a regular basis. It will cost approximately $200 for a complete V-8 engine balance.

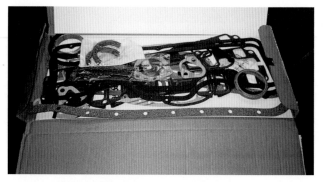

This is the Fel-Pro FS8007PT-3 complete gasket set for Chevrolet 348-ci V-8 engines.

GASKETS
The Fel-Pro FS8007PT-3 complete gasket set for the Chevrolet 348-ci V-8 engines is available at most automotive supply stores, and the current retail price is $65.

B. CONNECTING RODS AND PISTON SUMMARY
- GM 3774771 forged-steel, heat-treated I-beam connecting rods, pressed-in wrist pin. Connecting rod length, 6.135 inches (center to center); connecting rod weight: 789 grams each. Connecting rod ratio: 1.89 (with 3.25-inch stroke crankshaft). **$40**
- Connecting rods shot peened, Magnafluxed, aligned, resized, pin fitted, and balanced. New ARP 134-6403 Wave Loc connecting rod bolts, ARP2000 alloy, 220,000 psi, 3/8 inch in diameter, installed. **$320**
- New Clevite 77 CB-743P-10 connecting rod bearings, 0.010 inch oversize, installed allowing for 0.002-inch connecting rod clearance and 0.012-inch side clearance per pair of connecting rods. Connecting rod bolts torqued to 45 ft-lbs using Molykote and allowing for 0.006-inch stretch. **$50**
- New Egge Parts House L2049.8-030 cast-aluminum slipper-skirt pistons, 0.030 inch oversize, gabled-roof design, 9.5:1 compression ratio. Piston weight: 831 grams each. Pressed-in, heat-treated, and case-hardened 4340 chrome-moly steel straight-wall wrist pins. Wrist pin length, 3.250 inches; wrist pin diameter, 0.990 inch; wrist pin weight, 174 grams. Piston groove width: top compression ring, 5/64 inch; second compression ring, 5/64 inch; oil ring, 3/16 inch. New Sealed Power (Federal-Mogul) E-243K-30 moly top-ring piston ring set, 0.030 inch oversize, installed within manufacturer's recommended arc. Top compression ring gap, 0.015 inch; second compression ring gap, 0.015 inch; oil ring gap, 0.015 inch. New displacement: 352.5 ci (5.8 liters). **$329.41**
- Complete V-8 engine balance. New Fel-Pro FS8007PT-3 complete gasket set installed. **$265**

- Connecting Rods and Pistons Total: $1,004.41

CHAPTER 4
LUBRICATION SYSTEM

A. LUBRICATION SYSTEM
OIL PUMP AND PICKUP SCREEN

The engineers at General Motors did a superb job of designing the oiling system for the OHV Chevrolet V-8 engines; thus it is the one system that should not be modified in a street performance engine. The GM 3755420 standard-volume oil pump, with the GM 3754942 oil pump pickup screen attached, was installed in the Chevrolet 348-ci V-8 engines, and it delivered 35-psi oil pressure at 2,000 rpm. Always install a new oil pump—never a used one—when assembling an engine.

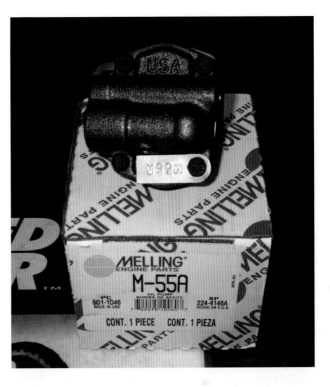

This is a Melling M55A standard-volume oil pump with a higher oil pressure (60 to 70 psi) spring installed. This oil pump is for the small-block Chevrolet V-8 engine, although it can be used in the Chevrolet 348-ci V-8 engine.

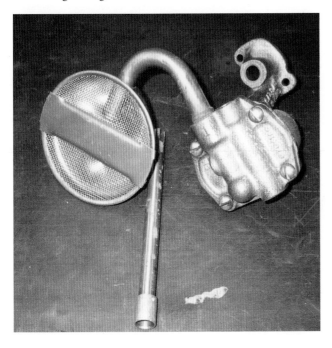

Here is the GM 3755420 standard-volume oil pump, with the attached 3754942 oil pump pickup screen, and the 3740477 oil pump driveshaft used in Chevrolet 348-ci V-8 engines.

The Melling M55 standard-volume oil pump, used in the small-block Chevrolet V-8 engines, will fit a Chevrolet 348-ci V-8 engine. You can install the Melling M55HV high-volume oil pump; however, this pump is unnecessary for anything other than a wild street performance engine or race engine. A high-volume oil pump only provides a greater volume of oil, not an increase in oil pressure. The Melling M55A oil pump is a standard-volume oil pump, except it has a higher oil pressure spring, similar to the GM 3848907 high-pressure (60–70 psi) oil pump with the GM 3848911 spring (color-coded white)

used in the early small-block Corvette LT-1 and Camaro Z-28 engines. The current retail price for a Melling M55, M55HV, or M55A oil pump is $20.

When using a new oil pump in a street performance engine, mill or ground pressure balance grooves into the oil pump body and the underside of the top; also check it for end clearance. The recommended end clearance (between the top of the gears and the top of the oil pump body) is 0.00025 inch. If there is excessive end clearance, sand the top of the oil pump body on top of a thick piece of glass. If there is inadequate end clearance, sand the tops of the oil pump gears on top of a thick piece of glass.

The GM 3754942 oil pump pickup screen used in the Chevrolet 348-ci V-8 engine was also used in the 1955–1957 Corvettes and Chevrolet passenger cars with the small-block 265-ci and 283-ci V-8 engines. Tack weld the oil pump pickup screen to the oil pump body to prevent the oil pump pickup screen from coming loose.

The distance from the bottom of the oil pump pickup screen to the bottom of the oil pan should be 1/2 to 3/4 inch. Check the clearance by installing the oil pump with the attached pickup screen on the rear main bearing cap, laying the oil pan gaskets in position, and placing some putty on the oil pump pickup screen. Then lay the oil pan in position on the engine block and press down firmly on it. Remove the oil pan, and measure the thickness of the compressed putty. If the clearance is not correct, adjust the oil pump pickup screen until you obtain the correct clearance. Always match the oil pump pickup screen to the oil pan.

Check the oil pump passage from the rear main bearing cap into the engine block to ensure it is perfectly aligned. If it is not, use a high-speed grinder with a carbide bit to correct the situation. Attach the oil pump to the rear main bearing cap with the GM 3754998 oil pump bolt. If this bolt is damaged or missing, use the ARP 230-7001, the Manley Performance

Parts 42339, or the Milodon 17050 oil pump stud kits (for the small-block Chevrolet V-8 engines). These stud kits are manufactured using heat-treated 8740 steel and are available at your local speed-parts store. The current retail price for one is $6.

The GM 3740477 oil pump driveshaft was installed in the Chevrolet 348-ci V-8 engines. This driveshaft has a steel sleeve (for attaching to the oil pump) and is 6.693 inches long (including the steel sleeve). Do not use the nylon sleeve included with most aftermarket oil pumps. If the stock oil pump driveshaft is damaged or missing, install the ARP 135-7901 oil pump driveshaft (for the big-block Chevrolet V-8 engines). This driveshaft is 6.702 inches long (including the steel sleeve) and is manufactured using heat-treated chrome-moly steel rated at 170,000 psi. Although the ARP 135-7901 oil pump driveshaft is 0.009 inch longer than the GM 3877672 oil pump driveshaft, there should not be any negative effect. The ARP 135-7901 oil pump driveshaft is available at most high-performance parts stores for the current retail price of $14.

OIL PAN

The GM 3798527 stamped-steel oil pan was installed on the Chevrolet 348-ci V-8 engines, and it is internally baffled with a rear sump. This oil pan has a 4-quart capacity, although 5 quarts of oil are used when including the canister-type oil filter. I am not aware of any aftermarket oil pan currently available for the 348-ci engines. The oil pan will most likely be covered in grease and possibly even rusty. If this is the case, hot tank the oil pan, remove any dents, and send it out to be Redi-Stripped. The result will be an oil pan that is exceptionally clean and will look like new when it is painted.

For the engine described here, the GM 3758390 dipstick tube and GM 3740414 dipstick were installed in the left side of the oil pan. Also, the GM 3711724 oil filler tube and GM 6419440 oil filler tube/crankcase breather cap were installed in the front of the intake manifold above the breather port in the front of the engine block.

WINDAGE TRAY

The Chevrolet 348-ci V-8 engines were not factory equipped with a windage tray. Installing a windage tray will aid with oil control, reduce aeration of the oil, and minimize oil slosh. The GM 3797749 windage tray, designed for the 400- and 425-horsepower Chevrolet 409-ci V-8 engines, can be fitted to the Chevrolet 348-ci V-8 engine. GM 3815534 windage tray studs, four in total, are required for installation. The current retail price for the GM 3797749 windage tray is $15, and the four GM 3815534 windage tray studs are $30.

OIL FILTER

The Chevrolet 348-ci V-8 engines incorporated a full-flow oil system. The GM 5573837 oil filter adapter, with the GM 5574278 oil filter canister, were installed as part of that system. The oil filter canister must be removed to change the oil

The internal baffle in the GM 3798527 stamped-steel oil pan for Chevrolet 348-ci V-8 engines is shown here.

Here are the AC-Delco PF-141 oil filter, GM 5574278 oil filter canister, and GM 5573837 oil filter adapter used with Chevrolet 348-ci V-8 engines.

filter, which is an AC-Delco PF-141. Unless the engine is for a numbers-matching vehicle, the Trans-Dapt 1024 oil filter adapter converts the canister-type oil filter to the post-1967 spin-on oil filter, such as the Fram PH-8A. The current retail price for the Trans-Dapt 1024 oil filter adapter is $10.

B. LUBRICATION SYSTEM SUMMARY

• New Melling M55A standard-volume oil pump with high-pressure spring and pressure balance grooves, installed with GM 3754942 oil pump pickup screen. Oil pump pickup screen tack welded to oil pump body. Oil pump end clearance: 0.00025 inch. Oil pump cover gasket installed using silicone sealant, and oil pump cover bolts torqued to 80 in-lbs using Loctite. GM 3877672 oil pump driveshaft, 6.693 inches long (including steel sleeve), installed. GM 3754998 oil pump bolt installed using Loctite and torqued to 65 ft-lbs. **$123.54**

• GM 3798527 stamped-steel oil pan, 4-quart capacity, internally baffled, installed with oil pan bolts torqued to 15 ft-lbs using Loctite. Oil pan gaskets and rear oil seals installed using silicone sealant. GM 3758390 dipstick tube and GM 3740414 dipstick installed. Oil pan, dipstick tube, and dipstick painted with PPG 60914 orange high-gloss polyurethane. GM 5573837 oil filter adapter installed with bolts torqued to 20 ft-lbs using Loctite. Oil filter adapter gasket installed using silicone sealant. GM 5574278 oil filter canister with new GM 5573980 O-ring installed with new AC-Delco PF-141 oil filter. Engine lubricated with 5-quart Pennzoil HD-30 weight motor oil. **$291.93**

• Lubrication System Total: $415.47

CHAPTER 5
CAMSHAFT AND CYLINDER HEADS

A. CAMSHAFT AND CYLINDER HEADS
CAMSHAFT BEARINGS

The camshaft bearings used in the Chevrolet 348-ci V-8 engines are the same dimensions as those in the small-block Chevrolet V-8 engines. However, there are some differences. The oil holes in the 348-ci camshaft bearings are larger, and the rear camshaft bearing has an oiling groove located around the middle of the inside diameter, similar to the rear camshaft bearing in the big-block Chevrolet 396-ci, 409-ci, and the early 427-ci V-8 engines. The camshafts in all these engines have a groove around the middle of the rear journal. The purpose of the groove in the rear camshaft bearing and the rear camshaft journal is to provide valve lifter oiling.

The Clevite 77 SH-398S and the Federal-Mogul 1177M camshaft bearings are available for the Chevrolet 348-ci V-8 engine, and the current retail price for a set is $50.

The camshaft bearings should be removed using a camshaft bearing installation tool, and they must be installed using this tool in order to avoid damage to the camshaft bearing housings and the camshaft bearings. Camshaft bearings installation is best left to an engine building shop.

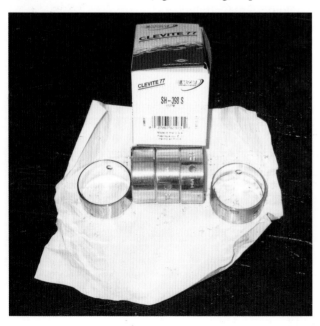

A set of Clevite 77 SH-398S camshaft bearings for the Chevrolet 348-ci V-8 engines is shown here. The oiling groove around the middle of the rear bearing on the right is barely visible.

CAMSHAFT

The camshaft is quite possibly the single most important part, and certainly the heart, of an engine. Camshaft advice is probably the cheapest commodity available today, with every "expert" offering it. However, the camshaft manufacturers employ the people who know most about camshafts, and there are some excellent companies located in North America. Every engine builder has a preference for a certain camshaft grinder, which is fine, provided that the correct camshaft is selected for an engine.

A basic understanding of camshaft technology is helpful, even for a novice engine builder. I will give a brief explanation of a few of the most common terms used when referring to camshafts. If you would like a more in-depth explanation, look in the catalogs most camshaft companies distribute, for they have a section on camshaft terminology and the mathematics associated with camshafts.

ADVERTISED DURATION

Duration is the number of crankshaft degrees the intake and exhaust valves are held open. The advertised duration of a camshaft could mean anything. When camshaft manufacturers specify that a camshaft has a duration of so many degrees, they do not specify at which point of tappet (camshaft lifter) lift that duration is calculated. This could be 0.004-inch lift, 0.006-inch lift, 0.007-inch lift, 0.010-inch lift, 0.020-inch lift, or any lift imaginable. It seems as though none of the camshaft manufacturers use a similar method to calculate the duration, making it nearly impossible to compare different camshafts from different companies.

DURATION AT 0.050-INCH LIFT

A number of years ago, Harvey J. Crane Jr. (the founder of Crane Cams) started to measure the duration at 0.050 inch of tappet (camshaft lifter) lift. This is now the standard to use when comparing camshafts.

VALVE LIFT

This is the maximum net lift of the valve, expressed in decimals of an inch. The net valve lift in an OHV engine is calculated by multiplying the camshaft lobe lift by the rocker arm ratio, and then subtracting the valve lash if solid (mechanical) lifters (tappets) are used. There is no valve lash when hydraulic lifters (tappets) are used.

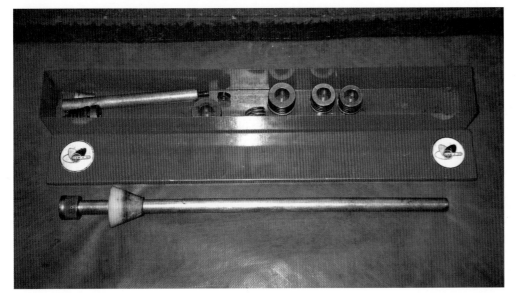

This is a Cam-A-Go camshaft bearing installation tool. Camshaft bearings should be removed and installed with this type of tool.

OVERLAP

Overlap is defined as the number of crankshaft degrees the intake and exhaust valves are held open together. A crankshaft with a lot of overlap creates a rough idle, less fuel economy, higher emissions, and is not recommended for street performance use.

LOBE SEPARATION ANGLE

The lobe separation angle (also known as "lobe centerline angle") is the angle between the intake and exhaust lobes at the maximum lift point. A large lobe separation angle (110–118 degrees) will result in a smoother idle and greater power range. A smaller lobe separation angle (104–110 degrees) will result in a rougher idle and a narrower power range. The engines described in this book will be driven on the street, which dictates that they must have a camshaft with a large lobe separation angle. This will ensure the engine idles properly and has vacuum at idle.

Only a new camshaft should be installed in a street performance engine. If installing a used camshaft, you must have the valve lifters (tappets) that were used with that camshaft matched exactly to the lobes of the camshaft, the same way they were installed in the engine. If the valve lifters are mixed up, the camshaft will be destroyed when the engine is started. Buying a used camshaft is a real gamble. The camshaft might have been reground, or one or more of the lobes might have gone flat. You can take a used camshaft to a reputable camshaft company for inspection, but why bother? New camshafts are not expensive, and you know exactly what you are buying. Always install a new camshaft with new valve lifters. If a new camshaft is installed with used valve lifters or new valve lifters are installed with a used camshaft, camshaft failure is guaranteed.

The GM 3744901 hydraulic lifter camshaft was installed as standard in the Chevrolet 348-ci V-8 engines with a 9.5:1 compression ratio. It has an advertised duration of 266

Here is a thoroughly tired GM 3744901 hydraulic lifter camshaft used in the Chevrolet 348-ci V-8 engines with a 9.5:1 compression ratio. Notice the groove around the rear camshaft journal, which provides valve lifter oiling.

degrees intake and 274 degrees exhaust. The lobe separation angle is 113 degrees, and the net valve lift is 0.3987 inch for the intake and exhaust. The valve lash is zero. General Motors did not provide the camshaft timing information for duration at 0.050-inch lift for this camshaft or the next two that will be mentioned.

Chevrolet introduced the Police Cruiser 348-ci V-8 engine in April 1958 as an option. The engine came equipped with the GM 3755946 solid (mechanical) lifter camshaft and an 11.0:1 compression ratio. This camshaft has an advertised duration of 287 degrees intake and exhaust, a lobe separation angle of 111 degrees, and the valve lift is 0.4058 inch intake and 0.4120 inch exhaust. The valve lash is 0.012 inch intake and 0.018 inch exhaust. The Police Cruiser camshaft was, and still is, known also as the 348 Duntov camshaft (named after Zora Arkus-Duntov), due to the similarity in the timing events with the GM 3736097 solid (mechanical) lifter camshaft for the small-block Corvette 283-ci V-8 engines. The GM 3764664 high-lift solid (mechanical) lifter camshaft was available as an option from 1959 to 1961 for the Chevrolet 348-ci V-8 engines with an 11.0:1 compression ratio. This camshaft had an advertised duration of 287 degrees intake and exhaust, a lobe separation angle of 117 degrees, and the valve lift was 0.4076 inch intake and 0.4139 inch exhaust. The valve lash was 0.012 inch intake and 0.018 inch exhaust.

The three camshafts listed above are no longer available from General Motors. A stock replacement hydraulic lifter camshaft for the base Chevrolet 348-ci V-8 engines with a 9.5:1 compression ratio is the Sealed Power (Federal-Mogul) CS-171 camshaft. The advertised duration is 272 degrees intake and 280 degrees exhaust; the duration at 0.050-inch lift is 190 degrees intake and 198 degrees exhaust; the lobe separation angle is 112 degrees; and the net valve lift is 0.400 inch

intake and 0.412 inch exhaust. The valve lash is zero. This camshaft is apparently better suited for a truck than a passenger car, as the torque peaks at 3,000 rpm and the horsepower peaks at 4,000 rpm. The current retail price for this camshaft is $150, and it is the one installed in the engine described here.

In the late 1950s, many companies manufactured camshafts for the Chevrolet 348-ci V-8 engines: W. G. "Racer" Brown, Crower Cams & Equipment, Engle Racing Cams, Harman & Collins, Chet Herbert, Howard's Racing Cams, Iskenderian Racing Cams, (Frank) McGurk Engineering, Potvin Auto Equipment Company, Schneider Racing Cams, Clay Smith Racing Cams, and Weber Cam Grinding Company. Cast alloy billet, solid roller lifter camshafts, and even a "cheater" camshaft (Weber HC-1100 hydraulic lifter camshaft) were available. There are very few sources today for an off-the-shelf Chevrolet 348-ci V-8 camshaft.

Crane Cams (see Resources) has been manufacturing camshafts for decades and is a well-respected company. The Crane Cams 150291, grind H-218/300-2S-12, is a hydraulic lifter camshaft with an advertised duration of 288 degrees intake and 300 degrees exhaust. The duration at 0.050-inch lift is 218 degrees intake and 230 degrees exhaust, the lobe separation angle is 112 degrees, and the net valve lift is 0.525 inch intake and 0.543 inch exhaust. The valve lash is zero. This camshaft has 0.1263 inch more intake lift and 0.1443 inch more exhaust lift than the GM 3744901 hydraulic lifter camshaft. This additional valve lift should help the engine breathe a lot better; however, make certain to check the valve-to-piston clearance. The power range is 2,200–5,000 rpm, and the current retail price for the Crane Cams 150291 hydraulic lifter camshaft is $160. If the Crane Cams 150291 hydraulic lifter camshaft had been installed in the engine being described, the estimated output would have been 297 horsepower at 5,000 rpm and 350 ft-lbs, and torque at 3,500

This is the Sealed Power (Federal-Mogul) CS-171 hydraulic lifter camshaft for Chevrolet 348-ci V-8 engines. The valve lifters are a new old stock (NOS) set of GM 5232720 hydraulic lifters.

ft-lbs. The torque curve is almost straight from 2,000 to 4,000 rpm, indicating this is a good choice of camshaft for the Chevrolet 348-ci V-8 engines.

The Crane Cams 150411, grind 3755946, blueprinted replacement factory muscle car solid (mechanical) lifter camshaft has an advertised duration of 256 degrees intake and 262 degrees exhaust. The duration at 0.050-inch lift is 222 degrees intake and 225 degrees exhaust, the lobe separation angle is 112 degrees, and the net valve lift is 0.3905 inch intake and 0.3941 inch exhaust. The valve lash (hot) is 0.012 inch intake and 0.018 inch exhaust. This camshaft is a direct replacement for the GM 3755946 Police Cruiser camshaft, and the power range is 2,500–5,500 rpm. The current retail price for the Crane Cams 150411 solid (mechanical) lifter camshaft is $160. If the Crane Cams 150411 solid lifter camshaft had been installed in the engine being described, the estimated output would have been 302 horsepower at 5,000 rpm and 377 ft-lbs torque at 3,500 rpm. The torque curve is almost straight from 2,000 to 4,000 rpm, indicating this is another good choice of camshaft for the Chevrolet 348-ci V-8 engine.

Competition Cams (see Resources) is another well-known camshaft manufacturer. It has new solid (mechanical) or hydraulic flat tappet (valve lifter) camshaft cores and new steel billet solid (mechanical) roller lifter camshaft cores in stock for the 348-ci engines. The Competition Cams 48-000-5 flat tappet camshaft cores or the 48-000-9 steel billet roller camshaft cores can be custom ground according to the customer's requirements, provided the customer supplies all the pertinent information, such as: the general use and a full description of the vehicle; the bore and stroke; type of pistons; size of valves; combustion chamber volume; compression ratio; type of intake manifold; and carburetor cfm. There is little difference in price between a custom-ground and an off-the-shelf camshaft.

DEGREE CAMSHAFT

The tools required to degree a camshaft are: a 9-inch-diameter degree wheel, 1-inch travel dial indicator with a long stem, magnetic adjustable dial indicator stand, and a heavy-gauge wire pointer (such as coat hanger material). You must install the crankshaft, connecting rods and piston assemblies, camshaft, and intake and exhaust valve lifters for the No. 1 cylinder to degree the camshaft. The procedure described next is referred to as the "duration at 0.050-inch lift method".

Locate TDC for the No. 1 piston with a dial indicator. Install the degree wheel on the nose of the crankshaft, and attach the wire pointer to the engine block so it is as close as possible to the edge of the degree wheel. With the No. 1 piston at TDC, turn the degree wheel until the pointer is at the zero-degree mark on the wheel. Then securely clamp the degree wheel in position so it cannot move. Turn the crankshaft in one direction until the No. 1 piston reaches TDC; the wire pointer should be at the zero-degree position on the degree wheel. Rotate the crankshaft in the opposite direction until the No. 1 piston reaches TDC; the wire pointer should be at the zero-degree position on the degree wheel. The degree wheel is now perfectly positioned. Remove the dial indicator from the No. 1 piston.

Place the magnetic dial indicator stand on the deck of the engine block above the No. 1 intake valve lifter. Align the dial indicator so it passes through the deck and touches the top of the No. 1 intake valve lifter. The dial indicator must be at the same angle as the intake valve lifter to obtain an accurate reading.

Rotate the crankshaft in the normal direction of rotation until you locate the maximum lift point for No. 1 intake valve lifter. Rotate the crankshaft one revolution past the maximum lift point. The intake valve lifter is now in the center of the base circle. Set the dial indicator to the zero position. Turn the crankshaft until you reach 0.050 inch on the dial indicator. The degree wheel will now show the number of degrees BTC (before top center) for the No. 1 intake valve lifter. Rotate the crankshaft past the maximum lift point for the No. 1 intake valve lifter until the dial indicator again reaches 0.050 inch. The degree wheel will now show the number of degrees ABC (after bottom center) for the No. 1 intake valve lifter.

Remove the dial indicator and stand from the No. 1 intake valve lifter position, and set them up above the No. 1 exhaust valve lifter. Align the dial indicator so it passes through the deck and touches the top of the No. 1 exhaust valve lifter. The dial indicator must be at the same angle as the exhaust valve lifter to obtain an accurate reading.

Rotate the crankshaft in the normal direction of rotation until you locate the maximum lift point for the No. 1 exhaust valve lifter. Rotate the crankshaft one revolution past the maximum lift point. The exhaust valve lifter is now in the center of the base circle. Set the dial indicator to the zero position. Turn the crankshaft until you reach 0.050 inch on the dial indicator. The degree wheel will now show the number of degrees BBC (before bottom center) for the No. 1 exhaust valve lifter. Rotate the crankshaft past the maximum lift point for the No. 1 exhaust valve lifter until the dial indicator again reaches 0.050 inch. The degree wheel will now show the number of degrees ATC (after top center) for the No. 1 exhaust valve lifter.

All of the readings from the degree wheel for BTC, ABC, BBC, and ATC should be in accordance with the manufacturer's camshaft specification card (timing tag). If the camshaft is degreed according to those specifications, you should obtain maximum engine performance.

The second accepted method for degreeing the camshaft is referred to as the "intake centerline method". It requires the same tools used for the previous method.

Locate TDC for the No. 1 piston with the dial indicator. Install the degree wheel on the nose of the crankshaft, and attach the wire pointer to the engine block so it is as close as possible to the edge of the degree wheel. With the No. 1 piston at TDC, turn the degree wheel until the pointer is at the zero-degree mark on the wheel. Then securely clamp the degree wheel in position so it cannot move. Turn the crankshaft in one direction until the No. 1 piston reaches TDC; the wire pointer should be at the zero-degree position on the degree wheel. Rotate the crankshaft in the opposite direction until the No. 1 piston reaches TDC; the wire pointer should be at the zero-degree position on the degree wheel. The degree wheel is now perfectly positioned. Remove the dial indicator from the No. 1 piston.

Place the magnetic dial indicator stand on the deck of the engine block above the No. 1 intake valve lifter. Align the dial indicator so it passes through the deck and touches the top of the No. 1 intake valve lifter. The dial indicator must be at the same angle as the intake valve lifter in order to obtain an accurate reading.

Rotate the crankshaft in the normal direction of rotation until you locate the maximum lift point for the No. 1 intake valve lifter. Set the dial indicator to the zero position. Turn the crankshaft in the opposite direction of rotation back 0.100 inch on the dial indicator. Turn the crankshaft in the normal direction of rotation 0.050 inch on the dial indicator. The reading on the dial indicator is 0.050 inch before maximum intake valve lift. The degree wheel will now show the number of degrees BTC for the No. 1 intake valve lifter. Rotate the crankshaft in the normal direction of rotation past the maximum lift point for the No. 1 intake valve lifter until the dial indicator again reads 0.050 inch. The degree wheel will now show the number of degrees ABC for the No. 1 intake valve lifter.

Add the number of degrees BTC to the number of degrees ABC, and then divide the total by two. The result is the intake centerline. This should be the same as the intake centerline indicated on the manufacturer's camshaft specification card (timing tag). If it is not, adjust the camshaft timing gear until you obtain the correct result.

VALVE LIFTERS

The four basic types of valve lifters (or tappets, or cam followers) used in today's OHV V-8 street performance engines are: hydraulic lifter, solid (mechanical) lifter, hydraulic roller lifter, and solid (mechanical) roller lifter. None of these valve lifters are adjustable; the valve adjustment is carried out at the rocker arm or with the use of adjustable pushrods.

The most common type of valve lifter is the hydraulic lifter, and these were installed in the majority of engines delivered from the factory. This type seldom causes problems, provided the oil and oil filter are changed on a regular basis. The installation of hydraulic lifters avoids re-adjusting the valve lash on a regular basis. The oil in the hydraulic lifters acts as a shock absorber for the valvetrain, and these lifters' only negative aspect is the potential for pump-up at higher engine speeds.

The main benefit of using solid (mechanical) lifters is they stabilize the valvetrain at higher engine speeds. Crower Cams & Equipment offers a Coolface option for the Chevrolet V-8 solid lifters. This option has a 0.024-inch hole drilled in the center of the solid lifter face, which provides oil to lubricate

the camshaft lobe, thus ensuring a longer camshaft and valve lifter life. The Coolface option does not result in a significant loss of oil pressure. The biggest drawback when using solid lifters is they must be periodically adjusted. The solid (mechanical) and hydraulic lifters are referred to as "flat tappet", although the face of the valve lifter is actually convex. This permits the valve lifters to rotate, thereby encouraging even wear on the valve lifter face and the camshaft lobe.

The roller camshaft allows for more aggressive camshaft profiles. Roller lifters encounter less friction and thus wear less than solid lifters or hydraulic lifters. Most roller lifters are linked in pairs with a moveable bar to prevent the valve lifters from rotating. The only downside for roller camshafts is they are expensive. Hydraulic roller lifter camshafts work very well in street performance engines, even blown engines, and their valves do not require periodic adjustment, unlike solid roller lifters. This can be beneficial for some engines, where it is a nearly impossible task to remove the valve covers for valve lash adjustment because the engine compartment lacks space.

Match the camshaft and valve lifters, because one company's camshaft should not be used with another company's valve lifters. In most instances, this practice would void the camshaft manufacturer's warranty.

The GM 5232720 (old 5232670) hydraulic lifters are 2.005 inches long overall, 0.842 inch in diameter, weigh 98 grams each, and were installed by the factory with the GM 3744901 camshaft. When properly preloaded, they will operate at 7,000 rpm and were the same lifters used in the earlier small- and big-block Chevrolet V-8 engines. The GM 5231450 hydraulic lifters are available from Chevrolet dealers at a current retail price of $60 for a set of 16.

This is a GM 5262395 inertia-flapper (piddle valve) solid (mechanical) lifter used in small- and big-block Chevrolet V-8 engines.

These Iskenderian Racing Cams lightweight aluminum bars are part of the Chevrolet 348-ci V-8 engine's 240 Rev Kit. This is a racing item used to stabilize a roller lifter valvetrain when operating at extremely high rpm.

The Crane Cams 99277-16 anti-pump-up hydraulic lifters are used with the Crane Cams 150291, grind H-218/300-2S-12, camshaft. A stronger retainer ring is used in anti-pump-up hydraulic lifters. The Crane Cams 99277-16 have a maximum rpm range of 6,500–7,000, and the retail price for a set of 16 is $90.

The GM 5231585 solid (mechanical) lifters, also known as the "edge orifice valve lifters", were installed by the factory with the GM 3755946 and GM 3764664 camshafts. They restrict the overhead oiling to the rocker arms, thus you must make a modification to correct this situation if installing stock rocker arms. There is a wide recess around the middle of this valve lifter body, as well as a lubrication hole in the side of the valve lifter body approximately 1/8 (0.125) inch above the wide recess. Use a high-speed grinder with a carbide bit, and grind a vertical groove in the valve lifter body downward from the lubrication hole to the wide recess. The vertical groove should be approximately 1/16 (0.0625) inch wide and 1/32 (0.03125) inch deep. Do not perform this operation if roller rocker arms are going to be installed.

PUSHRODS

The GM 3755545 intake pushrods are 8.779 inches long overall, 5/16 inch in diameter, and weigh 53 grams each. The GM 3755543 exhaust pushrods are 9.121 inches long overall, 5/16 inch in diameter, and weigh 53 grams each. The GM 3755545 and GM 3755543 pushrods were used with the GM 3744901 hydraulic lifter camshaft, although they are no longer available from General Motors. (Photo: 5-20).

Federal-Mogul offers stock-style replacement pushrods for the 348-ci engines. The Federal-Mogul RP-3102 intake pushrods are 8.788 inches long overall, 5/16 inch in diameter, weigh 55 grams each, and were installed in the engine described here. The Federal-Mogul RP-3028 exhaust pushrods are 9.142 inches long overall, 5/16 inch in diameter, and weigh 56 grams each. The current retail price for a set of either the Federal-Mogul RP-3102 or RP-3028 pushrods is $45.

You should always install good quality pushrods in a street performance engine. Crower Cams & Equipment offers 5/16-inch- and 3/8-inch-diameter pushrods in a wide variety of lengths and with a wall thickness of 0.080 inch. These pushrods are manufactured using 4130 seamless chrome-moly steel, have

The Federal-Mogul RP-3102 intake pushrods on the left and the RP-3028 exhaust pushrods on the right are stock-style replacements for Chevrolet 348-ci V-8 engines.

This picture shows the GM 3704214 camshaft sprocket and Morse chain, which the factory installed in Chevrolet 348-ci V-8 engines.

a black oxide finish, and are heat treated to a surface hardness of 60RC. The current retail price for a set of 16 is $130.

TIMING CHAINS

Never install a used timing chain set when rebuilding an engine. The stock-type Morse timing chains will stretch over a period of time, resulting in erratic timing. This will eventually lead to internal engine damage and possibly the demise of the engine. The GM 3704214 camshaft sprocket with the Morse timing chain and crankshaft sprocket are no longer available from General Motors.

A timing chain set for a Chevrolet 348-ci V-8 engine can be created by using a GM 340236 camshaft sprocket, GM 3896959 crankshaft sprocket, and a Cloyes C494 Morse timing chain. The camshaft and crankshaft sprockets are for the earlier small-block Chevrolet V-8 engines. This setup was installed in the engine described here and costs about $50.

A better solution is to use a double-roller timing chain set. The Cloyes 93101 True Roller timing chain set, with a three-keyway crankshaft sprocket (for advancing or retarding the camshaft timing) is available for the Chevrolet 348-ci V-8 engine. The current retail price is $95, and Cloyes products are available at most automotive stores. I am not aware of any company that is currently manufacturing a gear drive for the Chevrolet 348-ci V-8 engine. Install a Manley Performance Parts (see Resources) 42114 camshaft gear-locking plate kit (with bolts) to ensure the camshaft gear remains securely in

The Manley Performance Parts 42114 camshaft gear locking plate kit and 42146 aluminum camshaft thrust button are pictured here.

place. Install the bolts using Loctite, and torque them to 20 ft-lbs. The installation of the Manley Performance Parts 42146 aluminum camshaft thrust button prevents the camshaft from walking, thus creating erratic timing. The thrust button fits on the end of the camshaft and rotates against the inside of the timing gear cover.

The GM 3736357 timing gear cover is used on the Chevrolet 348-ci V-8 engines. Glass bead the timing gear cover, and paint the inside with Glyptal G-1228A medium-gray gloss enamel. Position the timing tab on the GM 3736357 timing gear cover for use with a 6 1/4-inch-o.d. harmonic balancer. Years ago, the Weiand 7129 and Moon Equipment Company 187 die-cast finned aluminum timing gear covers were available. A small-block Chevrolet V-8 one-piece oil seal will fit the GM 3736357 timing gear cover. Unless the engine is for a numbers-matching car, install the timing gear cover using polished stainless-steel bolts, lock-washers, and AN flat washers.

CYLINDER HEADS

All Chevrolet 348-ci V-8 engines were equipped with cast-iron cylinder heads, which had a very unusual shape resembling a W. Each of these cylinder heads weighed 53 pounds (bare). The following is a list of the Chevrolet 348-ci V-8 cylinder head casting numbers:

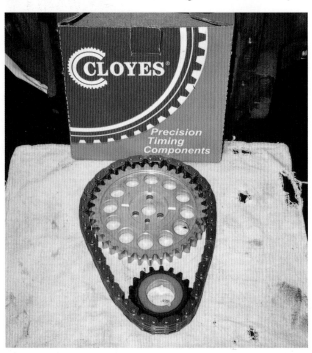

This stock-style timing chain set for a Chevrolet 348-ci V-8 engine consists of a GM 340236 camshaft sprocket, 3896959 crankshaft sprocket, and Cloyes C494 Morse timing chain. The camshaft and crankshaft sprockets are for the earlier small-block Chevrolet V-8 engines.

3732791: 1958–1960
3758379: 1959–1961
3759256: 1958
3759332: 1958–1960
3764702: 1960
3767738: 1959–1961
3781147: 1960–1961
3795586: 1961

These are the casting numbers I am aware of, but there may well be others. These cylinder heads have a very small combustion chamber volume, unlike the small-block Chevrolet 265-ci, 283-ci, 327-ci, 350-ci, 400-ci, and big-block Chevrolet 396-ci, 427-ci, and 454-ci cylinder heads. The 348-ci V-8 cylinder heads from 1958 to 1960 all had a 15-cc combustion chamber volume and were used with both the 9.5:1 and 11.0:1 compression ratio engines. The late 1960 and 1961 Chevrolet 348-ci V-8 cylinder heads with a 10.3-cc combustion chamber volume were used with the 9.5:1 and the 11.25:1 compression ratio engines. The combustion chamber volumes mentioned above do not include the combustion chamber volume of the engine block cylinders, which ranged from 70.4 to 76.3 cc (for each cylinder), depending on the year and RPO number.

The first revision of the Chevrolet 348-ci V-8 cylinder heads by General Motors came in 1959 with the addition of water passage cooling holes for the spark plugs. The cooling holes also had to be in the cylinder head gaskets that would be installed with the first revision cylinder heads. Exactly when in 1959 this revision was introduced is unclear, as the cylinder heads installed on the engine described here had casting dates of 12758 (December 7, 1958) and 12858 (December 8, 1958). This indicates they would have been installed on a 1959 Chevrolet engine, but they did not have the water passage cooling holes for the spark plugs.

The last revision of the 348-ci cylinder heads came in late 1960 with the introduction of the GM 3785085 cylinder heads, casting number 3781147. These cylinder heads were installed on the 1961 Special Turbo-Thrust and Special Super Turbo-Thrust

V-8 engines. Many engine builders believe they are the best 348-ci cylinder heads to use on a street performance engine, due to better port design and larger head diameter valves.

The GM 3759254 cylinder heads, casting number 3732791, have a combustion chamber volume of 15 cc, while the engine block cylinders' combustion chamber volume is 70.4 cc, making

Here is a picture of a GM 3759254 cylinder head, casting number 3732791, that has been surfaced. This is a first-design cylinder head, known by the fact there are no additional water passage cooling holes for the spark plugs. The felt pen circles (near the "V") indicate where these holes would have been located.

This 348-ci first-revision cylinder head, casting number 3758379, has the water passage holes (on each side of the "V") for the spark plugs.

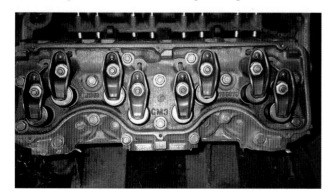

Here is a Chevrolet 348-ci V-8 cylinder head with a casting number of 3758379 and a casting date of J1659 (October 16, 1959). This is a first-revision cylinder head.

This is a pair of GM 3759254 cast-iron cylinder heads, casting number 3732791, for the Chevrolet 348-ci V-8 engine. The area beneath the valve covers has been painted with Glyptal G-1228A medium-gray gloss enamel. Each cylinder head weighs 53 pounds.

This GM 3890462 cylinder head is about to undergo a multi-angle blueprint valve grind on a Serdi 60 automatic centering by spherical and flat air cushion valve seat grinding machine. It is the ultimate in valve grinding.

the total combustion chamber volume 85.4 cc. A pair of these cylinder heads, installed on the engine described here, cost approximately $150 (bare) in good condition.

Used cylinder heads should be completely disassembled, hot tanked, and Magnafluxed. Pressure test older cylinder heads to be certain there are no hidden cracks. The cylinder heads should be Redi-Stripped, which will guarantee they are thoroughly clean. As soon as the cylinder heads return from being Redi-Stripped, mask off the outside with newspaper, place plastic plugs of the appropriate size over the valve guides, and paint the area of the cylinder heads beneath the valve cover with Glyptal G-1228A medium-gray gloss enamel. This paint will assist with oil return, as well as prevent the formation of rust on the surface of the cylinder heads if there is any moisture present. Smoothly ground the outside surface of the cylinder heads using a high-speed grinder with a carbide bit or small sanding discs. Make sure the entire surface is as smooth as possible. If installing cylinder heads in a numbers-matching car, omit this step.

Gasket match the intake and exhaust ports. Use some blue machinist's dye, and spray or brush it around the general area of each intake and exhaust port. Place the intake and exhaust manifold gaskets in position on the cylinder heads. Use a scribe to trace the outline of the gaskets around each port, and then use a high-speed grinder with a carbide bit to grind the excess material from around the scribe marks.

Clean up the intake and exhaust ports with a high-speed grinder with a carbide bit to remove any casting flash or rough spots. Do not go bananas with the grinder, just smooth them out, bearing in mind the ports do not have to be ground to a mirror-like finish.

In the 1950s and 1960s, many people would plane the deck surface of cylinder heads to raise the engine's compression ratio. Do not perform this outdated practice on the 348-ci cylinder heads, because it will probably not raise the compression ratio, due to the small combustion chamber size in the cylinder heads. Instead, have the cylinder heads surfaced by a reputable machine shop to guarantee the mating surface with the engine block is absolutely true. Do not confuse this procedure with having the cylinder heads planed.

No benefit will be derived from making modifications to the combustion chamber area in the 348-ci cylinder heads, other than a Serdi-machined multi-angle blueprint valve grind. Locate a machine shop that has a reputation for performing top-quality Serdi-machined multi-angle blueprint valve grinds. The Serdi 60 automatic centering by spherical and flat air cushion valve seat grinding machine is equipped with a boring bar, which machines the valve seats (or valve seat inserts), rather than the old-style method of grinding the valve seats with stones. The boring bar enables the valve seats to be blended in with the intake and exhaust port runners, which is also referred to as "pocket porting". A Serdi-machined multi-angle blueprint valve grind guarantees all the valves are perfectly centered in the valve seats and are all at the same depth in the valve seats. No other valve grind ensures this. Obviously, you must purchase the valves prior to this operation. A Serdi-machined multi-angle blueprint valve grind, performed on the cylinder heads described here, costs approximately $200.

Many engine builders today strongly advocate the installation of hardened exhaust valve seats for use with unleaded gasoline, while many others do not feel this is mandatory. The material used in the castings for the Chevrolet 348-ci V-8 cylinder heads is very hard (this was observed when the cylinder heads were surfaced), and the valve seats consist of the same material. The valve seats in the newer Chevrolet V-8 cylinder heads are manufactured using a much softer material. Provided the valve seats in 348-ci cylinder heads are in good condition (not cracked or pitted), which was the case with the cylinder heads described here, installing hardened exhaust valve seats is unnecessary. Some things are best left alone!

The pushrod holes in the cylinder heads will have to be opened up slightly if installing 3/8-inch-diameter pushrods. This is another job that should be left to an experienced machine shop to avoid striking water.

VALVES

The GM 3747307 intake valves for the Chevrolet 348-ci V-8 cylinder heads were manufactured using 864-5 high alloy steel with a 1 15/16-inch (1.9375-inch) head diameter, 3/8-inch (0.375-inch) stem diameter, and 5.10-inch overall length; they weighed 127 grams each. The GM 3747308 exhaust valves were manufactured using 21-N steel with a 1 21/32-inch (1.656-inch) head diameter, 3/8-inch (0.375-inch) stem diameter, 5.115-inch overall length, and weighed 124 grams each. These valves were installed in the majority of the 348-ci cylinder heads.

The GM 3785085 cylinder heads, casting number 3781147, installed on the late 1960 and 1961 Special Super Turbo-Thrust engines were fitted with aluminized valves. The GM 3781155 intake valves have a 2.070-inch head diameter and 3/8-inch stem diameter, and are 5.10 inches in overall length. The GM 3781156 exhaust valves have a

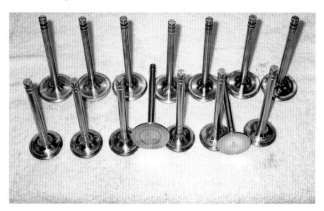

This picture shows a complete set of GM 3747307 intake valves with a 1 15/16-inch (1.9375-inch) head diameter and 3747308 exhaust valves with a 1 21/32-inch (1.656-inch) head diameter for the Chevrolet 348-ci V-8 cylinder heads. All the valves were polished prior to being ground.

1.725-inch head diameter and 3/8-inch stem diameter, and are 5.115 inches long overall. Installing these larger valves in other 348-ci cylinder heads originally equipped with smaller valves will be beneficial only at the top end of the rpm range.

Grind the valves on a Sioux Tools 2075HP Accu-chuck

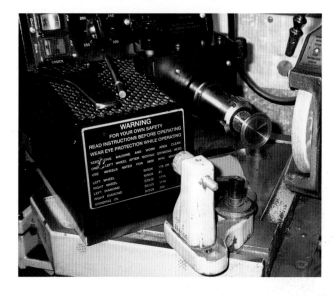

This small-block Ford stainless-steel intake valve is being ground on a Sioux Tools 2075HP accu-chuck valve grinder.

valve grinder, or similar machine, to obtain a quality multi-angle blueprint valve grind, which can consist of up to seven different angles. The most common valve grind consists of three different angles. The valves for the engine described here were in very good condition; as a result, they were reused. Clean and polish the valves in a lathe prior to grinding.

If new valves for the Chevrolet 348-ci V-8 cylinder heads are required, Egge Parts House and Show Cars Automotive (Dr. 409) are reliable sources. Complete sets of 16 are available for the current retail price of $225. Stainless-steel valves are more durable than the stock-type valves. Exhaust valves can be used as intake valves, but intake valves cannot be used as exhaust valves.

VALVE GUIDES, BUSHINGS, AND SEALS

The valve guides form part of the casting in the Chevrolet 348-ci V-8 cylinder heads, which means they are not removable. After almost 50 years of faithful service, the valve guides are usually worn, resulting in excessive valve stem clearance. Chevrolet specified the valve-stem-to-valve-guide clearance to be 0.001 to 0.003 inch for the intake valves and 0.0025 to 0.004 inch for the exhaust valves.

A street performance engine should have bronze valve guide liners installed due to their better endurance quality. The K-Line KL1842STA universal-length, 3/8-inch (0.375-inch) bronze bullet valve guide liners were installed in the cylinder heads described here. If 11/32-inch (0.34375-inch) stem diameter valves will replace the 3/8-inch (0.375-inch) stem diameter valves, the Manley Performance Parts 42158 bronze valve guide sleeves can be installed. The installation of bronze valve guide liners should be left to a reliable machine shop, and the recommended valve stem clearance is 0.0015 to 0.002 inch when using today's unleaded gasoline.

Valve stem seals for oil control should be installed in any

This photograph shows a K-Line KL1842STA bronze-bullet valve guide liner and an Enginetech S2890 Viton-material positive-seal valve stem seal for use with 3/8-inch stem diameter valves.

This picture shows (from the left) the GM 3732891 valve stem oil shield, 3743960 single valve spring with damper, 3729363 valve spring retainer, and 3947880 valve stem locks used with the 3744901 hydraulic lifter camshaft.

street performance engine. The Hastings silver seal Teflon/steel valve stem seals require machining of the valve guides for proper installation. These valve stem seals can be used in street engines, although they are more commonly used in race engines. The valve stem seal of choice for a street performance engine is the Enginetech Viton-material positive-seal valve stem seal. The valve guides do not usually have to be machined to install these valve stem seals. The Enginetech S2890 valve stem seals are for 3/8-inch stem diameter valves, and the Enginetech S2927 valve stem seals are for 11/32-inch stem diameter valves. They cost about $1 each.

VALVE SPRINGS
The GM 3743960 single valve springs with damper were installed in the Chevrolet 348-ci V-8 engines equipped with the GM 3744901 hydraulic lifter camshaft, but they are no longer available from General Motors. The specifications for the GM 3743960 valve spring are:
Installed height:
82 pounds at 1.646 inches valves closed
190 pounds at 1.230 inches valves open
1.345 inches o.d. and 0.700 inch inside diameter (i.d.)
1.930 inches long overall

In early 1959, McGurk Engineering offered high-performance valve spring kits for the Chevrolet 348-ci V-8 engines. These progressive wound-valve springs were installed with 82 pounds valves closed and 220 pounds valves open, and had a smaller outside diameter than the GM 3743960 valve springs. The kit consisted of the valve springs, heavy-duty valve spring retainers, valve stem locks, oil shields, and shims.

The Federal-Mogul VS522 single valve springs with damper are replacement valve springs for the Chevrolet 348-ci V-8

This Federal-Mogul VS522 single valve spring with damper is being measured on a Rinck-McIlwaine 0–500-pound precision valve spring tester at High Performance Engines.

engines equipped with the GM 3744901 hydraulic lifter camshaft, or an aftermarket camshaft with similar timing events. These valve springs were used in the engine described here. The specifications for the Federal-Mogul VS522 valve springs are:
Installed height:
90 pounds at 1.646 inches valves closed
220 pounds at 1.230 inches valves open
1.325 inches o.d. and 0.915 inch i.d.
1.970 inches long overall

The Crane Cams 99838 dual valve springs are compatible with the Crane Cams 150291 hydraulic lifter and 150411 solid (mechanical) lifter camshafts. The current retail price for a set of 16 valve springs is $90, and the specifications are:

Installed height:
110 pounds at 1.688 inches valves closed
320 pounds at 1.208 inches valves open
1.465/1.091 inches o.d. and 0.807 inch i.d.
Coil bind: 0.950 inch
Maximum valve lift: 0.560 inch

The valve spring retainers must be matched to the valve springs, and the valve stem locks must be matched to the valve spring retainers. The camshaft manufacturer's recommendation for these parts should be followed.

The GM 3732891 valve stem oil shields are cup-shape and were fitted over the top of the valve springs, beneath the valve spring retainers, for oil control. Provided the oil shields fit over the top of aftermarket valve springs, it does no harm to install them.

VALVE SPRING RETAINERS AND LOCKS

The GM 3729363 valve spring retainers were used with the GM 3743960 single valve springs with damper but are no longer available from General Motors. The Crane Cams 99948 heat-treated machined-steel valve spring retainers—7 degrees, 3/8-inch valve stem, black oxide finish—are matched to the Crane Cams 99838 dual valve springs. The current retail price for a set of 16 is $57.

The GM 3947880 valve stem locks, 7 degrees, were used in the Chevrolet 348-ci V-8 engines. Aftermarket valve stem locks are available today with a 7-degree or 10-degree style. The standard 7-degree valve stem locks are used in mild street performance or stock engines, and they are manufactured using heat-treated stamped alloy steel, which is a step above the factory valve stem locks. The current retail price for a set of 32 Crane Cams 99042-1 stamped-steel 7-degree valve stem locks is $10.

The machined-steel 7-degree valve stem locks are recommended for use in a street performance engine, as they are stronger than the stamped-steel version. A set of 32 Crane Cams 99098-1 machined-steel 7-degree valve stem locks, installed in the engine described here, costs $32. The 10-degree valve stem locks are manufactured using heat-treated chrome-moly and are twice as strong as the 7-degree valve stem locks. This type of valve stem lock should be used in serious street performance and race engines.

ROCKER ARMS

The Chevrolet 348-ci V-8 cylinder heads had GM 3814692 pressed-in rocker arm studs, which are fine for stock or mild street performance engines. If modifying the engine or installing roller rocker arms, have an experienced machine shop remove the pressed-in rocker arm studs and install screw-in rocker arm studs. Cracking a rocker arm stud boss is a certainty if performed by the less experienced. The ARP 134-7101 high-performance series rocker arm stud kit (for the small-block Chevrolet V-8 engines), 3/8 inch in diameter and rated at 170,000 psi, can be installed in the 348-ci cylinder heads. The current retail price is $30.

This is a set of ARP 134-7101 high-performance series 3/8-inch-diameter rocker arm studs. They are rated at 170,000 psi.

Here is a pair of GM 3732893 stamped-steel rocker arms, 1.75 ratio, for the Chevrolet 348-ci V-8 engines. These two have truly had their day!

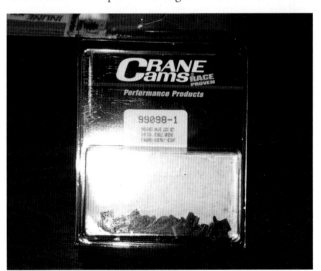

A set of Crane Cams 99098-1 machined-steel 7-degree valve stem locks for 3/8-inch stem diameter valves is pictured here.

This is a pair of Federal-Mogul R-827 replacement stamped-steel rocker arms, 1.75 ratio, complete with rocker arm balls and self-locking nuts, for the Chevrolet 348-ci V-8 engines.

The GM 3732893 stamped-steel, heat-treated rocker arms with the GM 5723552 rocker arm balls and self-locking nuts were installed in the Chevrolet 348-ci V-8 cylinder heads. These rocker arms have a ratio of 1.75, which means they are not interchangeable with the small-block Chevrolet V-8 rocker arms with a 1.50 ratio, or the big-block Chevrolet V-8 rocker arms with a 1.70 ratio. The GM 3732893 rocker arms and GM 5723552 rocker arm balls are no longer available from General Motors.

The Federal-Mogul R-827 stamped-steel, heat-treated rocker arms are replacements for the 348-ci rocker arms and come with the rocker arm balls and self-locking nuts. The current retail price for a set of 16 Federal-Mogul R-827 rocker arms is $72. Poor-quality aftermarket rocker arms will have off-center holes, inaccurate ratios, and poor heat treating. Any aftermarket stamped-steel rocker arms should be carefully inspected prior to installation.

The best design of rocker arms is the roller rocker arms, which can handle large valve lifts and valve spring pressures, as well as reduce friction within the valvetrain. The Crane Cams 15750 Gold Race 1.70 ratio roller rocker arms are designed for a 3/8-inch-diameter rocker arm stud. They are CNC machined from billet-extruded aluminum and have a precision needle bearing fulcrum, an 8620 steel alloy roller

tip, and a slotted body for extra stud clearance. The Crane Cams 15750 roller rocker arms are for the Chevrolet 348-ci V-8 engine, and the current retail price for a set of 16, complete with 4140 chrome-moly steel poly-loc nuts and setscrews, is $400.

The Manley Performance Parts 42107 rocker arm nuts for 3/8-inch-diameter studs are a practical item to install on any stud-mounted rocker arm assembly. The ends of the rocker arm studs must be ground flat to properly lock these poly-loc nuts. There is a setscrew in the end of the nut that jams against the end of the rocker arm stud after the valve lash has been set, thus ensuring the nut will not loosen. You must check the clearance between the tops of the poly-loc nuts and the undersides of the valve covers. The current retail price for a set of 16 is $35.

The Chevrolet 348-ci V-8 cylinder heads were not equipped with pushrod guide plates. If installing 3/8-inch-diameter pushrods, a set of guide plates will have to be modified to fit the 348-ci cylinder heads. Adding pushrod guide plates would also require pushrods with hardened tips. The pushrod guide plates are mounted under the rocker arm studs.

Some engine owners make the classic mistake of assembling their own cylinder heads, even though they lack experience in this area. The assembly of cylinder heads should be left to a professional, like T-Bone, "the wizard of all cylinder heads," to carry out at a premium shop, such as High Performance Engines.

CYLINDER HEAD BOLTS

The GM 3735721 long cylinder head bolts and GM 3735722 short cylinder head bolts were installed in the Chevrolet 348-ci V-8 engines. There are 20 long cylinder head bolts, which are 7/16 inch NC by 3.98 inches long, and there are 16 short cylinder head bolts, which are 7/16 inch NC by 3.32 inches long. Provided they are not badly corroded or have damaged threads, the Chevrolet cylinder head bolts—which are good quality—can be glass beaded and the exterior bolts painted, while the bolts inside the valve covers can be coated with graphite. The cylinder head bolts in the 348-ci engines are torqued to 65 ft-lbs. General Motors no

A set of Crane Cams 15750 Gold Race 1.70-ratio aluminum roller rocker arms for a Chevrolet 348-ci V-8 engine is pictured here.

Here is a complete set of Chevrolet 348-ci V-8 cylinder head bolts. There are 20 of the GM 3735721 long (3.98-inch) bolts and 16 of the GM 3735722 short (3.32-inch) bolts. Guess which ones are installed outside the valve covers.

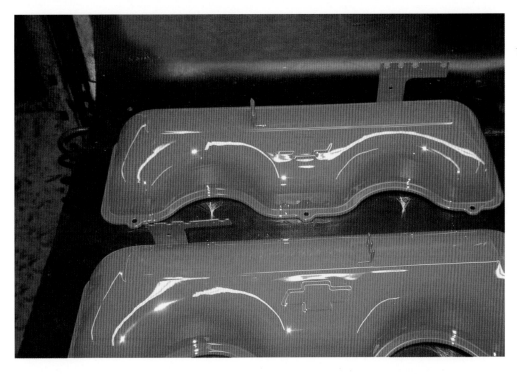

This pair of GM 5774089 stamped-steel valve covers has been painted with PPG 60914 orange high-gloss polyurethane.

longer lists these cylinder head bolts.

The ARP 135-3602 high-performance series cylinder head bolt kit for the 409-ci engines will fit the 348-ci engines. The 12-point head bolts are manufactured using heat-treated chrome-moly steel rated at 180,000 psi, and the current retail price is $85.

VALVE COVERS

The GM 5774089 stamped-steel valve covers were installed on the Chevrolet 348-ci V-8 engines with the GM 3877670 valve cover hold-down tabs. The tabs had a small rubber gasket attached, which was positioned against the valve cover lip. The valve covers installed on the 348-ci engines with a hydraulic lifter camshaft were painted Chevrolet orange. If using the stock-style valve covers, glass bead them, remove any dents, and paint the underside with Glyptal G-1228A medium-gray gloss enamel. This will prevent any rust from forming if there is moisture present.

In the late 1950s, some aftermarket valve covers were available for the 348-ci engines. The Edelbrock (see Resources) 4140 polished die-cast finned aluminum valve covers were quite common, but they are no longer manufactured. The popular Moon Equipment Company NN-48 No Name polished die-cast finned aluminum valve covers are now produced under the new company name of Mooneyes USA (see Resources), with MP650 as the new part number. The current retail price for a polished pair is $265. The Offenhauser (see Resources) 5042 die-cast finned aluminum valve covers are still available, and the current retail price for an unpolished pair is $190, while a fully polished pair costs $245. To give aftermarket valve covers a touch of class, install them with stainless-steel studs with polished acorn nuts, lockwashers, and AN flat washers.

B. CAMSHAFT AND CYLINDER HEADS SUMMARY

- New Clevite 77 SH-398S camshaft bearings installed allowing for 0.002-inch camshaft clearance and 0.002-inch end play. No. 1 bearing: SH-398, housing bore diameter: 2.019 to 2.0210 inches. No. 2 bearing: SH-399, housing bore diameter: 2.009 to 2.011 inches. Nos. 3 and 4 bearings: SH-400, housing bore diameter: 1.999 to 2.00 inches. No. 5 bearing: SH-401, housing bore diameter: 2.009 to 2.011 inches. Camshaft journal diameter: 1.870 inches. **$50**

- New Federal-Mogul CS-171 cast-iron alloy hydraulic lifter camshaft with advertised duration, 272 degrees intake and 280 degrees exhaust; duration at 0.050-inch lift: 190 degrees intake, and 198 degrees exhaust; lobe separation angle: 112 degrees; net valve lift: 0.400 inch intake and 0.412 inch exhaust; valve lash: zero. Camshaft degreed. **$160**

- NOS GM 5232720 hydraulic lifters, 2.005 inches long overall by 0.842 inch in diameter, installed. Lifter weight: 98 grams each. **$60**

- New Federal-Mogul RP-3102 intake pushrods, 5/16 inch in diameter by 8.788 inches long overall, installed. Intake pushrod weight: 55 grams each. New Federal-Mogul RP-3028 exhaust pushrods, 5/16 inch in diameter by 9.142 inches long overall, installed. Exhaust pushrod weight: 56 grams each. **$45**

- New GM 340236 camshaft sprocket, new GM 3896959 crankshaft sprocket, and new Cloyes C494 Morse-style timing chain set installed with GM 106751 camshaft gear woodruff key and new Manley Performance Parts 42114 camshaft gear locking plate kit using Loctite on bolts and torqued to 20 ft-lbs.

New Manley Performance Parts 42146 aluminum camshaft thrust button installed. GM 3736357 timing gear cover installed with bolts torqued to 15 ft-lbs using Loctite. Timing gear cover gasket installed using silicone sealant. Inside of timing gear cover painted with Glyptal G-1228A medium-gray gloss enamel, and exterior surface painted with PPG 60914 orange high-gloss polyurethane. **$136.92**

- GM 3759254 cast-iron cylinder heads, casting number 3732791, casting dates 12758 (December 7, 1958) and 12858 (December 8, 1958). Combustion chamber volume: 15 cc; cylinder combustion chamber volume: 70.4 cc; total combustion chamber volume: 85.4 cc. Cylinder head weight (bare): 59 pounds each. **$150**

- Cylinder heads hot tanked, Magnafluxed, Redi-Stripped, and pressure tested. Intake and exhaust ports gasket matched; cylinder heads surfaced; new K-Line KL1842STA universal-length 3/8-inch-diameter bronze bullet valve guide liners installed; and new Enginetech S2890 Viton-material positive-seal valve stem seals, 3/8 inch diameter, installed. Serdi-machined multi-angle blueprint valve grind performed. Area beneath valve covers painted with Glyptal G-1228A medium-gray gloss enamel, and exterior surface painted with PPG 60914 orange high-gloss polyurethane. Cylinder heads installed with GM 3735721 long cylinder head bolts, 7/16 inch NC by 3.98 inches long, and GM 3735722 short cylinder head bolts, 7/16 inch NC by 3.32 inches long, using Permatex aviation form-a-gasket and torqued to 65 ft-lbs. **$758.30**

- GM 3747307 864-5 alloy steel intake valves, 1.9375-inch head diameter by 3/8-inch stem diameter by 5.10 inches long overall. Intake valve weight: 127 grams each. GM 3747308 21-N steel exhaust valves, 1.656-inch head diameter by 3/8-inch stem diameter by 5.115 inches long overall. Exhaust valve weight: 124 grams each. Valves polished and installed with Serdi-machined multi-angle blueprint valve grind. **$212.31**

- New Federal-Mogul VS522 single valve springs with damper and an installed height: 90 pounds at 1.646 inches valves closed, and 220 pounds at 1.230 inches valves open; 1.325 inches o.d. and 0.915 inch i.d.; 1.970 inches long overall; installed with NOS GM 3729363 heat-treated steel valve spring retainers, 7-degree, 3/8-inch valve stem, and new Crane Cams 99098-1 heat-treated machined-steel valve stem locks, 7-degree, 3/8-inch valve stem, black oxide finish, stock height. GM 3732891 valve stem oil shields installed. **$48**

- New Federal-Mogul R-827 heat-treated stamped-steel rocker arms (with rocker arm balls and self-locking nuts), 1.75 ratio, installed with GM 3814692 pressed-in rocker arm studs. **$72**

- GM 5774089 stamped-steel valve covers installed with GM 3877670 valve cover hold-down tabs using Loctite with bolts torqued to 15 ft-lbs. Valve cover gaskets installed using silicone sealant. Underside of valve covers painted with Glyptal G-1228A medium-gray gloss enamel, and exterior surface painted with PPG 60914 orange high-gloss polyurethane. **$90**

- **Camshaft and Cylinder Heads Total: $1,782.53**

CHAPTER 6
INTAKE SYSTEM

A. INTAKE SYSTEM
INTAKE MANIFOLD

The GM 3772265 cast-iron single four-barrel carburetor intake manifold, casting number 3732757 and casting date A3158 (January 31, 1958), was installed on the engine described here. This intake manifold, which had a low-profile design, was produced from 1958 to 1961 for the Chevrolet 348-ci V-8. It does not have the best runner layout, to put it politely.

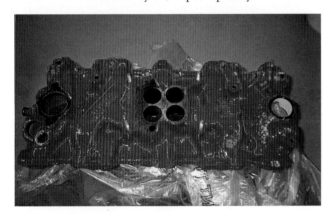

This is a GM 3772265 cast-iron intake manifold, casting number 3732757, used on Chevrolet 348-ci V-8 engines. It is not the greatest of designs.

The casting numbers for the Chevrolet 348-ci four-barrel intake manifolds are:

3732757: 1958–1961, cast iron
3749948: 1958–1961, cast iron (three x two-barrel)
3753748: 1960–1961, aluminum
3760436: 1958–1959
3767579: 1961, cast iron
3770084: 1958–1959
3772265: 1960–1961
3780540: 1958–1959, aluminum
3797775: 1959–1960, aluminum
3844472: 1962–1965 truck, cast iron

These are the casting numbers I am aware of, but there may well be others. One of the first options Chevrolet offered for the 348-ci engines was the triple carburetor cast-iron intake manifold, casting number 3749948, and produced from 1958 to 1961.

There were a number of aftermarket intake manifolds available for the Chevrolet 348-ci V-8 engines in the 1950s. Listed here are those designed for the different types of Holley 94 and

This GM 3749948 (casting number) cast-iron triple carburetor intake manifold was used on 1958–1961 Chevrolet 348-ci V-8 engines.

Stromberg 97 carburetors. The Edelbrock 1945 aluminum intake manifold was a staggered design for mounting four x two-barrel carburetors. The Edelbrock C-68 6007 aluminum intake manifold accepted six x two-barrel carburetors. The Weiand WCL6 aluminum log manifold was designed for six x two-barrel carburetors, and the Weiand WCL4 aluminum log manifold accepted four x two-barrel carburetors.

Offenhauser is probably the only company today that is still manufacturing intake manifolds for the 348-ci engines. The Offenhauser 3925 Pacesetter aluminum intake manifold with heat riser passage accepts six x two-barrel Holley 94 or Stromberg 97 carburetors. The Offenhauser 5025 Pacesetter aluminum intake manifold with heat riser passage is designed for four x two-barrel carburetors with a three- or four-bolt pattern. The Offenhauser 5263 Pacesetter aluminum intake manifold without heat riser passage has large ports and is designed for four x two-barrel carburetors using a four-bolt pattern. The current retail price of these three models is $250, unpolished. The Offenhauser 5492 dual quad aluminum low-profile intake manifold is drilled for Holley or Carter AFB carburetors and is available for the current retail price of $240, unpolished. The Offenhauser 5695 dual quad aluminum high-rise intake manifold is drilled for Holley or Carter AFB carburetors, and the current retail price is $285, unpolished.

Also during the 1950s, the Cragar CS-1 338-5 aluminum intake manifold adapted a GMC 4-71 blower to the 348-ci engines. The Cragar 337-5 complete street GMC 4-71 blower kit with intake manifold, pulleys, brackets, and a blower belt was offered as well. The Weiand WCI-671 aluminum intake manifold, for mounting a GMC 6-71 blower, or the Weiand WCI-DK complete street blower kit

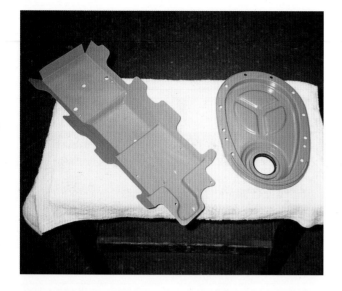

This picture shows the inside of the GM 3814817 oil splash shield for the 3772265 cast-iron four-barrel carburetor intake manifold, casting number 3732757, and the inside of the 3736357 timing gear cover painted with Glyptal G-1228A medium-gray gloss enamel.

The GM 3814817 oil splash shield has been reattached to the GM 3772265 cast-iron intake manifold, casting number 3732757. It is unfortunate no one will ever see this color combination after the engine is assembled!

with a GMC 6-71 blower, intake manifold, pulleys, brackets, and a blower belt could be purchased.

The Blower Drive Service (see Resources) 8036 aluminum blower intake manifold for mounting a GMC 6-71 or GMC 8-71 blower is available today for those 348-ci engine owners without a weak heart. The Blower Drive Service 356-3S1/2 complete blower kit consists of the GMC 6-71 or GMC 8-71 blower, intake manifold, pulleys, brackets, blower belt, and all the necessary gaskets and bolts.

The GM 3772265 cast-iron intake manifold, casting number 3732757, has the GM 3814817 large stamped-steel oil splash shield attached to the underside by six special rivets. The purpose of this oil splash shield was to act as an oil separator, preventing oil from being pulled through the crankcase vent tube at the rear of the intake manifold. It also served as a heat shield, reflecting the heat off the underside of the intake manifold, thereby keeping the air/fuel mixture cooler. Remove the six special rivets using a small cold chisel and a hammer.

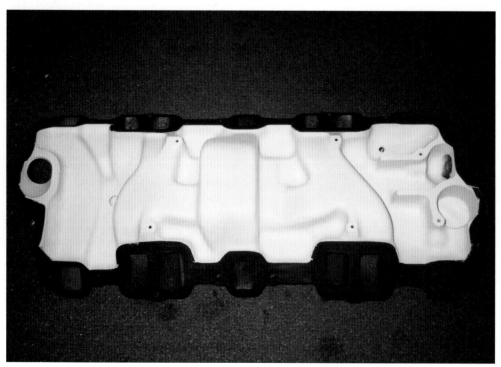

The underside of this GM 3772265 cast-iron intake manifold, casting number 3732757, has been painted with VHT SP-101 white high-temperature coating. This is an old drag racing trick used to reflect the heat off of the underside of the intake manifold.

Gently tap around the head of the rivets to loosen them, and then pull them out with a pair of pliers. This procedure just takes a little patience. You will be amazed at the different types of debris—possibly including deceased critters—attached to the underside of the intake manifold and heat shield!

The intake manifold and oil splash shield should be hot tanked and Redi-Stripped. Immediately after they return from being Redi-Stripped, mask off the ports and the outside of the intake manifold with newspaper, and paint the underside of the intake manifold with VHT SP-101 white high-temperature coating. This old drag racing trick should, in theory, reflect the heat off the underside of the intake manifold, thus ensuring a cooler air/fuel mixture. It certainly does no harm, and the white paint looks great in photographs! Afterward, paint the oil splash shield with Glyptal G-1228A medium-gray gloss enamel to assist with oil return. Reattach the heat shield to the intake manifold using Loctite on the six special rivets, and then firmly hammer them in place.

Used intake manifolds can be a problem because of hidden cracks, improper repairs, stripped threads, and gasket surfaces that are not true. Unless a specific intake manifold is required for a numbers-matching car or you desire an extremely rare aftermarket model, always purchase a new intake manifold. In many instances, new intake manifolds have a better runner layout than the original factory designs. The price for a used 348-ci cast-iron four-barrel carburetor intake manifold is approximately $50, and the price for a used aluminum or after-market intake manifold is determined by the market forces.

Gasket match the ports in the intake manifold, and remove any casting flash in the runners. Use silicone sealant to install the intake manifold gaskets, and secure the intake manifold in position with polished stainless-steel bolts and AN flat washers (unless the engine is for a numbers-matching car). Use Loctite on the bolts, and torque them to 25 ft-lbs. Install the carburetor studs using anti-seize compound.

Attach the GM 3740642 crankcase vent tube to the rear of the intake manifold, and support the right side (passenger side) of the engine block with the GM 3741636 crankcase vent tube bracket.

CARBURETOR

The Chevrolet 348-ci V-8 engines were equipped with three types of four-barrel carburetors: Rochester 4 Jet, Will Carter four-barrel (WCFB), and Carter aluminum four-barrel (AFB). I will not list all the different models and part numbers of these carburetors; there are many good books available containing this information if you are interested. In the 1950s and early 1960s, most shop manuals did not contain the cfm airflow ratings of carburetors, making it difficult to compare the different models. However, the Internet has produced some otherwise unpublished information about carburetors.

The Rochester 4 Jet carburetors did not have a part number cast into the body; instead, they were identified by a thin triangular piece of metal attached to one of the carburetor top screws. This tag had the part number stamped on it, but

This Carter AFB 9635 Competition Series carburetor has an airflow rating of 625 cfm and an electric choke.

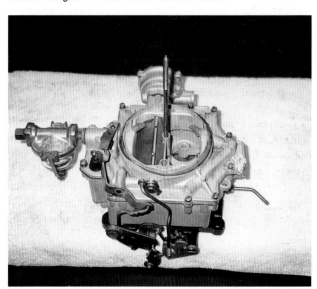

Here is a 486-cfm Rochester 7011108 (GM 3780698) 4GC Jet carburetor that has been completely refurbished and appears almost new.

without it, it was almost impossible to determine which carburetor it was. The Rochester 4G is the four-barrel carburetor with a manual choke, and the Rochester 4GC is the four-barrel carburetor with an automatic choke. The Rochester 4G and 4GC carburetors were produced from 1952 to 1967 and are not considered performance carburetors. There were three different carburetors with airflow ratings of 486, 553, and 692 cfm. Niehoff has complete tune-up kits available for the Rochester 4G and 4GC carburetors.

The WCFB carburetor was manufactured from 1952 to 1962 and has an identification number cast into its body. The WCFB carburetor has an estimated airflow rating of 385 cfm, thus it is not a performance carburetor. These carburetors were manufactured with manual and automatic chokes, and Niehoff has complete tune-up kits available.

The Carter AFB was introduced in 1957 and is still going strong today, although it has been improved. This performance carburetor is available with airflow ratings of 500, 600, and 750 cfm with a manual choke, or 500 and 625 cfm with an electric choke. The current retail price for a Carter AFB Competition Series is $225–$245, depending on the model.

The 348-ci engines equipped with the three x two-barrel carburetor setup used the Rochester 2G and 2GC Jet carburetors. The 2G had a manual choke and was used for the end carburetors. The 2GC had an automatic choke and was used as the center carburetor. Niehoff complete tune-up kits are available for the Rochester 2C and 2GC Jet carburetors. One of the best sources for completely rebuilt Rochester carburetors is Vintage Speed (see Resources). The factory equipped the three x two-barrel carburetors with vacuum-actuated progressive linkage, which was less than impressive. The Moon Equipment Company VLB-3 mechanical progressive linkage was one of the first kits to convert the carburetor linkage.

Unless a Rochester 4 Jet, WCFB, or early Carter AFB is required for a numbers-matching car, a modern four-barrel carburetor will offer fuel economy, throttle response, and fewer emissions. Edelbrock Performer four-barrel carburetors have the same basic design as the Carter AFB and have airflow ratings from 600 to 800 cfm. These carburetors have no gaskets below the fuel bowl level and are available with manual or electric chokes. The current retail price for an Edelbrock Performer four-barrel carburetor is $260 to $330, depending on the model.

Holley offers the widest range of four-barrel carburetors, everything from fuel economy and throttle response to all-out gas-guzzling drag race monsters. The prices vary accordingly. The Carter AFB, Edelbrock Performer, and Holley carburetors are available at the nearest speed-equipment outlet. Niehoff complete carburetor tune-up kits are available at most automotive parts stores.

To calculate what size of carburetor(s) you should install on an engine, use the following formula:

(cubic inches x maximum rpm)/3456 = carburetor cfm x 85 percent (volumetric efficiency)

Let's use a 348-ci engine operating at a maximum of 5,000 rpm as an example. Based on the above formula, the cfm requirement is 503.5 at 100 percent volumetric efficiency. At 85 percent volumetric efficiency, which is used for high-performance engines, the actual requirement is 428 cfm.

A Rochester 7011108 (GM 3780698) 4GC Jet carburetor installed on the engine described here has an airflow rating of 486 cfm. The original tag was on the carburetor, indicating it was the correct one for this particular engine—or someone put the right tag on the carburetor! Bud Bennett, the illustrious owner of a local speed shop, rebuilt the carburetor. It was disassembled, cold tanked, and glass beaded. The body

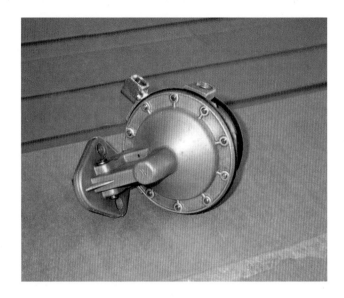

This AC 4432 (GM 5631637) mechanical fuel pump was used on the base 1958 Chevrolet 348-ci V-8 engine.

This photograph shows the GM 3704817 fuel pump pushrod and GM 3719599 fuel pump mounting plate used on Chevrolet 348-ci V-8 engines.

was chemically recoated, and a Niehoff CK-320 complete tune-up kit installed. The assembled carburetor looks like new with the original chromate finish. The GM 3756841 choke tube assembly connects the automatic choke on the carburetor to the top of the right side exhaust manifold. According to the formula mentioned above, this Rochester carburetor meets the airflow requirements for a Chevrolet 348-ci V-8 engine.

FUEL PUMP

The AC 4432 (GM 5631637) mechanical fuel pump was installed on the 1958 Chevrolet 348-ci V-8 engines equipped with the hydraulic lifter camshaft. This fuel pump produces 5 1/4 to 6 1/2 psi fuel pressure. Using the AC 4432 fuel pump on a stock engine is acceptable and has a retail cost of $85, outright.

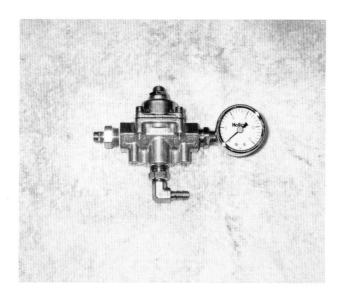

The Holley 12-803 fuel pressure gauge, 4 1/2 to 9 psi, and the Holley 26-500 fuel pressure gauge, 0 to 15 psi, are shown here.

The mechanical fuel pumps used for the 348-ci engines are the same as the small-block Chevrolet V-8 mechanical fuel pumps. Unless the engine is for a numbers-matching car, install an aftermarket high-performance mechanical fuel pump. The Holley 12-327-11 mechanical fuel pump delivers 110 gallons per hour of fuel at 6–8 psi. This silver-finish mechanical fuel pump costs $66.

When using multiple carburetors, install an electric fuel pump. The mechanical fuel pump can be left intact and operated with the electric fuel pump, or you can remove it and block off the mechanical fuel pump opening. Mount the electric fuel pump as close to the fuel tank as possible to push the fuel and not pull it.

The AC 4432 mechanical fuel pump is operated by the

GM 3704817 fuel pump pushrod, which is 1/2 inch in diameter by 5 3/4 (5.75) inches long. This pushrod is the same one used in all the small- and big-block Chevrolet V-8 engines. The aftermarket pushrods are manufactured with hardened steel for race purposes; soon after installment they will cause excessive wear in a street camshaft. Stick with the stock Chevrolet fuel pump pushrod for street performance use. Bolt the GM 3719599 fuel pump mounting plate to the engine block, and then bolt the mechanical fuel pump to the plate. This is the same fuel pump mounting plate used on the Chevrolet 327-ci V-8 engines.

FUEL PRESSURE REGULATOR AND GAUGE

If using an electric fuel pump, closely fit a fuel pressure regulator to a four-barrel carburetor. If using two four-barrel carburetors, then install two fuel pressure regulators (one for each carburetor). The Holley 12-803 fuel pressure regulator can be adjusted from 4 1/2 to 9 psi and has a silver finish. The current retail price is $23.

Install a fuel pressure gauge between the fuel pressure regulator(s) and the carburetor(s) to simplify the adjustment of the fuel pressure regulator(s). The Holley 26-500 fuel pressure gauge will indicate 0–15 psi of fuel pressure and has a 1 1/2-inch-diameter face in a chrome case. The current retail price is $20.

Never—and I repeat never—install copper fuel or brake lines in an automobile. Copper is very soft and fatigues easily; it could lead to a fracture, which will result in a disaster of major proportions. All-steel brake and fuel lines installed in a car must be double flared. Stainless-steel tubing is the best material to use for fuel and brake lines, although regular versions cannot be double flared. However, double-annealed stainless-steel tubing can be double flared and bends easily. The only source for the latter tubing I am aware of is Summit Racing Equipment (see Resources). The Summit Racing Equipment SUM-220238 stainless-steel tubing is 3/8 inch in

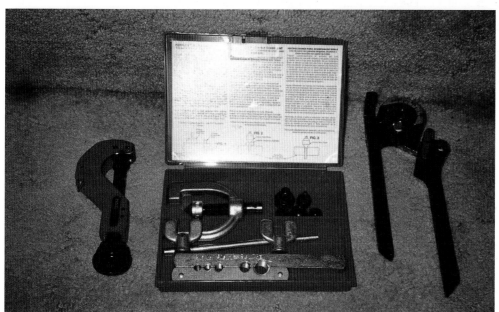

These are the tools required for double flaring steel tubing. On the left is a Sears 951252 tubing cutter, in the middle is a Summit Racing Equipment 900310 double flaring kit, and on the right is a Performance Tools W80675 precision tubing bender. All steel fuel and brake lines must be double flared.

diameter by 0.028 inch wall, and the SUM-220256 stainless-steel tubing is 5/16 inch in diameter by 0.028 inch wall. This aircraft-quality tubing is only available in 20-foot-long coils and costs $20 for a coil. A tubing cutter, tubing bender, and double flaring kit are required for the installation of steel tubing fuel lines. These tools are not expensive and are available in most automotive stores.

A fuel filter must be installed as close to the carburetor as possible. The Carter (GM 854328) glass bowl fuel filter was attached to the Rochester 7011108 (GM 3780698) 4GC Jet carburetor, and the GM 3741171 fuel line, 3/8 inch o.d., was plumbed from there to the fuel pump.

AIR CLEANER

The GM 1553498 single-snorkel oil bath air cleaner was installed on the base Chevrolet 348-ci V-8 engines. This air cleaner is required for a numbers-matching vehicle. There are hundreds of different air cleaners available today, in all shapes and sizes and manufactured using chrome-plated stamped steel, cast aluminum, or billet aluminum. The cost of air cleaners varies depending on how exotic the material and design are. The air filter, though, is often overlooked yet quite important. Always install a quality air filter, such as those manufactured by K & N, which are guaranteed for a million miles. Happy cruising! The K & N air filters are reasonably priced and available in many different dimensions. Visit your local automotive parts store to purchase one.

B. INTAKE SYSTEM SUMMARY

- GM 3772265 cast-iron single four-barrel intake manifold, casting number 3732757, installed with bolts torqued to 25 ft-lbs using Loctite. Intake manifold gaskets installed using silicone sealant. Underside of intake manifold painted with VHT SP-101 white high-temperature coating, and exterior surface painted with PPG 60914 orange high-gloss polyurethane. GM 3814817 intake manifold oil splash shield painted with Glyptal G-1228A medium-gray gloss enamel. GM 3740642 crankcase vent tube and GM 3741636 crankcase vent tube bracket painted with PPG DCC 9300 black semi-gloss polyurethane and installed using Loctite on bolts. **$474.62**

- Rebuilt Rochester 7011108 (GM 3780698) 4GC carburetor, automatic choke, 486 cfm, installed using anti-seize compound on intake manifold studs. Carburetor replated and new Niehoff CK-320 complete tune-up kit installed. GM 1553498 single-snorkel oil bath air cleaner painted with PPG DGHS 9000 black high-gloss polyurethane and installed. Carter (GM 854328) glass bowl fuel filter installed with GM 3741171 fuel line, 3/8 inch o.d. GM 3756841 choke tube assembly installed. **$653.75**

- GM 3704817 fuel pump pushrod, 1/2 inch in diameter by 5.75 inches long, installed using Molykote. GM 3719599 fuel pump mounting plate installed with bolts torqued to 20 ft-lbs using Loctite. Fuel pump mounting plate gasket installed using silicone sealant. NOS AC 4432 (GM 5631637) fuel pump, 5 1/4 to 6 1/2 psi, installed with bolts torqued to 20 ft-lbs using Loctite. Fuel pump gasket installed using silicone sealant. Inside of fuel pump mounting plate painted with Glyptal G-1228A medium-gray gloss enamel, and exterior surface painted with PPG 60914 orange high-gloss polyurethane. **$105**

- GM 3711724 crankcase breather/oil filler tube and GM 6419440 crankcase breather/oil filler tube cap painted with PPG DCC 9300 black semi-gloss polyurethane and installed. **$30**

- Intake System Total: **$1,263.37**

CHAPTER 7
IGNITION SYSTEM

A. IGNITION SYSTEM
DISTRIBUTOR

The GM 1110948 single-point vacuum advance distributor was installed in the 1958–1960 Chevrolet 348-ci V-8 engines equipped with a hydraulic lifter camshaft. The distributor advance was 12 degrees at 1,600 rpm and 24 degrees at 4,000 rpm. The GM 3770598 distributor clamp used on the 348-ci engines is the same one used on the small-block Chevrolet 327-ci V-8 engines. The GM 3758904 vacuum advance line was installed on the 348-ci engines.

Aftermarket dual-point distributors were available by early 1959 for the 348-ci engines. The Spaulding 10 Flamethrower distributor was popular because of its similarity to a magneto, such as the Scintilla Vertex model. This distributor was available with or without vacuum advance.

Anyone building an engine nowadays should install a modern electronic distributor to guarantee accurate timing and reliability. The GM 1110948 distributor can be converted using a Pertronix Performance Products 1181 Ignitor solid-state electronic system. The current retail price is $75, and Pertronix Performance Products are available at most automotive supply stores.

The Mallory (Mr. Gasket) 3734501 Unilite mechanical (centrifugal) advance distributor is triggered by a self-contained, photo-optic infrared LED system and will fit a 348-ci engine. This distributor is machined from 6061 T-6 billet alu-minum. It has an upper sealed ball bearing unit, and the shaft is heat treated and centerless ground. The Mallory 3734501 distributor will operate to 10,000 rpm, which is something a street performance Chevrolet 348-ci V-8 engine will not and should not see. The current retail price is $300, and Mallory products are available at most speed-equipment shops.

The MSD 8393 vacuum advance distributor is referred to as "ready to run", because it has a built-in inductive ignition module and will fit the 348-ci engines. The MSD distributors are machined from 6061 T-6 billet aluminum to within plus or minus 0.001 inch. It has an upper sealed ball bearing unit, the shaft is polished and tuftrided, and this distributor will operate to 10,000 rpm. The current retail price is $340, and MSD ignition components are available at most performance outlet stores.

COIL AND IGNITION CONTROL

The GM 1115091 ignition coil was installed on the base 1958 Chevrolet 348-ci V-8 engines equipped with the hydraulic lifter camshaft and a 9.5:1 compression ratio. The ignition coil was mounted using the GM 1929496 ignition coil bracket, which is the same ignition coil bracket used on the small-block Chevrolet 327-ci V-8 engines. The ignition system used with 348-ci engines is 12 volt, negative ground.

The MSD 8200 Blaster 2 chrome ignition coil is a good addition for any street performance engine. This coil has an

This GM 1110948 single-point distributor has been converted using a Pertronix Performance Parts 1181 Ignitor solid-state electronic system.

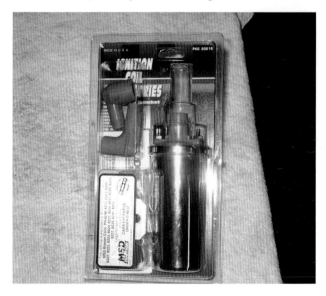

An MSD 8200 Blaster 2 chrome ignition coil, 45,000 volts, is shown here. This ignition coil is compatible with ignition control boxes.

This is the MSD 6A 6200 multiple-spark ignition control box.

A set of prefabricated Lectric Limited 1302-000 spark plug wires, for the Chevrolet 348-ci V-8 engines equipped with a four-barrel carburetor, is pictured here.

output of 45,000 volts, and it is compatible, unlike some coils, with a multi-spark discharge ignition control box. The current retail price is $34.

The Mallory 6852M Hyfire VI-A microprocessor-controlled CD ignition is a very reliable unit and costs $115. The Mallory 6853M Hyfire VI-AL multiple-spark ignition system, with adjustable rev limiter, is an excellent control box for use on a blown street performance engine. Its current retail price is $170.

The MSD 6A 6200 multiple-spark ignition control box is another reliable unit and costs $150. The MSD 6AL 6420 multiple-spark ignition control box is equipped with rpm limiter modules and is also a great addition for a blown street performance engine. The current retail price is $196.

SPARK PLUG WIRES AND SPARK PLUGS

The Chevrolet 348-ci V-8 engines were equipped with black 7-millimeter spark plug wires, that had dull orange-colored 135-degree spark plug boots with "Radio GM TVRS" on the wires. Lectric Limited (see Resources) manufactures exact replica spark plug wire sets for the Chevrolet 348-ci V-8 engines and sells one set for $65. The Lectric Limited 1302-000 spark plug wire set is for single four-barrel carburetor engines, and the Lectric Limited 1304-000 is for engines equipped with a tri-power intake system. The spark plug wires manufactured by General Motors prior to January 1961 were not date coded (see Chapter 17).

A great product for a street performance Chevrolet 348-ci V-8 engine (not being built up to stock appearance) is the Taylor/Vertex 70053 Pro Series 8-millimeter high-performance black spark plug wire set—Spiro Pro Kelvar resistor core, 135-degree boots. This universal set has the current retail price of $55 and is available at most speed equipment outlets. The Spectre 4245 chrome/plastic professional spark plug wire separator kit adds a nice detailing touch.

The AC-44 spark plugs were installed in the 1958 and 1959 Chevrolet 348-ci V-8 engines, and these currently cross-reference to Autolite 65 (3/4-inch reach), Champion RJ8C, and NGK GR4. The AC-44N spark plugs were installed in the 1960 and 1961 engines, and these currently cross-reference to Autolite 65, Champion RJ12YC, and NGK GR4. The AC-43N spark plugs were used only in the 1961 engines rated at 340 and 350 horsepower, and these currently cross-reference to Autolite 65, Champion RJ12YC, and NGK XR4. General Motors specified the spark plug gap to be 0.033 to 0.038 inch. They are

This is a set of Taylor/Vertex 70053 Pro Series 8-millimeter high-performance black spark plug wires, Spiro Pro Kevlar resistor core, 135-degree boots.

This is the GM 1102115 12-volt generator with the optional GM 5685600 power steering pump installed.

Here is a GM 1107889 12-volt starting motor, with the 1985846 snout, used on the Chevrolet 348-ci V-8 engines.

torqued to 25 ft-lbs in cast-iron cylinder heads using a slight smear of anti-seize compound. The AC spark plugs are available from your local Chevrolet dealer and the Autolite, Champion, and NGK spark plugs can be purchased at most automotive parts outlets.

GENERATOR

The GM 1102115 12-volt generator installed on the 1958 Chevrolet 348-ci V-8 engines is a very unusual unit, as the GM 5685600 power steering pump is attached to rear of the generator. The generator is installed using the GM 3725274 bottom-mounting bracket and GM 3746138 front-mounting bracket, and adjusted with the GM 3743080 generator brace.

STARTING MOTOR

The GM 1107688, 1107687, 1107711, 1107712, and 1107889 are some of the starting motors installed on the Chevrolet 348-ci V-8 engines. These starting motors are mounted using three horizontal bolts, unlike the starting motors installed on most small- and big-block Chevrolet V-8 engines, which require two vertical bolts. The GM 1985846 snout attaches to the GM 1107711 and 1107889 starting motors.

B. IGNITION SYSTEM SUMMARY

- GM 1110948 single-point distributor with vacuum advance converted using new Pertronix Performance Products 1181 Ignitor solid-state electronic module.

New AC-Delco D-308R distributor cap, new Niehoff DR-493 rotor, and NOS GM 1116118 vacuum advance control installed. Distributor advance: 16 degrees at 850 rpm and 24 degrees at 3,100 rpm. Distributor installed with GM 3770598 distributor clamp. NOS GM 1115091 ignition coil, 12 volts, installed with GM 1929496 ignition coil bracket. Distributor clamp and ignition coil bracket painted with PPG DCC 9300 black semi-gloss polyurethane. GM 3758904 vacuum advance line installed. **$338.58**

- New Lectric Limited 1302-000 black 7-millimeter resistor core spark plug wire set, 135-degree boots, installed. New NGK GR4 V-power resistor-type spark plugs, 18 millimeter, installed with 0.035-inch gap and torqued to 25 ft-lbs using anti-seize compound. **$74.95**

- Rebuilt GM 1102115 generator, 12 volts, with GM 5685600 power steering pump attached, installed with GM 3725274 bottom mounting bracket, GM 3746138 front mounting bracket, and GM 3743080 generator adjustment brace. Generator, brackets, and brace painted with PPG DCC 9300 black semi-gloss polyurethane. **$300**

- Rebuilt GM 1107889 starting motor, 12 volts, with GM 1985846 snout attached, installed with bolts torqued to 25 ft-lbs using anti-seize compound. Starting motor painted with PPG DCC 9300 black semi-gloss polyurethane. **$175**

- Ignition System Total: **$888.53**

CHAPTER 8
COOLING AND EXHAUST SYSTEMS

A. COOLING AND EXHAUST SYSTEMS
WATER PUMP

The GM 3774213 cast-iron short-style water pump, casting number 3732750, was installed on the Chevrolet 348-ci V-8 engines. It cannot be interchanged with the small- and big-block Chevrolet V-8 water pumps, although the shaft and impeller from a small-block Chevrolet V-8 water pump will fit. Rebuilt 348-ci water pumps are still available at many automotive parts stores, and the current retail price for one is $150 outright. The GM 3704172 water pump pulley, single groove, 7 inches o.d., was used with a GM 3774213 water pump. The GM 3755892 V-belt connected the crankshaft pulley, water pump pulley, and generator pulley.

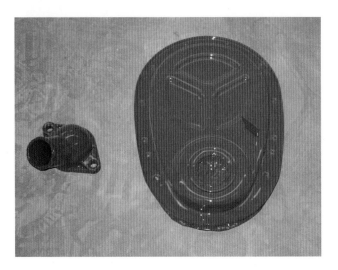

The GM 3837223 cast-aluminum water outlet elbow and 3736357 timing gear cover have been painted with PPG 60914 orange high-gloss polyurethane.

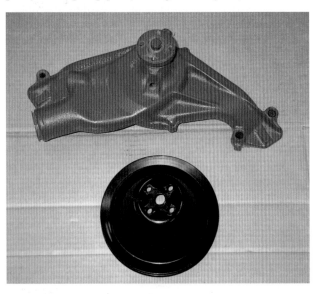

The GM 3774213 water pump, casting number 3732750, and 3704172 single-groove water pump pulley for the 348-ci engines are pictured here.

The GM 3837223 cast-aluminum water outlet elbow used on the 348-ci engines is the same one used on the Chevrolet 327-ci V-8 engines. Any street performance engine should have a thermostat installed. Removing the thermostat will cause the coolant in the engine to move too fast for the heat to be dissipated. In the summer months or in hot climates, use little to no anti-freeze if possible. Antifreeze traps heat in the engine cooling system and restricts heat from dissipating quickly, which results in an above-average engine temperature on hot days. Use a minimal amount of antifreeze, or a substitute, to lubricate the water pump. The GM 1513321 electrical water temperature sending unit is installed in the intake manifold.

You should not encounter any cooling problems with a street performance engine, provided the engine block, cylinder heads, and radiator are clean; the water pump is in good working order; and a mechanical or electric fan is installed. A fan shroud is often overlooked, yet it is an integral part of the cooling system and will aid in cooling the engine. The GM 3730342 four-blade fan, 17 inches in diameter, and the GM 814241 aluminum 2-inch-wide fan spacer were installed on the base 348-ci engines. The GM 3789562 five-blade fan with the GM 3916139 thermal fan clutch was used on the 348-ci engines equipped with air conditioning. The GM 3747299 front bracket and GM 3742450 rear bracket were used to mount the air conditioning compressor.

The special high-performance Chevrolet 348-ci V-8 engines incorporated the GM 3765198 idler pulley to provide constant tension to the crankshaft pulley/water pulley/generator pulley V-belt.

EXHAUST MANIFOLDS

The exhaust manifolds installed on the Chevrolet 348-ci V-8 engines are cast iron with a center-dump design. Today these exhaust manifolds would be considered "block huggers,"

The GM 3730342 four-blade fan, 17 inches in diameter, was used on the 348-ci engines not equipped with air conditioning.

because they were designed to fit almost against the sides of the engine block to clear the frame. The GM exhaust manifolds with casting number 3732793 on the left side and the GM exhaust manifolds with casting number 3732794 on the right side are for the 1958–1961 348-ci engines. The GM exhaust manifolds with casting number 3767583 on the left side and the GM exhaust manifolds with casting number 3767584 on the right side are for the 1959–1961 high-performance Chevrolet 348-ci V-8 engines.

The cast-iron exhaust manifolds have a tendency to rust, which gives any engine an unsatisfactory appearance. The exhaust manifolds should be metallic-ceramic coated to protect them. This may not be a numbers-matching approach, but it does reduce the under-hood temperature.

Install a set of tubular exhaust headers to pick up some additional horsepower. In the late 1950s, the Hedman Hedders H-CH5 center dump and H-CHU5 single-tube exhaust headers were available for the 348-ci engines. The Hooker Headers 2171 tubular exhaust headers have 1 7/8-inch-diameter primary tubes and a 3-inch-diameter collector. These uncoated exhaust headers are available today for approximately $400. The Sanderson Headers CC409 block-hugger exhaust headers have 1 7/8-inch-diameter primary tubes, a 3-inch-diameter collector, and cost $350. Exhaust headers should be metallic-ceramic coated and the gaskets installed using Permatex ultra copper high-temperature silicone sealant. Torque the exhaust manifold or exhaust header bolts to 25 ft-lbs using Loctite for cast-iron cylinder heads. Most speed-equipment outlets sell exhaust headers.

The semi-gloss, cast-iron finish, metallic-ceramic-coated exhaust manifolds shown here are for a 348-ci engine. They have casting numbers of 3732793 and 3732794.

LABOR

The labor costs for checking clearances, gapping piston rings, degreeing the camshaft, painting and detailing, trial assembly of motor, final assembly of motor, and the initial startup of the engine have not been included in Section B of the previous chapters. I will include that cost at end of this chapter.

B. COOLING AND EXHAUST SYSTEMS SUMMARY

- Rebuilt GM 3774213 cast-iron water pump, casting number 3732750, installed with bolts torqued to 25 ft-lbs using Loctite. Water pump gaskets installed using silicone sealant. Water pump painted with PPG 60914 orange high-gloss polyurethane. GM 3704172 water pump pulley, single groove, 7 inches o.d.; GM 3814241 aluminum fan spacer, 2 inches long; and GM 3730342 fan, four blades, 17 inches in diameter, installed with bolts torqued to 25 ft-lbs using Loctite. NOS GM 3755892 crankshaft pulley, water pump pulley, and generator pulley V-belt installed. New GM 1513321 temperature sending unit installed using pipe thread sealant. GM 3837223 cast-aluminum water elbow and new Gates 33006S Green Stripe Superstat 160-degree (Fahrenheit) superior performance thermostat installed with bolts torqued to 20 ft-lbs using anti-seize compound. Water outlet elbow gasket installed using silicone sealant. Water outlet elbow painted with PPG 60914 orange high-gloss polyurethane. **$225**

- GM casting numbers 3732793 and 3932794 cast-iron exhaust manifolds installed with bolts torqued to 25 ft-lbs using Loctite. Exhaust manifold gaskets installed using Permatex ultra copper high-temperature silicone sealant. Semi-gloss cast-iron finish, metallic-ceramic coating applied to exhaust manifolds. **$285**

- Labor for checking clearances, gapping piston rings, degreeing the camshaft, painting and detailing, trial engine assembly, final engine assembly, and initial startup of engine. **$1,200**

- Cooling and Exhaust Systems Total: $1,710
- Engine Grand Total: $9,009.87

Note: The estimated output of this engine is 251 horsepower at 4,000 rpm and 375 ft-lbs torque at 3,000 rpm (see Dyno Printouts).

Chevrolet 348-ci Turbo-Thrust V-8 Engine Summary:
$1,237.56 Engine block
$708 Crankshaft
$1,004.41 Connecting rods and pistons
$415.47 Lubrication system
$1,782.53 Camshaft and cylinder heads
$1,263.37 Intake system
$888.53 Ignition system
$1,710 Cooling and exhaust systems
$9,009.87 Total

CHAPTER 9
MISSING PARTS

FLEXPLATE AND BELL HOUSING

The GM 3760392 flexplate, 168 teeth by 14 1/8 inches o.d., was installed on the Chevrolet 348-ci V-8 engines equipped with an automatic transmission. The 168-tooth flexplate used on the small-block Chevrolet V-8 engines will fit the 348-ci engines. Install the flexplate using good-quality flexplate bolts, such as the ARP 100-2901 high-performance series, rated at 170,000 psi and having a 12-point head. The current retail price for a set is $10. Torque the flexplate bolts to 60 ft-lbs using Loctite.

The GM 3751080 cast-iron automatic transmission adapter, casting number 3742366, was bolted to the back of the 348-ci engine block to install a two-speed Powerglide automatic transmission. The Powerglide automatic transmission case used in the 1958 Chevrolet Bel Air was manufactured with cast iron. Bolt the starting motor plate, like the GM 3754194, to the bottom front of the automatic transmission adapter. Use stainless-steel hex-head bolts, AN flat washers, and nylocks to install the starting motor plate, and torque the bolts to 25 ft-lbs using anti-seize compound.

FLYWHEEL AND BELL HOUSING

The GM 3986390 (early 1958) and GM 3889694 (late 1958) flywheels were installed on the Chevrolet 348-ci

This is a GM 3751080 cast-iron automatic transmission adapter, casting number 3742366, for the Chevrolet 348-ci V-8 engines. The casting date is L1657 (December 16, 1957).

This is a GM 3760392 flexplate used on the Chevrolet 348-ci V-8 engines.

The GM 3754194 starting motor plate is bolted to the bottom front of the GM 3751080 cast-iron automatic transmission adapter.

V-8 engines. The 168-tooth flywheel used on the small-block Chevrolet V-8 engines will fit the 348-ci engines. Install the flywheel using good quality bolts, such as the ARP 100-2801 high-performance series flywheel bolts, rated at 170,000 psi with a 12-point head. Torque the flywheel bolts to 60 ft-lbs using Loctite. If substituting a manual (standard) transmission, check the rear end of a 348-ci crankshaft used with an automatic transmission to ensure it has been machined for the installation of a pilot bearing. The GM 3750809, casting number 3741311, and the GM 3755533, casting number 3771733, bell housings are cast iron. The GM 3785644, casting number 3779553, bell housing is aluminum. These bell housings are for use with a standard (manual) transmission.

CHAPTER 10
ASSEMBLY

ASSEMBLY

Note: Certain procedures, such as engine block and cylinder head cleaning, clearances, oil pump end gear clearance, wrist pin fitting, and piston ring gaps, are not mentioned in the assembly chapters of this book. These tasks were carried out prior to the final engine assembly. Also refer to Chapters 20 and 30.

ENGINE BLOCK

Clean the camshaft bearings with clean solvent using a clean, lint-free cloth. Install the camshaft bearings dry in the engine block using a camshaft bearing installation tool (this is a must!), taking special care to line up the oil holes in the camshaft bearings with the oil holes in the engine block. Do not lubricate the camshaft bearing bosses.

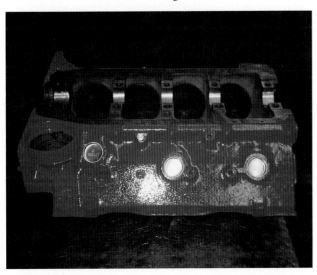

This Chevrolet 348-ci V-8 engine block has been painted with PPG 60914 orange high-gloss polyurethane and thoroughly cleaned. The brass freeze plugs have been installed, and it is now ready for assembly.

Install the six brass freeze plugs in the sides of the engine block, install the two brass freeze plugs in the front of the engine block, and install the rear camshaft boss plug using Permatex aviation form-a-gasket. Install the four oil gallery line plugs, 1/4 inch NPT, in the front and rear of the engine block; install the three oil gallery line plugs, 1/8 inch NPT, in the left side of the engine block; and install the water jacket drain plugs, 1/4 inch NPT, using pipe thread sealant. Install the 1/4-inch-NPT plug in the front of the fuel pump boss, and install the 1/8-inch-NPT plug in the top front of the engine block

(above the timing gear cover) using pipe thread sealant.

Lubricate the camshaft bearings and camshaft bearing journals with Clevite 77 bearing guard. Generously apply camshaft lubricant (provided by the camshaft manufacturer) on the lobes of the camshaft. Gently slide the camshaft into the engine block, taking care not to nick the camshaft bearings.

CRANKSHAFT

Install the rear main bearing oil seal in the engine block using silicone sealant. Clean the main bearings with clean solvent using a clean, lint-free cloth. Line up the locking tang (tab) on the main bearings with the notch in the main bearing saddles, and install the main bearings in the engine block dry. Do not

The crankshaft has been installed, and the main bearing cap bolts have been torqued to 100 ft-lbs. The camshaft is visible just below the crankshaft.

lubricate the main bearing saddles in the engine block. Install the rear main bearing oil seal in the rear main bearing cap using silicone sealant. Line up the locking tang (tab) on the main bearings with the notch in the main bearing caps, and install the main bearings in the main bearing caps dry. Do not lubricate the main bearing caps. Apply Clevite 77 bearing guard to the face of all the main bearings.

Place the crankshaft gear woodruff key in the crankshaft using anti-seize compound. Gently tap the woodruff key into position using a hammer.

Gently lower the crankshaft into the main bearing saddles; take special care not to nick the main bearings. Place the main

The crankshaft and camshaft gears with the timing chain have been installed. The oil slinger is on the snout of the crankshaft.

bearing caps in the correct order in the engine block, with the locking tang (tab) in the engine block and the locking tang (tab) in the main bearing caps on the same side. Lubricate the main bearing cap bolts with Molykote, and torque them to 100 ft-lbs. The crankshaft should now turn freely in the engine block. Check the crankshaft end play.

Apply some anti-seize compound to the snout of the crankshaft, and slide the crankshaft gear onto the crankshaft snout. The crankshaft gear and camshaft gear have a dot or a line on them, which are the timing marks and face outward from the engine block. Line up the timing marks on the crankshaft and camshaft gears, and slip the timing chain over the gears. Position the camshaft gear on the camshaft. The timing marks should be vertically in line with each other. Install the three camshaft gear bolts and locking plate using Loctite, and torque them to 20 ft-lbs. Bend the tabs on the locking plate over the heads of the camshaft gear bolts. Install the camshaft thrust button in the front of the camshaft gear. Slide the oil slinger onto the snout of the crankshaft.

CONNECTING RODS AND PISTONS

The pistons may have an arrow on the piston top or an "F" on the side of the pistons, indicating which side faces the front of the engine block. Remember this when assembling the connecting rods and pistons. The pistons used with this engine have a pressed-in wrist pin. The pistons and connecting rods have previously been assembled, and the pistons rings have been properly gapped.

Install the piston rings on the pistons using a piston ring expander tool, and rotate each of the piston rings on the pistons within the manufacturer's recommended arc, also

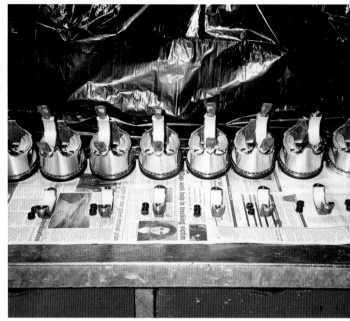

The pistons and connecting rods have been assembled, and the piston rings and connecting rod bearings have been installed.

known as "preferred ring gap location".

Clean the connecting rod bearings with clean solvent using a clean, lint-free cloth. Install the connecting rod bearings dry in the connecting rods and the connecting rod caps. Do not lubricate the connecting rods or connecting rod caps. Line up the locking tang (tab) on the connecting rod bearings with the notch in the connecting rods and connecting rod caps, and install them. Apply Clevite 77 bearing guard to the connecting rod bearings.

All the piston and connecting rod assemblies have been installed, and the connecting rod bolts have been torqued to 45 ft-lbs, allowing for 0.006-inch stretch.

Apply motor oil to the inside of the piston ring compressor, and place the latter around the piston. Place plastic connecting rod bolt protectors on the connecting rod bolts. Tighten the piston ring compressor around the piston, and insert the connecting rod into the cylinder (with the connecting rod locking tang facing outward from the crankshaft). Gently tap the piston down into the cylinder using the handle of a rubber hammer or a piece of wood. Guide the connecting rod around the crankshaft journal as you push the piston downward. Do not try and rush this job, as it is easy to break a piston ring when installing the pistons because of the counter bore at the top of the cylinders. After the connecting rod is on the crankshaft journal, install the connecting rod cap with the locking tang on the same side as the locking tang in the connecting rod. Install the connecting rod nuts using Molykote, and torque them to 45 ft-lbs allowing for 0.006-inch stretch. Repeat this procedure for the rest of the connecting rod and piston assemblies.

Install the crankshaft bolt in the crankshaft snout, and turn the crankshaft. The rotating assembly should turn over smoothly. Use a feeler gauge to check the side clearance per pair of connecting rods. Degree the camshaft (refer to Chapter 5).

LUBRICATION SYSTEM

Position the oil pump on the rear main bearing cap. Install the oil pump bolt using Loctite, and torque it to 65 ft-lbs.

Use silicone sealant to install both the timing gear cover gasket and then the one-piece oil seal in the timing gear cover. Install the timing gear cover bolts using Loctite, and torque them to 15 ft-lbs.

Place some putty on the oil pump pickup screen, and position the oil pan on the engine block without the oil pan gaskets. Push down firmly on the oil pan, and then remove it. Measure the thickness of the compressed putty. The correct oil-pump-

The Melling M55A standard-volume oil pump, with the GM 3754942 oil pump pickup screen, has been installed.

The timing gear cover, oil pan, fuel pump, and oil filter canister have all been installed. It is time to flip this 348-ci engine over.

pickup-screen-to-oil-pan clearance should be 1/2 to 3/4 inch. If the clearance is correct, carry on. If the clearance is not correct, adjust the oil pump pickup screen arm until you obtain the correct clearance. Install the oil pan gaskets using silicone sealant. Place the oil pan in position, and install the oil pan bolts, lockwashers, and AN flat washers using Loctite, and torque them to 15 ft-lbs. Install the dipstick tube in the oil pan using silicone sealant, and install the dipstick.

Install the oil filter adapter gasket using silicone sealant. Install the oil filter adapter using Loctite on the bolts, and torque them to 20 ft-lbs. Insert the oil filter in the oil filter canister, and fill the oil filter with motor oil. Install the oil filter canister, and tighten the bolt snugly. Do not overtighten the bolt.

Install the oil pressure gauge fitting in the engine block using pipe thread sealant. Install a temporary oil pressure gauge. Pour the required amount of motor oil in the engine.

CAMSHAFT AND CYLINDER HEADS

After the cylinder heads have been thoroughly cleaned, apply some motor oil to the valve stems, and install the valves in the cylinder heads. Install the valve stem oil seals. Install the valve springs with valve stem oil shields and the valve spring retainers using a liberal amount of motor oil. Use an OHV spring compressor to compress the valve springs to install the valve stem locks. Make sure to install the valve springs at the manufacturer's recommended height; shim the valve springs as required.

Lubricate the body of each valve lifter (tappet) with motor oil and the face of each valve lifter with the camshaft assembly lubricant supplied by the camshaft manufacturer. Install all the valve lifters. Place some putty on the crown of the No. 1 piston top. Place the cylinder head gasket in position on the engine block, and install the cylinder head. Install four cylinder head bolts (one for each corner), and snugly tighten them. Install the intake and exhaust pushrods for the No. 1 cylinder. Install the intake and exhaust rocker arms for the No. 1 cylinder, and adjust the

The numbers on the cylinder head bolts show the factory-recommended torque sequence for Chevrolet 348-ci V-8 engines.

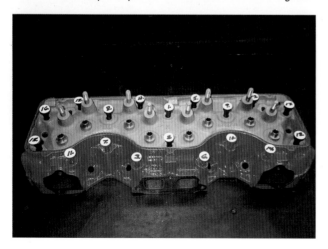

The assembled cylinder heads have been installed with the cylinder head bolts torqued to 65 ft-lbs.

valve lash according to the camshaft manufacturer's specifications (timing tag). Rotate the crankshaft until the exhaust valve for the No. 1 cylinder starts to open, and adjust the valve lash for the No. 1 intake valve. Rotate the crankshaft until the intake valve for the No. 1 cylinder starts to close, and adjust the valve lash for the No. 1 exhaust valve. The valve lash with hydraulic lifters is zero. Turn the adjusting nut on the rocker arm down an additional quarter-turn after the pushrod starts to depress the hydraulic lifter (tappet) plunger. Rotate the crankshaft at least two full turns. Remove the cylinder head. Measure the thickness of the compressed putty. The absolute minimum intake-valve-to-piston-top clearance is 0.100 inch, and the absolute minimum exhaust-valve-to-piston-top clearance is 0.125 inch (with the cylinder head gasket) when using forged-steel connecting rods.

Remove the putty from the No. 1 piston top, and clean the piston top with wax-and-grease remover. Place the cylinder head gaskets, and then the cylinder heads in position on the engine block. Install the cylinder head bolts using Permatex aviation form-a-gasket. Torque the cylinder head bolts to 65 ft-lbs using the factory-recommended torque sequence.

Install all the intake and exhaust valve pushrods. Install all the rocker arms using Molykote on the rocker arm stud threads. Adjust the valve lash, which was explained in the second paragraph of this subsection.

Gap the spark plug plugs to 0.035 inch, and install them in the cylinder heads. Torque the spark plugs to 25 ft-lbs (for cast-iron cylinder heads).

Install the valve cover gaskets. Place the valve covers in position on the cylinder heads. Install the valve cover, and hold

The valve covers have been temporarily installed. After the engine has been started and the cylinder head bolts retorqued, the valve covers will be permanently installed.

down the tabs, gaskets, and valve cover bolts. The valve cover gaskets and bolts will be installed permanently after the engine has been initially started.

INTAKE SYSTEM

Install the intake manifold gaskets using silicone sealant. Place the intake manifold in position on the cylinder heads. Install the intake manifold bolts using Loctite, and torque them to 25 ft-lbs. Place the thermostat in the intake manifold. Install the water outlet elbow gasket using silicone sealant. Place the water outlet elbow in position, install the bolts using anti-seize compound, and torque them to 20 ft-lbs.

Install the fuel pump pushrod in the engine block using Molykote. Install the fuel pump mounting plate gasket using

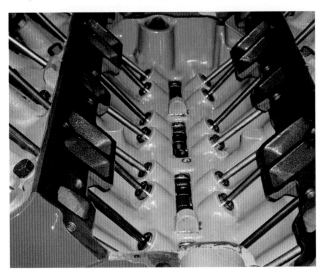

This is a good photograph of the valve lifter gallery showing the valve lifters, pushrods, and Glyptal G-1228A medium-gray gloss enamel.

silicone sealant. Install the fuel pump mounting plate and bolts using Loctite, and torque the bolts to 20 ft-lbs. Install the fuel pump gasket using silicone sealant. Install the fuel pump and bolts using Loctite, and torque the bolts to 20 ft-lbs.

Install the carburetor studs in the intake manifold using anti-seize compound. Install the carburetor-to-intake-manifold gasket. Place the carburetor in position on the intake manifold, and tighten the stud nuts snugly. Do not overtighten them. Install the fuel-pump-to-carburetor fuel line using pipe thread sealant on the fuel line fittings.

Install the crankcase breather tube in the rear of the intake manifold. Install the bolt using anti-seize compound, and tighten the bolt snugly. Slide the crankcase breather tube bracket over the crankcase breather tube, and bolt it into position using Loctite. Install the crankcase breather/oil filler tube in the front of the intake manifold using a slight smear of silicone sealant around the neck of the tube. Install the crankcase breather/oil filler tube cap. Install the electrical temperature sending unit in the intake manifold using pipe thread sealant.

Install the water pump gaskets using silicone sealant. Position the water pump on the front of the engine block, install the water pump bolts using Loctite, and torque them to 25 ft-lbs. Place the water pump pulley, fan spacer, and fan on the water pump. Install the fan bolts using Loctite, and torque them to 25 ft-lbs.

IGNITION SYSTEM

Install the harmonic balancer on the crankshaft snout using a harmonic balancer installation tool (this is a must!). Torque the harmonic balancer bolt and flat washer to 85 ft-lbs using Loctite. Install the crankshaft pulley on the harmonic balancer, and torque the bolts to 30 ft-lbs using Loctite.

Rotate the crankshaft until the engine is set with the No. 1 piston at 10 degrees before TDC, and insert the distributor

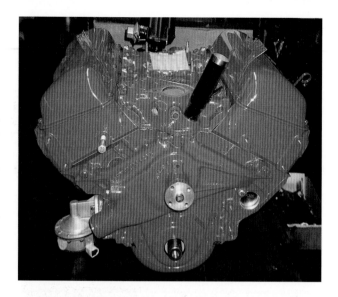

The intake manifold has been installed with the bolts torqued to 25 ft-lbs. The distributor has also been installed.

The GM 3774213 water pump, casting number 3732750, and the 3755820 single-groove crankshaft pulley have been installed.

The Rochester 7011108 4GC four-barrel carburetor is installed with the Carter glass bowl fuel filter.

front of the engine block. Place the spark plug boots over the spark plugs. Slide the distributor cap boots over the ends of the spark plug wires, and install the distributor cap terminals. Crimp the distributor cap terminals. Insert the distributor wires in the distributor cap in the correct firing order, which is 1, 8, 4, 3, 6, 5, 7, and 2. Install the ignition-coil-to-distributor-cap wire.

Install the generator brackets using Loctite on the bolts, and torque them to 25 ft-lbs. Install the generator on the mounting brackets and bolts using anti-seize compound. Install the crankshaft pulley/water pump pulley/generator pulley V-belt, and adjust the tension with the generator.

The engine has been installed in the 1958 Chevrolet Bel Air. The GM 3755820 single-groove crankshaft pulley is installed.

in the intake manifold. Connect the end of the distributor shaft with the oil pump driveshaft. Rotate the distributor until the rotor is aligned with the No. 1 spark plug lead position. Install the distributor clamp, and snugly tighten the distributor clamp bolt using anti-seize compound.

Insert the ignition coil in the ignition coil bracket, and snugly tighten the ignition coil bracket screw using anti-seize compound. Position the ignition coil and bracket on the intake manifold, and install the ignition coil bracket bolts using Loctite. Snugly tighten the bolts.

Lay out the spark plug wires, and cut them to length for each cylinder. The cylinders on the left side are numbered 1, 3, 5, and 7 from the front of the engine block. The cylinders on the right side are numbered 2, 4, 6, and 8 from the

The spark plug wires and generator have been installed. The engine is almost ready for the initial startup.

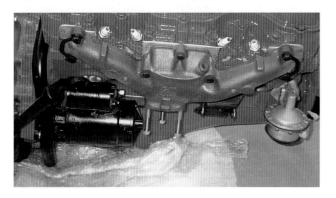

The GM 3732794 right exhaust manifold is metallic-ceramic coated with a semi-gloss cast-iron gray color. The studs are stainless steel.

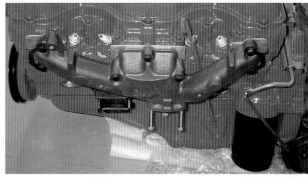

The GM 3732793 left exhaust manifold has been installed with the bolts torqued to 25 ft-lbs. Notice the French locks on the end bolts.

The Powerglide two-speed automatic transmission has been bolted to the back of the Chevrolet 348-ci V-8 engine. Installation is about to begin.

This is a left side view of the completed Chevrolet 348-ci V-8 engine. All the detail work in the engine compartment is excellent.

There should be 3/4 to 1 inch of slack in the V-belt when the generator brace is tightened.

Install the exhaust manifold gaskets using Permatex ultra copper high-temperature silicone sealant. Place the exhaust manifolds in position on the cylinder heads, install the bolts using Loctite, and torque them to 25 ft-lbs.

Install the automatic transmission adapter on the rear of the engine block using Loctite on the bolts, and torque the bolts to 30 ft-lbs. Place the flexplate on the crankshaft flange, install the flexplate bolts using Loctite, and torque them to 60 ft-lbs.

Install the starting motor plate on the front of the bell housing adapter using anti-seize compound on the bolts, and torque the bolts to 25 ft-lbs. Position the starting motor in the bell housing adapter, install the bolts using anti-seize compound, and torque them to 25 ft-lbs.

Install a pair of mufflers and a radiator with some water in it. Wire up the ignition system, and hook up a battery with a starter switch. Start the engine, and adjust the timing and carburetor. Allow the engine to run at approximately 2,000 rpm for 30 minutes to break in the camshaft. After the engine is at full operating temperature, shut it off and allow it to cool. Remove the valve covers, and retorque the cylinder heads. Install the valve cover gaskets using silicone sealant. Install the valve cover, hold-down tabs and gaskets, and bolts using Loctite, and torque them to 15 ft-lbs.

This clean Chevrolet 348-ci V-8 engine is well built and almost a numbers-matching model. The dyno results for this engine would have been far more impressive if a street performance camshaft had been installed and some cylinder head work had been performed. Possibly a blower?

SECTION II: BLOWN CHEVROLET 409-CI V-8 ENGINE

CHAPTER 11
ENGINE BLOCK

This blown (supercharged) OHV (overhead valve) 1963 Chevrolet Truck 409-ci V-8 was installed in a 1964 Chevy II Nova two-door coupe. The short block was built by High Performance Engines, and the final assembly was carried out in early November 2005 by the owner.

A. ENGINE BLOCK
PURCHASE AND MAGNAFLUX

The 1963 Chevrolet Truck 409-ci V-8, RPO (regular production option) L80, engine specifications are:

    409.1-ci (6.7-liter) displacement
    Stock bore: 4.3125 inches
    Stock stroke: 3.500 inches
    Stock compression ratio: 7.75:1
    One x four-barrel carburetor
    252 horsepower at 4,000 rpm and 390 ft-lbs torque at 2,400 rpm

The Chevrolet 409-ci V-8 engine is also referred to as a "W" design, due to the unique shape of the cylinder heads with the valves staggered diagonally. Having the same external dimensions as the Chevrolet 348-ci V-8 engine, the 409-ci engine is basically a bored and stroked version of it. Offered as an option for the 1961–1965 Chevrolet passenger cars, a recorded 43,755 owners selected this engine. It was also installed in heavy-duty trucks from 1961 to 1965. The 409-ci engine was one of the first true muscle car engines, and it was the terror of the super-super stock (SS/S) class at drag strips in the early 1960s. In 1961, shortly after it was released, a 409-ci Chevrolet Impala two-door hardtop, driven by Don "Dyno" Nicholson, won the National Hot Rod Association (NHRA) Winternationals in its class at Pomona, California. It had a top speed of 109.88 miles per hour and a low elapsed time (ET) of 13.19 seconds.

The Chevrolet 409-ci V-8 passenger car engine remained unchanged from 1961 to 1965, with the exception of three different compression ratios and revised cylinder heads with larger head diameter valves (this is explained in the Cylinder Heads section of Chapter 15).

Here is a 3857656 casting number, indicating this Chevrolet 409-ci V-8 engine block was installed in 1964–1965 vehicles.

This picture shows the casting number 3830814 on a 1963 Chevrolet 409-ci V-8 engine block that has been parallel decked.

The engine block casting date is located above the oil filter boss, and the casting number is located at the top left rear (driver's) side of the engine block (where the bell housing bolts on). The casting numbers are:

3788068: 1962–1963
3795623: 1961
3830814: 1963–1964
3839752: 1962–1963
3839754: 1965
3844422: 1963–1965
3857656: 1964–1965
3860386: 1962–1964

These are the casting numbers I am aware of, but there may well be others. The 409-ci engine block weighs the same as a

The casting date J12 (October 12, 1963) is seen here above the oil filter boss.

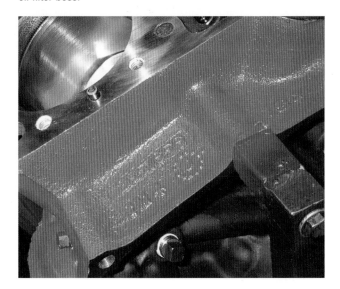

This Chevrolet 409-ci V-8 engine block has a casting number of 3857656. The counterbore at the top of the cylinder is visible.

348-ci engine block, which is 175 pounds (bare). The popularity of the 409-ci engines is on the rise, which will result in higher prices for original parts. The current cost of a good used engine block is approximately $250. The 409-ci Truck engine blocks are not as popular, thus they cost approximately $150. A Chevrolet Truck 409-ci V-8 engine block with a casting number of 3830814 and a casting date of J12 (October 12, 1963) was used as the basis for the engine described here.

The number 297 is located at the top right rear (where the bell housing bolts on) of the engine block described here. Supposedly, this number represents the 297th day of the year, which is October 24. However, this theory does not jive with the casting number J12 (October 12). Another rumor put to rest! The acronym CFD is occasionally found at the top rear (where the bell housing bolts on) of the 409-ci engine blocks, and this stands for Central Foundry Division (Saginaw, Michigan).

The engine block casting number of 3830814 is the same as the famous 1963 Chevrolet 427-ci V-8 engine RPO Z11, more commonly referred to as the "Mark II Mystery Motor". Created only for the NASCAR circuit, this 427-ci engine (4.3125-inch bore by 3.650-inch stroke) was the forerunner of the 1965–1991 big-block Chevrolet V-8 Mark IV engines. The Z-11 engine ratings were 430 horsepower at 6,000 rpm and 425 ft-lbs torque at 4,200 rpm. Also part of the package was a 13.5:1 compression ratio, two x four-barrel carburetors, and improved high-port cylinder heads,

This is the 1963 Chevrolet Truck 409-ci V-8 engine block, casting number 3830814, casting date J12 (October 12, 1963), whose buildup is described in this section. Notice the exhaust valve relief near the top of the cylinder bores.

along with a solid (mechanical) lifter camshaft.

The most powerful 409-ci engine Chevrolet ever offered for passenger cars was the 1963 and 1964 Turbo-Fire model, RPO L-80. The ratings for this engine were: 425 horsepower at 6,000 rpm and 425 ft-lbs torque at 4,200 rpm. An 11.0:1 compression ratio, two x four-barrel carburetors, revised cylinder heads with bigger head diameter valves, and a solid (mechanical) lifter camshaft were required in order to achieve those numbers.

CLEANING
> Refer to Chapter 1.

DETAILING THE ENGINE BLOCK
> Refer to Chapter 1.

RETAP AND CHAMFER BOLT HOLES
> Refer to Chapter 1.

REDI-STRIP THE ENGINE BLOCK
> Refer to Chapter 1.

GLYPTAL
> Refer to Chapter 1.

MACHINING
> Refer to Chapter 1.

CYLINDER BORING

Purchase the pistons beforehand, and deliver them to the machine shop with the engine block. The machine shop will then measure each piston with a micrometer, and bore the cylinders accordingly to ensure there is adequate piston-to-bore clearance (after cylinder honing), measured below the bottom of the wrist pin perpendicular to the wrist pin. Chevrolet specified the piston-to-cylinder-bore clearance for the 409-ci engines to be 0.0009 to 0.0015 inch for cast-aluminum pistons and 0.003 to 0.0036 inch for forged-aluminum pistons. Always adhere to the piston manufacturer's specifications for the piston-to-cylinder-bore clearance.

The engine block is usually bored to within 0.003 to 0.004 inch of the final bore, and then the cylinders are honed and deglazed, resulting in the final bore. The 409-ci engine blocks have a cylinder bore size of 4.3125 inches, which is 0.1875 inch (3/16 inch) larger than the 348-ci engine blocks. The 409-ci engine blocks can be safely bored 0.060 inch oversize, equaling 4.3725 inches. If building an engine similar to the one described here, then the maximum cylinder bore size for a used 409-ci engine block is 4.3425 (0.030 inch oversize) for the cylinders to be bored to 4.3525 inches (0.040 inch oversize). With a bore size of 4.3525 inches (0.040 inch oversize), the cylinder walls have enough material left for the engine block to be bored one additional time in the future.

The engine block described here was bored to 4.3525 inches (0.040 inch oversize), and the cylinders were honed and

Here is a set of 409-ci two-bolt main bearing caps that have been shot peened to assist with removing stress. An ARP 135-5402 main bearing cap stud kit is also pictured.

deglazed, allowing for 0.006 to 0.008 inch piston-to-bore clearance. Ross Racing Pistons recommends this clearance range for its forged-aluminum blower pistons. Refer to Chapter 1 for more information about cylinder boring, cylinder honing, and deglazing.

The deck surface of the Chevrolet 409-ci V-8 engine blocks is machined at a 16-degree angle, which is similar to the deck surface of the Chevrolet 348-ci V-8 engine blocks. The 409-ci passenger car pistons have a 16-degree angle on one side of the crown only, which makes them flush with the deck surface when the piston is at TDC (top dead center). The flat-top section of the piston is on the lower side, which means there is a 16-degree angle in the cylinder. This 16-degree wedge shape is the combustion chamber. The 409-ci Truck engine blocks have a relief cut into the top of the cylinder walls near the outer edge of the engine block for exhaust valve clearance, which is similar to the Chevrolet 348-ci engine blocks. The 409-ci passenger car engine blocks also have this exhaust valve relief. The 409-ci engine blocks have a counter-bore near the top of the cylinders, which is similar to the 348-ci engine blocks. Refer to Chapter 1 for information about the exhaust valve relief and counterbore.

ALIGN HONE AND ALIGN BORE

The diameter of all the main bearing housing bores in the Chevrolet 409-ci V-8 engine blocks is 2.687 to 2.688 inches. Refer to Chapter 1 for information about align honing and align boring engine blocks. The engine block described here was align honed.

If an engine is being equipped with a blower (supercharger) and the boost is going to exceed 5 pounds, replace the GM 3828570 main bearing cap bolts with studs. Main bearing cap stud kits are not currently available for the 409-ci engine; however, the main bearing cap studs used in the big-block Chevrolet 396- to 454-ci V-8 engines are compatible. The ARP 135-5402 main bearing cap stud kit without a windage tray, for two-bolt main bearing caps, currently sells for $50. The ARP 235-5502 main bearing cap stud kit with a windage tray, for two-bolt main bearing caps, is $60. Both of the ARP stud sets are rated at 190,000 psi.

The Chevrolet 409-ci V-8 engines cannot be converted to accept splayed four-bolt main bearing caps. The installation of splayed main bearing cap bolts (or studs) would penetrate the oil line inside the 409-ci engine block on the left side above the oil pan rail. Main bearing cap support bridges should be fabricated for additional support of the bottom end of a blown 409-ci engine block when the boost exceeds 5 pounds.

PARALLEL DECK

Refer to Chapter 1 for information about parallel decking. The engine block described here was parallel decked.

SHOT PEEN

> *Refer to Chapter 1.*

DEGLAZE

> *Refer to Chapter 1.*

O-RINGS

> *Refer to Chapter 1.*

CLEANING AND PAINTING

> *Refer to Chapter 1.*

B. ENGINE BLOCK SUMMARY

- 1963 Chevrolet Truck 409-ci V-8 engine block, casting number 3830814, casting date J12 (October 12, 1963), RPO L80. Stock bore, 4.3125 inches; stock stroke, 3.500 inches; two-bolt main bearing caps; 7.75:1 compression ratio; one x four-barrel carburetor; 252 horsepower at 4,000 rpm and 390 ft-lbs torque at 2,400 rpm. Engine block weight (bare): 175 pounds. **$150**

- Engine block hot tanked and Redi-Stripped; engine block and main bearing caps Magnafluxed; main bearing caps shot peened; all threads retapped; cylinder head bolt holes chamfered; valve lifter bosses deglazed, allowing for 0.0015-inch valve lifter clearance; and No. 5 main bearing cap oil pump cavity polished. New brass freeze plugs, 1.75 inches o.d., and new camshaft rear boss plug, 2.109 inches o.d., installed using Permatex aviation form-a-gasket. Front oil gallery line plugs (two) tapped for 1/4-inch-NPT plugs. New stainless-steel oil gallery line plugs and new stainless-steel water jacket drain plugs installed using pipe thread sealant. A 0.030-inch hole drilled in lower face of front camshaft boss for additional oiling. Exterior surface of engine block painted with Plasti-Kote 200 Chevrolet orange high-gloss engine enamel. **$406.67**

- Engine block bored 0.040 inch oversize, and cylinders honed and deglazed using Sunnen 800-series 400-grit stones with torque plate, final bore: 4.3525 inches. Piston to bore clearance: 0.006 inch measured below bottom of wrist pin perpendicular to the wrist pin. **$125**

- Engine block align honed. **$200**

- Engine block parallel decked to 0.008-inch average, below deck. **$120**

- Engine Block Total: **$1,001.67**

CHAPTER 12
CRANKSHAFT

A. CRANKSHAFT
PURCHASE

Good-quality forged-steel crankshafts were installed in all the Chevrolet 409-ci V-8 engines and are acceptable for a blown street performance engine. The 409-ci crankshafts have a stock stroke of 3.500 inches, which is 0.250 (1/4) inch longer than a Chevrolet 348-ci V-8 crankshaft's stroke. The main bearing journal diameter is 2.4985 to 2.4995 inches, the connecting rod journal diameter is 2.1998 to 2.2000 inches, and the crankshaft weight is 67 pounds. Show Cars Automotive (Dr. 409, see Resources) have 409-ci crankshafts in stock with main bearing journals ground 0.010 inch undersize and the connecting rod journals ground 0.010 inch undersize. The current retail price for one of these 409-ci crankshafts is $250.

The casting numbers for the Chevrolet 409-ci V-8 crankshafts are:

3733223: 1962–1965
3787072
3788072: 1961
3795589: 1961–1962
3829027: 1963
3838396
3838416: 1964–1965

These are the casting numbers I am aware of, but there may well be others. Refer to Chapter 1 for information regarding used crankshafts. In the early 1960s, Mickey Thompson and Crankshaft Company produced quality stroker crankshafts for the 409-ci engines. They offered strokes of 3.675 inches (1/8

This GM 3833147 forged-steel crankshaft has a casting number of 3838416. The 409-ci crankshafts are internally balanced.

inch longer), 3.750 inches (1/4 inch longer), 3.875 inches (3/8 inch longer), and 4.00 inches (1/2 inch longer). Practically none of those original stroker crankshafts have survived today.

The Chevrolet 409-ci V-8 crankshaft snouts are threaded for the GM 454960 bolt (7/16 inch NF) and GM 3739422 flat washer, unlike the Chevrolet 348-ci V-8 crankshafts. The 409-ci crankshaft bolt is similar to the bolt used in the small-block Chevrolet 350-ci crankshaft snouts. You should install a good quality harmonic balancer bolt kit, such as the ARP 134-2501 model, which currently costs $18.

Installing a big-block Chevrolet 454-ci V-8 Mark IV crankshaft in a 409-ci engine block is a common method to add cubic inches, which translates into more power. The 454-ci

This is a GM 3963523 forged 1053 steel crankshaft, casting number 3520, for a bigblock Chevrolet 454-ci V-8 engine. Many years ago, Bud Child (the founder of High Performance Engines) spent hours detailing and removing weight from this crankshaft, which included knife-edged counterweights.

The tip of the pen is pointing at the 0.125-inch (1/8-inch) chamfer on the connecting rod journal of this Eagle Specialty Products 4454400226135 crankshaft.

Mark IV crankshafts have a 4.00-inch stroke, a two-piece rear oil seal, and are externally balanced. The main bearing journal diameter for the No. 1 journal is 2.7492 inches; Nos. 2, 3, and 4 main bearing journals are 2.7498 inches; and the No. 5 main bearing journal is 2.750 inches. The connecting rod journal diameter is 2.1990 to 2.200 inches.

Reduce the main bearing journal diameter of the 454-ci crankshaft to the 2.4985- to 2.4995-inch size of the 409-ci main bearing journals. The diameter of the 409-ci crankshaft snout is 1.250 inches, which is the same diameter as the crankshaft snout of a small-block Chevrolet 350-ci V-8 crankshaft. The 1.6025-inch-diameter of the 454-ci crankshaft snout must be reduced to the 409-ci crankshaft snout diameter to fit the crankshaft gear, harmonic balancer, and front one-piece oil seal. Cut new crankshaft gear and harmonic balancer keyways in the snout, and internally balance the 454-ci crankshaft. Reduce the diameter of the front and rear counterweights by approximately 1/4 inch to clear the Chevrolet 409-ci V-8 engine block. Only the ends of the front and rear counterweights will have to be machined, as they are an oval shape.

The GM 3963523 Chevrolet 454-ci V-8 Mark IV crankshaft, casting number 3520, is one of the best crankshafts to use. This crankshaft was manufactured using forged 1053 steel, the journals are nitrided, and the oil holes are cross-drilled. The crankshaft snout is tapped for a 1/2-inch-NF bolt. Today, a good used forged-steel 454-ci Mark IV crankshaft is hard to locate, and when found, the seller usually wants you to take out a second and third mortgage to cover the price.

The blower (supercharger) installed on the engine described here requires a decent forged-steel crankshaft. There are a number of companies currently manufacturing

An Eagle Specialty Products 4454400226135 forged nontwisted 4340 steel crankshaft with a 4.00-inch stroke, for 6.135-inch-long (center to center) connecting rods, is pictured here.

The main bearing journals of this Eagle Specialty Products 4454400226135 forged-steel crankshaft have been reduced to 2.4985 to 2.4995 inches, and the crankshaft snout diameter has been reduced to 1.250 inches for a Chevrolet 409-ci V-8 engine.

good quality crankshafts for the 454-ci engines; one such product is the Eagle Specialty Products 4454400226135 forged nontwisted 4340 steel crankshaft. This crankshaft has a 4.00-inch stroke, 2.750-inch-diameter main bearing journals, and 2.200-inch-diameter connecting rod journals for use with stock 6.135-inch-long (center to center) connecting rods. It is heat treated, stress relieved, shot peened, X-rayed, Magnafluxed, and sonic tested. Its oil holes are cross-drilled and chamfered, and all the journals have a 0.125-inch chamfer and are micro-polished. The crankshaft is internally balanced and weighs 70 pounds (before balancing). The current retail price for this crankshaft, installed in the engine described here, is $800.

HOT TANK AND SHOT PEEN
> *Refer to Chapter 2.*

MAGNAFLUX
> *Refer to Chapter 2.*

STRAIGHTEN, CHAMFER, AND POLISH
> *Refer to Chapter 2.*

REGRINDING AND CLEANING
> *Refer to Chapter 2.*

MAIN BEARINGS
The Chevrolet 409-ci V-8 crankshafts accept the same main bearings as the Chevrolet 348-ci V-8 crankshafts. Refer to Chapter 2 for information about main bearings and the rear oil seal. Chevrolet specified the main bearing clearance to be 0.0006 to 0.0032 inch and the crankshaft end play to be 0.006 to 0.010 inch. The No. 5 main bearing is the thrust bearing that controls the end play.

Although the crankshaft installed in the engine described here has a 0.125-inch (1/8-inch) radius on the main bearing journals, they were reduced in size, thus eliminating the radius and permitting the use of regular (nonchamfered)

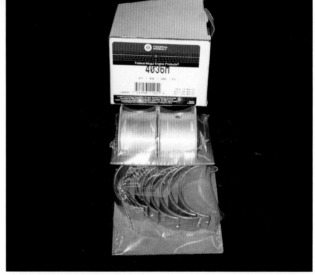

Pictured here is a set of Federal-Mogul 4036M main bearings, standard size, for a Chevrolet 409-ci V-8 engine.

main bearings. A set of Clevite 77 MS-458P main bearings, standard size, were installed.

HARMONIC BALANCER
The GM 3838371 harmonic balancer (crankshaft damper), 6 1/4 inches o.d., was installed on the standard-performance 409-ci engines. The GM 3796769 harmonic balancer, 7 inches o.d., was installed on the high-performance 409-ci engines. Both models are internally balanced. These harmonic balancers are no longer available from Chevrolet, although Show Cars Automotive (Dr. 409) sells stock replacement models for approximately $90–$120. A factory-type harmonic balancer should not be used on a street performance engine, especially a blown (supercharged) engine.

The Pro Race Performance Products 74265 race and street harmonic balancer is a decent-looking product, manufactured in Australia, for small-block Chevrolet supercharged (blown) engines. This all-steel model meets SFI Specification

This is a GM 3838371 harmonic balancer, 6 1/4 inches o.d., used on the standard-performance Chevrolet 409-ci V-8 engines. It is an internally balanced model.

A GM 3796769 harmonic balancer, 7 inches o.d., is shown on the left, and a 3858533 double-groove crankshaft pulley, 6 3/4 inches o.d., is pictured on the right.

18.1, is 6.61 inches o.d., and weighs 10.37 pounds. The current retail price for this harmonic balancer is $225.

The GM 3858533 and 3850831 double-groove crankshaft pulleys, 6 3/4 inches o.d., were installed on the Chevrolet 409-ci V-8 engines. The GM 3834720 cast-iron pulley was installed on the power steering pump.

B. CRANKSHAFT SUMMARY

- New Eagle Specialty Products 4454400226135 forged nontwisted 4340 steel crankshaft; 4.00-inch stroke; main bearing journals reduced to 2.500 inches in diameter;

Here is a Pro Race Performance Products 74265 race and street harmonic balancer designed for blown small-block Chevrolet engines. The GM 3980267 front one-piece oil seal is shown as well.

2.200-inch-diameter connecting rod journals; internally balanced; heat treated; stress relieved; shot peened; X-rayed; Magnafluxed; sonic tested; oil holes cross-drilled and chamfered; 0.125-inch (1/8-inch) connecting rod journal chamfered; and journals micro-polished. Crankshaft snout reduced to 1.250 inches in diameter. Crankshaft weight: 70 pounds. **$800**

- New Clevite 77 MS-458P main bearings, standard size, installed, allowing for 0.002-inch crankshaft clearance and 0.007-inch end play. New ARP 135-5402 main bearing cap stud kit, 190,000 psi, torqued to 100 ft-lbs using Molykote. **$195**

- New Pro Race Performance Products 74265 race and street harmonic balancer, 6.61 inches o.d., meets SFI Specification 18.1, installed with new ARP 235-2501 harmonic balancer bolt kit, 1/2 inch NF, 190,000 psi, using Loctite and torqued to 85 ft-lbs. Harmonic balancer weight: 10.37 pounds. Oil slinger painted with Glyptal G-1228A medium-gray gloss enamel. New GM 3858533 double-groove crankshaft pulley, 6 3/4 inches o.d., installed with new stainless-steel hex-head bolts, lockwashers, and flat washers using Loctite and torqued to 25 ft-lbs. Crankshaft pulley painted with Plasti-Kote 203 universal black engine enamel. **$275**

- Crankshaft Total: $1,270

CHAPTER 13
CONNECTING RODS AND PISTONS

A. CONNECTING RODS AND PISTONS PURCHASE

The GM 3814126 drop-forged steel I-beam connecting rods were installed in the Chevrolet 409-ci V-8 engines. These good quality forgings are acceptable for use in a street performance

This GM 3814126 drop-forged steel I-beam connecting rod is for a 409-ci engine. The piston is a cast-aluminum Jahns 1138C Powr Slot.

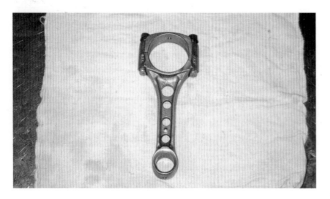

This GM 3856240 forged-steel I-beam connecting rod was used in a 427-ci drag boat engine. The wrist pin bushing is offset to raise the wrist pin height, and the dowel alignment pin in the cap locates the connecting rod bearing. This connecting rod has been debeamed and lightened to the point of scaring most sane people.

engine. The length (from the center of the big end to center of the small end) is 6.009 to 6.011 inches, which is 0.125 (1/8) inch shorter than the 348-ci connecting rods, and the diameter of the crankshaft end (the big end) is 2.3242 to 2.3252 inches. They weigh 783 grams and are designed for a pressed-in wrist pin with a diameter of 0.9895 to 0.9898 inch. The connecting rod bolts are 3/8 inch in diameter.

A big-block 454-ci crankshaft and connecting rods were installed in the engine described here. Refer to Chapter 3 for information about the connecting rods and aluminum connecting rods.

The Scat Enterprises 2-454-6135-220 H-beam full-floating connecting rods are manufactured in the United States using 4340 forged steel. They are 6.135 inches long (center to center) and have bronze alloy wrist pin bushings. The wrist pin end (small end) and crankshaft end are honed to plus/minus 0.0002-inch tolerance, a dowel alignment sleeve is fitted to ensure precise connecting rod cap alignment, and they have been Magnafluxed, shot peened, and stress relieved. The ARP 12-point connecting rod bolts are manufactured using 8740 steel, 7/16 inch in diameter, have 190,000 psi, and on average weigh 761 grams. A set of the Scat Enterprises 2-454-6135-220 H-beam connecting rods, installed in the engine described here, is $380. These connecting rods are completely adequate for

This is a set of Scat Enterprises 2-454-6135-220 forged 4340 steel H-beam connecting rods for a big-block Chevrolet V-8 crankshaft with a 4.00-inch stroke and 6.135-inch-long (center to center) connecting rods.

installation in a blown (supercharged) street performance engine and are available at speed-equipment stores. Connecting rods manufactured by Crower Cams & Equipment Company or Cunningham Rods (see Resources) should be considered for an engine producing some serious horsepower.

The GM 3969804 and 3963552 big-block Chevrolet V-8 connecting rods are fitted with 7/16-inch-diameter bolts and nuts. The Scat Enterprises 2-454-6135-220 H-beam connecting rods are fitted with 7/16-inch-diameter 12-point cap screw bolts. You have to notch the bottom of the cylinder bores in a 409-ci engine block (or a 348-ci engine block) to provide adequate clearance for the 7/16-inch-diameter connecting rod bolts and nuts, or the 7/16-inch-diameter cap screw bolts.

MAGNAFLUX AND SHOT PEEN
> *Refer to Chapter 3.*

ALIGN, RESIZE, AND REBUSH
> *Refer to Chapter 3.*

DEBEAM
> *Refer to Chapter 3.*

CONNECTING ROD BEARINGS
The Chevrolet 409-ci V-8 crankshafts accept the same size connecting rod bearings as the Chevrolet 348-ci V-8 crankshafts and big-block Chevrolet 454-ci V-8 crankshafts. Refer to Chapter 3 for information about connecting rod bearings. Chevrolet specified the connecting rod bearing clearance to be 0.0007 to 0.0028 inch and the side clearance per pair of connecting rods to be 0.016 to 0.020 inch.

The crankshaft installed in the engine described here has a 0.125-inch (1/8-inch) radius on the connecting rod journals, dictating the installation of chamfered connecting rod bearings. The Clevite 77 CB-743H chamfered connecting rod bear-

ings are available in standard size, 0.001 inch oversize, 0.010 inch oversize, and 0.020 inch oversize for $121. The Federal-Mogul 8-7200CH chamfered connecting rod bearings are available in standard size, 0.001 inch oversize, 0.009 inch oversize, 0.010 inch oversize, 0.020 inch oversize, 0.021 inch oversize, and 0.030 inch oversize for $113.

PISTONS
The GM 3799873 pistons installed in the Chevrolet 409-ci V-8 engines with a 10.0:1 compression ratio (or lower) were manufactured using cast aluminum, with the dome being approximately two-thirds flat and one-third gabled-roof (pent-roof) design. These pistons weigh 861 grams each. Chevrolet specified the cast-aluminum piston-to-cylinder-bore clearance to be 0.0009 to 0.0015 inch. Forged-aluminum pistons were installed in the 409-ci engines with an 11.0:1 and 11.25:1 compression ratio, and approximately

The GM 3788108 cast-aluminum piston on the left is for a 409-ci Truck engine. The GM 3819376 forged-aluminum piston on the right is for 409-ci engines with an 11.0:1 compression ratio.

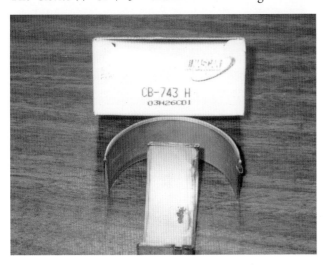

Here is a pair of Clevite 77 CB-743H chamfered connecting rod bearings, standard size, for crankshafts that have a radius on the journals.

This is a Jahns 1138C Powr Slot cast-aluminum piston, 0.060 inch oversize, for a 409-ci engine. Jahns advertised this unique oval slot piston as being capable of delivering up to 40 additional horsepower. Compare this piston to the Ross Racing Pistons forged-aluminum pistons shown in this chapter. How times have changed!

one-half of the dome was flat and one-half gabled-roof design. These pistons weigh 851 grams each.

It is rumored that Mickey Thompson supplied the forged-aluminum pistons used in the 1961 engines. Chevrolet specified the forged-aluminum piston-to-cylinder-bore clearance to be 0.003 to 0.0036 inch. The 1961 pistons had an intake valve relief milled across the entire top of the gabled-roof area of the dome. The 1962–1965 GM 3819375 and 3819376 forged-aluminum pistons had a single intake valve relief milled in the top of the gabled-roof area of the dome. The cast- and forged-aluminum 409-ci pistons came with a pressed-in wrist pin having the same dimension and weight as the pressed-in wrist pin used in 348-ci pistons. The wrist pin is 3.265 inches long, 0.9896 inch in diameter, a straight-wall design, and weighs 169 grams. Chevrolet specified the clearance in the piston to be 0.00045 to 0.00055 inch for a pressed-in wrist pin.

The Chevrolet 409-ci V-8 pistons are no longer available from General Motors. Egge Parts House is one of the few sources for purchasing aftermarket, off-the-shelf 409-ci cast-aluminum pistons. The Egge Parts House L2191 pistons are for the standard-performance 409-ci engines, and the Egge Parts House L2170 pistons are for the high-performance 409-ci engines. These pistons are available in standard size, 0.020 inch oversize, 0.030 inch oversize, 0.040 inch oversize, 0.060 inch oversize, and 0.080 inch oversize. The current retail price for a set of these pistons with pressed-in wrist pins is $355. Cast-iron piston rings are available with these pistons, which is entirely suitable for stock or mild street performance use. A set of the Egge Parts House SRH645 cast-iron piston rings is available for $61.

Always install new pistons when rebuilding an engine. On the rare occasion when you examine and find used pistons in very good condition, you should have them dye checked to ensure there are no hidden cracks. This procedure is routinely carried out with race car pistons.

Ross Racing Pistons has off-the-shelf stocking pistons for the Chevrolet 409-ci V-8 engine. The Ross Racing Pistons 83561

forged 2618 T-61 aluminum pistons are complete with straight-wall wrist pins, double Spiro Lox retainers, a bore size of 4.3425 inches (0.030 inch oversize), a 10.5:1 compression ratio, a stock 3.500-inch stroke, a stock 6.010-inch-long connecting rod (center to center), and they weigh 817 grams each. The full-floating wrist pins are 2.930 inches long, 0.990 inch in diameter, and weigh 153 grams each. The current retail price for a set of these pistons with wrist pins and double Spiro Lox retainers is $645. The combination of these pistons with a Chevrolet Truck 409-ci V-8 engine block and cylinder heads might reduce the compression ratio enough to use a blower, provided the boost is guaranteed not to exceed 5 pounds.

Use forged-aluminum blower pistons in an engine that will have more than 5 pounds of boost. Blower pistons have a

This is a set of Ross Racing Pistons forged 2618 T-61 aluminum blower pistons for the 409-ci engine described here. The pistons are complete with full-floating wrist pins and double Spiro Lox retainers.

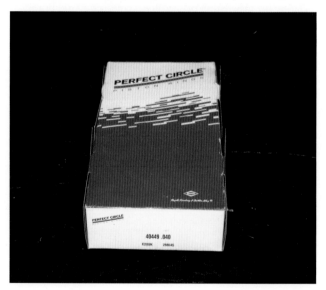

Pictured here is a Perfect Circle 40449-040 moly-coated ductile iron top piston ring set, 0.040 inch oversize, for a Chevrolet 409-ci V-8 engine.

Here is a set of Bill Miller Engineering forged-aluminum racing pistons for a small-block Buick V-8 drag-racing engine. The pistons are being dye checked.

thicker crown area, thicker ring lands, large internal radii, and bigger wrist pin bosses to handle the higher operating temperatures and additional cylinder pressure. The top compression ring on a blower piston should be at least 0.250 inch below the top of the piston. A set of Ross Racing Pistons forged 2618 T-61 aluminum custom blower pistons, complete with full-floating wrist pins and double Spiro Lox retainers, was installed in the engine described here. These pistons are 0.040 inch oversize (4.3525 inches); they have a compression ratio of 8.0:1, a dome height of 0.425 inch, and weigh 683 grams each. The piston groove width is: top compression ring, 5/64 inch; second compression ring, 5/64 inch; and oil ring, 3/16 inch. The current retail price for the Ross Racing Pistons blower pistons, wrist pins, and double Spiro Lox retainers is $715.

Ross Racing Pistons has its own moly piston ring sets manufactured exclusively for its pistons. The top compression rings are ductile SG iron and molybdenum inlaid, are barrel lapped to ensure quick seating, and are coated with zinc phosphate for added corrosion resistance. The second compression rings are cast iron and also zinc phosphate coated. The oil rings consist of a stainless-steel expander and chromium-plated carbon rails. The current retail price of a set of the Ross Racing Pistons moly piston rings, used for the engine described here, is $140.

Moly-coated piston rings should be used in a blown engine due to the higher operating temperatures and additional cylinder pressure. The moly piston rings are much more flexible than cast-iron piston rings. Refer to Chapter 3 for information about piston rings, gapping piston rings, and checking the valve-to-piston clearance. A Perfect Circle 40449-040 moly-coated ductile iron top piston ring set, 0.040 inch oversize and installed in the engine described, is $75.

If the second compression ring gap is smaller than the top compression ring gap, there is less blowby; however, this could cause the top compression ring to flutter. Ross Racing Pistons recommends a larger second compression ring gap than the top compression ring gap to prevent piston ring flutter. The piston ring gap, which Ross Racing Pistons recommends for its moly piston ring sets, is 0.004 inch by the cylinder bore for the top compression ring, plus 0.004 inch for blown engines and 0.005 inch by the cylinder bore for the second compression ring, plus 0.004 inch for blown engines. The piston ring gap for the engine described here is: 0.021 inch for the top compression ring, 0.026 inch for the second compression ring, and 0.016 inch for the oil ring.

BALANCING
> *Refer to Chapter 3.*

GASKETS
The Fel-Pro FS8007PT-3 and Victor-Reinz FS1195VC complete gasket sets for the Chevrolet 409-ci V-8 engines cost $65 and are available at most automotive supply stores.

The Victor-Reinz FS1195VC complete gasket set for a Chevrolet 409-ci V-8 engine is pictured here.

B. CONNECTING RODS AND PISTONS SUMMARY

- New Scat Enterprises 2-454-6135-220 forged 4340 steel H-beam connecting rods, 6.135 inches long (center to center), installed. Connecting rods Magnafluxed, shot peened, stress relieved; bronze alloy wrist pin bushings installed; dowel alignment sleeve fitted for precise connecting rod cap alignment; and connecting rods balanced. Wrist pin bushings honed, allowing for 0.0015-inch wrist pin clearance. ARP 12-point connecting rod bolts, 7/16 inch in diameter, 190,000 psi, installed. Connecting rod weight: 761 grams. Connecting rod ratio (with 4.00-inch stroke crankshaft): 1.53. **$380**

- New Clevite 77 CB-743H chamfered connecting rod bearings, standard size, installed allowing for 0.002-inch connecting rod clearance and 0.017-inch side clearance per pair of connecting rods. Connecting rod bolts torqued to 45 ft-lbs using Molykote and allowing for 0.006-inch stretch. **$121**

- New Ross Racing Pistons forged 2618 T-61 aluminum custom blower pistons, 0.040 inch oversize, 8.0:1 compression ratio, 0.425-inch dome height, installed. Piston weight: 683 grams. Full-floating, heat-treated, and case-hardened 4340 chrome-moly steel straight-wall wrist pins. Wrist pin length, 2.930 inches long; wrist pin diameter, 0.990 inch; and wrist pin weight, 153 grams. Piston groove width: top compression ring, 5/64 inch; second compression ring, 5/64 inch; and oil ring, 3/16 inch. New Perfect Circle 40449-040 moly-coated ductile iron top piston ring set installed within manufacturer's recommended arc. Top compression ring gap, 0.020 inch; second compression ring gap, 0.018 inch; and oil ring, 0.016 inch. New displacement: 476.2 ci (7.8 liters). **$790**

- Complete V-8 engine balance. New Victor-Reinz FS1195VC complete gasket set installed. **$265**

- Connecting Rods and Pistons Total: **$1,556**

A. LUBRICATION SYSTEM
OIL PUMP AND PICKUP SCREEN

The GM 3821979 standard-volume oil pump, with the GM 3756254 oil pump pickup screen attached, was installed in 1961 Chevrolet 409-ci V-8 engines, and it delivered 45 psi at 2,000 rpm. The GM 3848907 oil pump installed in 1962–1965 Chevrolet 409-ci V-8 engines delivered 50 psi at 2,000 rpm. The GM 3764553 oil pump driveshaft was used with these oil pumps. Always install a new oil pump when assembling an engine; never install a used one.

The 409-ci oil pump driveshafts have a nylon sleeve and are the same length as the 348-ci oil pump driveshafts. A Melling M55HV high-volume oil pump and a Melling IS-77 oil pump driveshaft (for a big-block Chevrolet 454-ci V-8 engine) were installed in the engine described. Refer to Chapter 4 for information about oil pumps, oil pump pickup screens, oil pump stud kits, and oil pump driveshafts.

This picture shows a GM 3821979 standard-volume oil pump with an attached 3756254 oil pump pickup screen installed in a 409-ci engine.

OIL PAN

The GM 3799873 stamped-steel oil pan was installed on Chevrolet 409-ci V-8 engines, and it is internally baffled with a rear sump. This oil pan has a 4-quart capacity, although when including the canister-type oil filter, it uses 5 quarts. The high-performance 409-ci engines were fitted with the GM 3816322 stamped-steel oil pan with a 5-quart capacity, although when including the canister-type oil filter, it uses 6 quarts. The GM 3854792 oil pan was installed on 409-ci engines in 1965. The dipstick in the 409-ci oil pans is located on the right side, and there were five different lengths with three chrome models.

The internal baffle in the passenger car oil pans is short and

Here is a Melling M55HV high-volume oil pump and a Melling IS-77 oil pump driveshaft. These items will fit a 409-ci engine.

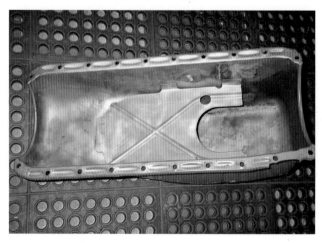

Shown here is a Chevrolet Truck 409-ci V-8 oil pan. The baffle in this oil pan is slightly higher and longer than the baffle in the passenger car oil pans.

This fine piece of workmanship is a Stef's Fabrication Specialties 1085 Nostalgia Series 5-quart aluminum oil pan with matching oil pump pickup screen. The windage tray, internal baffle with trap door, and magnetic oil drain plug are all installed.

in a lower position (similar to the 348-ci passenger car oil pans) compared to the longer baffle positioned higher up in the truck oil pans. The oil drain plug in the passenger car oil pans is located at the bottom front of the sump, horizontal to the ground. The oil drain plug in the truck oil pans is located at the bottom front of the sump, vertical to the ground. Refer to Chapter 4 for more information about oil pans.

Stef's Fabrication Specialties (see Resources) is one of the few companies that market off-the-shelf oil pans for Chevrolet 409-ci V-8 engines. The Stef's Fabrication Specialties 1085 Nostalgia Series race car aluminum oil pan is a high-quality product. This oil pan is internally baffled with a trapdoor system and has an attached windage tray, a capacity of 5 quarts of oil, a magnetic oil drain plug, and a matching oil pump pickup screen. The current retail price is $250.

WINDAGE TRAY
> *Refer to Chapter 4.*

The GM 3797749 windage tray was installed in the 400- and 425-horsepower engines using GM 3815534 main bearing cap studs (four). A windage tray is not normally used with the truck oil pans.

OIL FILTER
> *Refer to Chapter 4.*

B. LUBRICATION SYSTEM SUMMARY

- New Melling M55HV high-volume oil pump installed with Stef's Fabrication Specialties oil pump pickup screen. Oil pump pickup screen tack welded to oil pump body. Oil pump end clearance: 0.00025 inch. Oil pump cover gasket installed using silicone sealant, and oil pump cover bolts torqued to 80 in-lbs using Loctite. New Melling IS-77 oil pump driveshaft, 6.702 inches long (including steel sleeve), installed. GM 3754998 oil pump bolt installed using Loctite and torqued to 65 ft-lbs. **$123.54**

- New Stef's Fabrication Specialties 1085 Nostalgia Series race car aluminum oil pan with internal baffle and trapdoor, windage tray, and magnetic oil drain plug installed with new stainless-steel hex-head bolts, lockwashers, and AN flat washers using Loctite and torqued to 15 ft-lbs. Oil pan gaskets and rear oil seals installed using silicone sealant. GM 5573837 oil filter adapter installed with bolts torqued to 20 ft-lbs using Loctite. Oil filter adapter gasket installed using silicone sealant. GM 5574278 oil filter canister and new GM 5573980 O-ring installed with new AC-Delco PH-141 oil filter. Engine lubricated with 6 quarts of Pennzoil HD-30 weight motor oil. **$416.93**

- Lubrication System Total: **$540.47**

CHAPTER 15
CAMSHAFT AND CYLINDER HEADS

A. CAMSHAFT AND CYLINDER HEADS
CAMSHAFT BEARINGS

The camshaft bearings used in the Chevrolet 409-ci V-8 engines are the same as those used in the Chevrolet 348-ci V-8 engines. Refer to Chapter 5 for information pertaining to camshaft bearings. A set of Clevite 77 SH-398S camshaft bearings was installed in the engine described here.

This is a set of Federal-Mogul 1107 camshaft bearings for the Chevrolet 409-ci V-8 engine.

CAMSHAFT

The following is a list of Chevrolet data for some of the camshafts used in the 409-ci V-8 engines. The camshaft lift is not specified for the advertised duration, which in some cases is questionable. The duration at 0.050-inch lift is not included with any of these camshafts, because this standard of measurement was not in use during the early to mid-1960s. As a result of this, and the fact the information is over 40 years old, it is provided without any guarantee of its accuracy.

The 1963–1965 engines rated at 340 horsepower were equipped with the GM 3744430 hydraulic lifter camshaft. The advertised duration is 312 degrees intake and 320 degrees exhaust, the lobe separation angle is 113 degrees,

the valve lift is 0.401 inch intake and 0.412 inch exhaust, and the valve lash is zero.

The 1961 engine rated at 360 horsepower was equipped with the GM 3796076 solid (mechanical) lifter camshaft.

This GM 3744430 hydraulic lifter camshaft was installed in the 1963–1965 Chevrolet 409-ci V-8 engines rated at 340 horsepower.

This is a NOS GM 3837735 solid (mechanical) lifter camshaft for the famous Chevrolet 427-ci V-8 engine, RPO Z11. This camshaft was also installed in the 400- and 425-horsepower 409-ci engines.

Here is the Iskenderian Racing Cams 409 (241) hydraulic lifter camshaft, grind number 296HYD, that will be installed in the engine described here. Notice the oiling groove around the rear bearing journal.

The advertised duration is 346 degrees intake and 305 degrees exhaust, the lobe separation angle is 120 degrees, the valve lift is 0.440 inch intake and exhaust, and the valve lash (hot) is 0.008 inch intake and 0.018 inch exhaust.

The 1962 engines rated at 380 and 409 horsepower were equipped with the GM 3830690 solid (mechanical) lifter camshaft. The advertised duration is 398 degrees intake and 353 degrees exhaust, the valve lift is 0.440 inch intake and exhaust, and the valve lash (hot) is 0.008 inch intake and 0.018 inch exhaust.

The 1963 engines rated at 400 and 425 horsepower were equipped with the GM 3837735 solid (mechanical) lifter camshaft. The advertised duration is 444 degrees intake and 416 degrees exhaust, the valve lift is 0.5069 inch intake and 0.5185 inch exhaust, and the valve lash (hot) is 0.012 inch intake and 0.020 inch exhaust. This camshaft was also used in the 1963 Chevrolet 427-ci V-8 engine, RPO Z11.

The 1964 engines rated at 400 and 425 horsepower were equipped with the GM 3822930 solid (mechanical) lifter camshaft. The advertised duration is 322 degrees intake and 320 degrees exhaust, the lobe separation angle is 113.5 degrees, the valve lift is 0.5069 inch intake and 0.5185 inch exhaust, and the valve lash (hot) is 0.018 inch intake and 0.030 inch exhaust.

The 1965 engine rated at 400 horsepower was equipped with the GM 3837736 solid (mechanical) lifter camshaft. The advertised duration is 325 degrees intake and exhaust, the lobe separation angle is 113.5 degrees, the valve lift is 0.557 inch intake and exhaust, and the valve lash (hot) is 0.018 inch intake and 0.030 inch exhaust.

During the early 1960s, just about every camshaft manufacturer in the United States offered some type of grind for the Chevrolet 409-ci V-8 engine. Crane Cams is one that has continued to supply blueprinted replacement factory muscle car camshafts for the 409-ci engines. The Crane Cams 150801, grind number F-228/3067-2-12, is a replacement for the GM 3796076 solid (mechanical) lifter camshaft. The advertised duration is 290 degrees intake and 300 degrees exhaust, the duration at 0.050-inch lift is 228 degrees intake and 238 degrees exhaust, the lobe separation angle is 112 degrees, the net valve lift (with 1.75 ratio rocker arms) is 0.515 inch intake and 0.538 inch exhaust, and the valve lash (hot) is 0.022 inch intake and exhaust. The power range is 2,500–6,000 rpm.

The Crane Cams 150431, grind number 3830690, is a replacement for the GM 3830690 solid (mechanical) lifter camshaft. The advertised duration is 274 degrees intake and 281 degrees exhaust, the duration at 0.050-inch lift is 237 degrees intake and 241 degrees exhaust, the lobe separation angle is 113.5 degrees, the net valve lift (with 1.75 ratio rocker arms) is 0.482 inch intake and 0.485 inch exhaust, and the valve lash (hot) is 0.022 inch intake and 0.030 inch exhaust. The power range is 3,200–6,500 rpm.

The Crane Cams 150441, grind number 3837735, is a replacement for the GM 3837735 solid (mechanical) lifter camshaft used in the 409-ci (400- and 425-horsepower) engines and 427-ci Z-11 engine. The advertised duration is 296 degrees intake and exhaust, the duration at 0.050-inch lift is 250 degrees intake and exhaust, the lobe separation angle is 113.5 degrees, the net valve lift (with 1.75 ratio rocker arms) is 0.525-inch intake and 0.525 inch exhaust, and the valve lash (hot) is 0.030 inch intake and exhaust. The power range is 3,800–7,000 rpm.

An Iskenderian Racing Cams 409 (241), grind number 296HYD, hydraulic lifter camshaft was installed in the engine described here. The advertised duration is 296 degrees intake and exhaust, the duration at 0.050-inch lift is 234 degrees intake and exhaust, the lobe separation angle is 110 degrees, the net valve lift (with 1.75 ratio rocker arms) is 0.509 inch intake and exhaust, and the valve lash is zero. The power range is 2,500–6,000 rpm, and its current retail price is $145.

The specifications of a camshaft used in a blown engine are different than the specifications of a camshaft used in a naturally aspirated engine. A street performance blower camshaft should have a larger lobe separation angle, from 112 to 114 degrees. A camshaft with long duration and big overlap is not recommended. As far as I know, none of the major U.S. camshaft manufacturers sell an off-the-shelf blower camshaft for the Chevrolet 409-ci V-8 engine. Installing a camshaft that will deliver maximum performance is important, but an alternative is to have a camshaft custom ground. This will ensure the camshaft will be perfectly suited for a specific engine. A quality camshaft company, such as Crower

Cams & Equipment, can perform this job. Refer to Chapter 5 for more information about camshafts in general and custom-ground camshafts.

DEGREE CAMSHAFT
> *Refer to Chapter 5.*

VALVE LIFTERS
A set of the Iskenderian Racing Cams 202-HY Superlifters hydraulic valve lifters, anti-pump-up-style with Tru-Arc retainers, was installed in the engine described here. The current retail price for a set is $115. Refer to Chapter 5 for information about valve lifters.

PUSHRODS
The GM 3755545 intake pushrods used with the 409-ci hydraulic lifter camshafts are 5/16 inch in diameter by 8.756 inches long. The GM 3755543 exhaust pushrods are 5/16 inch in diameter by 9.121 inches long. The GM 3795627 intake pushrods used with the 409-ci solid (mechanical) lifter camshafts are 3/8 inch in diameter by 8.8125 inches long, and the GM 3795625 exhaust pushrods are 3/8 inch in diameter by 9.137 inches long. The 3/8-inch-diameter heavy-duty pushrods were heat treated with hardened tips. In late 1962, the 3/8-inch-diameter GM 3822934 exhaust pushrod length was increased to 9.176 inches. Refer to Chapter 5 for further information about pushrods.

A set of Manley Performance Parts 25718-8 intake pushrods was installed in the engine described here. These pushrods are manufactured using 4130 chrome-moly heat-treated steel, are 5/16 inch in diameter by 0.080 inch wall by

These Iskenderian Racing Cams 202-HY Superlifters hydraulic valve lifters are the anti-pump-up style with Tru-Arc retainers.

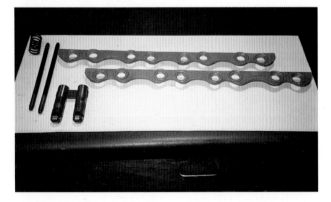

These parts are all manufactured by Iskenderian Racing Cams. The lightweight aluminum bars and the spring are part of the 241RR complete Rev Kit. The 272 solid (mechanical) roller lifter is 0.842 inches in diameter, and the 223 heat-treated chrome-moly steel pushrods are for a 409-ci engine. Both are 3/8 inch in diameter with an intake length of 8.796 inches and an exhaust length of 9.125 inches.

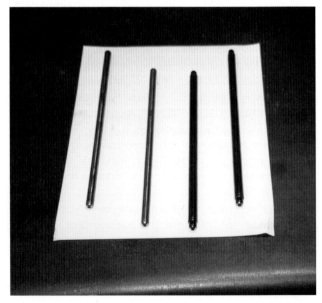

These are Chevrolet 409-ci V-8 pushrods, and starting from the left is a 5/16-inch-diameter by 8.756-inch-long intake, 5/16-inch-diameter by 9.121-inch-long exhaust, 3/8-inch-diameter by 8.8125-inch-long intake, and 3/8-inch-diameter by 9.137-inch-long exhaust.

The Manley Performance Parts 25718-8 intake pushrods on the left are 5/16 inch in diameter by 8.600 inches long, and the 25757-8 exhaust pushrods on the right are 5/16 inch in diameter by 8.950 inches long.

8.600 inches long, and have a black oxide finish. The Manley Performance Parts 25757-8 exhaust pushrods were also installed in this engine. These pushrods are manufactured using 4130 chrome-moly heat-treated steel, are 5/16 inch in diameter by 0.080 inch wall by 8.950 inches long, and have a black oxide finish. The current retail price for a set of these intake and exhaust pushrods is $105.

Many home engine builders make the classic mistake of purchasing a set of pushrods without first having mocked up the engine. This is a critical step with any custom-built engine and even with stock rebuilt engines. The pushrod lengths used in these engines may differ from the stock pushrod lengths provided by the factory. Camshaft manufacturers, such as Crower Cams & Equipment, sell adjustable checking pushrods with a minimum of plus or minus 0.250-inch (1/4-inch) adjustment travel in order to obtain the exact pushrod length. Accurate pushrod length is absolutely necessary to achieve the proper valvetrain geometry and check the valve-to-piston clearance. Adjustable checking pushrods are inexpensive items.

TIMING CHAINS

The Chevrolet 409-ci V-8 engines were equipped with a Morse timing chain set, which is no longer available from General Motors. Show Cars Automotive (Dr. 409) offers stock-style timing chain sets at a current retail price of $35. A Cloyes 93101 True Roller timing chain set, with a three-keyway crankshaft sprocket (for advancing or retarding the camshaft timing), was installed in the engine described here, as well as an Iskenderian Racing Cams 200-LP camshaft gear locking plate kit. Refer to Chapter 5 for information about timing chain sets, camshaft gear locking plate kits, and camshaft thrust buttons.

The Cloyes 92101 True Roller timing chain set has the three-keyway crankshaft sprocket used for advancing or retarding the camshaft timing.

The 409-ci camshaft sprocket is positioned using the GM 106751 woodruff key and GM 141195 pin.

The Pete Jackson 409-19C noisy dual-idler gear drive is available for Chevrolet 409-ci V-8 engines. Timing chains have a tendency to stretch over time, whereas a gear drive will not, thus ensuring continuous, accurate camshaft timing. The Peter Jackson 409-19C gear drive is $172 and is available at most speed-equipment outlets.

The GM 3736357 timing gear cover is used with the 409-ci 6 3/4-inch-diameter harmonic balancer, and the GM 3797799 timing gear cover is used with the 409-ci 7-inch-diameter harmonic balancer. A small-block Chevrolet one-piece oil seal will fit the 409-ci timing gear cover. Refer

Shown here is a Mr. Gasket 946G crankshaft bolt kit for a small-block Chevrolet V-8 engine, a GM 3736357 timing gear cover, and an Iskenderian Racing Cams 200-LP camshaft gear locking plate kit.

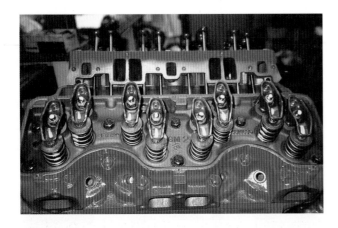

A pair of GM 3824370 cylinder heads—casting number 3814690, casting dates of 56 (May 6, 1962) and F662 (June 6, 1962)—are shown on a 409-ci engine with a casting number of 3857656 and a casting date of J23 (October 23, 1964). These large-port cylinder heads are one of the high-performance models.

A GM 3834370 high-performance cast-iron cylinder head is pictured here. The casting number is 3814690, casting date is F662 (June 6, 1962), and it has larger diameter pushrod holes and larger raised intake ports.

This is a GM 3819333 (casting number) cylinder head, casting date 117 (November 7, 1963), which was factory-equipped with 1.940-inch head diameter intake valves and 1.660-inch head diameter exhaust valves. This is a low-performance cylinder head.

to Chapter 5 for information about preparing timing gear covers. The original Moon Equipment Company 187 and Weiand 7129 die-cast finned-aluminum timing gear covers will fit a 409-ci engine.

CYLINDER HEADS

All the Chevrolet 409-ci V-8 engines were equipped with cast-iron cylinder heads that had a very unusual shape resembling a W. Each of these cylinder heads weighed 53 pounds (bare). The following is a list of Chevrolet 409-ci V-8 cylinder heads:

3795586: 1961
3814690: 1962–1963
3819333: 1962–1965 Truck
3830817: 1963–1965
3852583: 1963–1965

These are the castings numbers I am aware of, but there may well be others. Chevrolet 409-ci V-8 cylinder heads have a very small combustion chamber volume, similar to Chevrolet 348-ci V-8 cylinder heads.

The GM 3759254 cylinder heads, casting number 3795586, installed on the 1961 Chevrolet 409-ci V-8 engines, have the same casting number as the cylinder heads installed on the 1961 Chevrolet 348-ci V-8 engines, although there are some differences. The cylinder head used on the 409-ci engines has larger-diameter pushrod holes and bigger spring seat pockets. The GM 3795586 (casting number) cylinder heads were fitted with 2.066-inch head diameter intake valves and 1.720-inch head diameter exhaust valves, and have an estimated combustion chamber volume of 8.2 cc. The GM 3839747 cylinder heads, casting number 3830817, are a similar design and were fitted with the same valve size, although the combustion chamber volume is estimated to be 9.2 cc. The 409-ci cylinder heads with casting numbers 3795586 and 3830817 were considered standard performance models and were installed on all the 10.0:1 compression 409-ci engines and the 1961 engine with an 11.25:1 compression ratio.

The GM 3824370 cylinder heads, casting number 3814690, and GM 3852582 cylinder heads, casting number 3852583, were referred to as the "high-performance models". They have larger raised intake ports, 2.203-inch head diame-

heads have 1.940-inch head diameter intake valves, 1.660-inch head diameter exhaust valves, and a combustion chamber volume of approximately 7.9 cc.

The 1963 and 1964 Chevrolet 409-ci V-8 engines, rated at 425 horsepower and destined for street use, came equipped with double cylinder head gaskets (for each cylinder head) from the factory. Someone at General Motors was concerned about a novice driver's ability to handle all the horsepower on the street. So GM decided to lower the compression ratio, thus reducing the potential damage to the engine by reducing the power. Only a single cylinder head gasket (for each cylinder head) was installed for racing purposes. But after the owner finished racing for the day, and prior to driving home, did the owner reinstall the second cylinder head gasket? The average volume of a factory-equipped cylinder head gasket is estimated to be 7.1 cc.

A pair of GM 3189333 (casting number) cylinder heads was installed on the engine described here. A pair of these cylinder heads in good condition is approximately $150 (bare). The cylinder heads were surfaced and a Serdi-machined multi-angle blueprint valve grind performed. The intake and exhaust ports were fully ported, polished, and gasket matched. Refer to Chapter 5 for information about cylinder head preparation, Serdi-machined valve grinds, hardened exhaust valve seats, and pushrod holes.

The installation of good quality cylinder head gaskets is a necessity in a blown performance street engine, and thinner cylinder head gaskets will offer a better seal than thicker gaskets. The Fel-Pro 8007PT Permatorque cylinder head gaskets are approximately 0.040 inch thick. Even though these cylinder head gaskets are the Permatorque type, retorque the cylinder head bolts (or studs) after the initial startup of the engine, particularly with blown engines.

ter intake valves, 1.734-inch head diameter exhaust valves, and larger pushrod holes to accommodate 3/8-inch-diameter pushrods. The combustion chamber volume is approximately 10.3 cc. The GM 3852582 cylinder heads, casting number 3852583, were cast with reinforced valve spring pockets. The 409-ci cylinder heads with casting numbers 3814690 and 3852583 were installed on the 11.0:1 compression ratio engines. The GM 3852582 cylinder heads, casting number 3852583, are probably the most desirable type to use on a street performance engine.

The GM 3819333 (casting number) cylinder heads were installed on the Chevrolet Truck 409-ci V-8 engines with a 7.75:1 compression ratio. These low-performance cylinder

VALVES

The valves installed in the Chevrolet 409-ci V-8 cylinder heads were manufactured using aluminized alloy steel. The valve

This is a GM 3189333 (casting number) cylinder head that has been fully ported, polished, and gasket matched. Those are Scorpion Performance 1041 roller rocker arms. This cylinder head will be installed on the engine described here.

Manley Performance Parts 11310-8 Race Master stainless-steel intake valves—2.200-inch head diameter by 3/8-inch stem diameter—and 11310-8 Race Master stainless-steel exhaust valves—1.735-inch head diameter by 3/8-inch stem diameter—are installed in this GM 3189333 (casting number) cylinder head, which has also been surfaced.

stem diameter is 0.3710 to 0.3717 (3/8) inch, and the overall length is 5.105 to 5.125 inches. Chevrolet specified the intake-valve-stem-to-valve-guide clearance to be 0.010 to 0.033 inch and the exhaust-valve-stem-to-valve-guide clearance to be 0.015 to 0.032 inch. The GM 3814691 intake valves with a 2.203-inch head diameter were installed in the high-performance cylinder heads. The GM 3781155 intake valves with a 2.066-inch head diameter were installed in the standard-performance cylinder heads. The GM 3747307 intake valves with a 1.940-inch head diameter were installed in the truck cylinder heads. The GM 3817821 exhaust valves with 1.734-inch head diameter were installed in the high-performance cylinder heads. The GM 3781156 exhaust valves with 1.720-inch head diameter were installed in the standard-performance cylinder heads. The GM 3747308 exhaust valves with a head diameter of 1.660 inches were installed in the truck cylinder heads. Installing larger head diameter valves in the truck and standard-performance cylinder heads will prove to be beneficial only at the higher end of the rpm range.

General Motors no longer lists the valves for Chevrolet 409-ci V-8 engines. Show Cars Automotive (Dr. 409) sells replacement valves manufactured using 21-4N stainless steel. The intake valves are offered with different head sizes: 2.190, 2.075, and 1.940 inches. The exhaust valves are offered with different sizes: 1.750, 1.725, and 1.670 inches. The current retail price for each valve, in any of the sizes listed above, is $14.

Manley Performance Parts offers stainless-steel intake and exhaust valves for Chevrolet 409-ci V-8 engines. The Manley Performance Parts 11310-8 Race Master NK-842 stainless-steel intake valves have a 2.200-inch head diameter by 0.3715-inch stem diameter by 5.105 inches long overall. They are swirl polished, have hardened tips, and weigh 139 grams each. The Manley Performance Parts 11312-8 Race Master NK-842 stainless-steel intake valves have a 2.250-inch head diameter by 0.3715-inch stem diameter by 5.105-inch in overall length. They are swirl polished, have hardened tips, and weigh 141 grams each. The Manley

Performance Parts 11311-8 Race Master XH-426 stainless-steel exhaust valves have a 1.735-inch head diameter by 0.3715-inch stem diameter by 5.105-inch length. They are swirl polished, have hardened tips, and weigh 115 grams each. The Manley Performance Parts 11313-8 Race Master XH-426 stainless-steel exhaust valves have a 1.750-inch head diameter by 0.3715-inch stem diameter by 5.105-inch overall length. They are swirl polished, have hardened tips, and weigh 117 grams each. A set of eight of the Manley Performance Parts 11310-8 Race Master intake valves and a set of eight of the 11311-8 Race Master exhaust valves were installed in the engine described. The current retail price for one set is $200. The recommended valve-stem-to-valve-guide clearance in a street performance engine is 0.0015 to 0.002 inch for today's unleaded gasoline.

VALVE GUIDES, BUSHINGS, AND SEALS
K-Line KL1842STA bronze bullet valve guide liners, 3/8 inch in diameter, and Enginetech S2890 Viton positive-seal valve stem seals, 3/8 inch in diameter, were installed in the cylinder heads described here. Refer to Chapter 5 for a complete explanation of these parts.

VALVE SPRINGS
The GM 3795598 single valve springs with damper have an installed height of 128–148 pounds at 1.680 inches valves closed, and 267–291 pounds at 1.290 inches or 282–306 pounds at 1.250 inches valves open. The valve springs used in the Chevrolet 409-ci V-8 engines are no longer available from General Motors.

One of the best quality valve springs Chevrolet offered for the 409-ci engine was the GM 3822931 single valve spring with damper. It has an installed height of 140 pounds at 1.680 inches valves closed and 340 pounds at 1.200 inches valves open. The coil bind is 1.150 inches. These valve springs are manufactured using aircraft-quality chrome silicon steel, are centerless ground, and have been heat treated,

The Iskenderian Racing Cams 3105-D (outer) and 906-AM (inner) dual valve springs with damper, the 347-ST valve spring retainers, and the VL 3/8-inch valve stem locks are pictured here. The intake ports are nicely ported, polished, and gasket matched. The masking job is definitely slovenly.

shot peened, and Magnafluxed. These valves springs are no longer available from General Motors.

The valve springs used in a blown engine must have sufficient spring tension in the closed position to withstand the intake valves being pulled off the valve seats (or valve seat inserts) when the engine is under boost.

A set of Iskenderian Racing Cams dual valve springs with damper was installed in the engine described here. The valve spring assembly consists of the 3105-D outer valve spring and 906-AM inner valve spring. They are silicon chrome, aircraft-quality racing helical coil, oil tempered, and shot peened. The installed height is 135 pounds at 1.750 inches valves closed and 395 pounds at 1.225 inches valves open. The coil bind is 1.160 inches, and the maximum lift is 0.550 inches. The 3105-D outer valve spring is 1.490 inches o.d. and 1.076 inches i.d. with a natural color. The 906-AM inner valve spring is 1.005 inches o.d. and 0.730 inch i.d. with a blue color. The current retail price for a set of 16 of these inner and outer valve springs is $135.

The GM 3795664 valve stem oil shields are cup shaped and were fitted over the top of the valve springs, beneath the valve spring retainers, for the purpose of oil control. Provided the oil shields will fit over the top of aftermarket valve springs, it does no harm to install them.

Valve Spring Retainers and Locks

The GM 3729363 valve spring retainers and GM 3947880 valve stem locks were used with the GM 3795598 and 3822931 single valve springs with damper. The valve spring retainers are no longer available from General Motors. Iskenderian Racing Cams 347-ST valve spring retainers were installed in the engine described here with Iskenderian

Racing Cams 3105-D and 906-AM valve springs. These valve spring retainers are manufactured using 4130 chrome-moly heat-treated steel, they are 7 degrees for use with 0.3715-inch (3/8-inch) valve stems, and they have a black oxide finish. The current retail price for a set of 16 of these valve spring retainers is $55.

A set of 32 Iskenderian Racing Cams VL-3/8 valve stem locks was installed in the engine described here. These valve stem locks are manufactured using 4140 chrome-moly heat-treated steel, they are 7 degrees for use with 0.3175-inch valve stems, and they have a black oxide finish. The current retail price for these valve stem locks is $10. Refer to Chapter 5 for more information about valve stem locks.

ROCKER ARMS

The GM 3814692 rocker arm studs installed in the Chevrolet 409-ci V-8 cylinder heads are the pressed-in type. The length of the second design rocker arm studs was

The GM 3814692 rocker arm studs, 3732765 stamped-steel 1.75-ratio heat-treated rocker arms, 5723552 rocker arm balls with self-locking nuts, and 3795664 valve stem oil shields are pictured here.

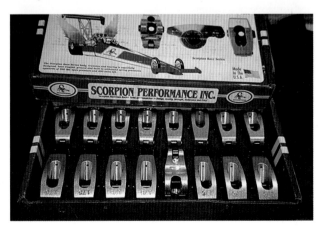

Here is a first-design set of Scorpion Performance 1041 roller rocker arms for Chevrolet 409-ci V-8 engines. These rocker arms have a 1.75 ratio.

increased by 0.150 inch, and they were pinned in position. Pressed-in rocker arm studs are fine for stock or mild street performance engines, but when modifying the engine or installing roller rocker arms, you should have them removed and have screw-in rocker arm studs installed. Leave this to the services of an experienced machine shop, otherwise cracking a rocker arm stud boss is a certainty. The ARP 134-7101 high-performance series rocker arm stud kit (for small-block Chevrolet V-8 engines), rated at 170,000 psi, 3/8 inch in diameter, can be installed in 409-ci cylinder heads, and the current retail price is $30.

The GM 3732765 stamped-steel heat-treated rocker arms, with a 1.75 ratio, and the GM 5723552 rocker arm balls and self-locking nuts were installed on the Chevrolet 409-ci V-8 cylinder heads. Refer to Chapter 5 for more information about stock-style and stock replacement rocker arms.

The rocker arms with the best designs are the roller rocker arms, which can handle large valve lifts and valve spring pressures, as well as reduce friction within the valvetrain. The Crane Cams 13750-16 Gold Race 1.70 ratio roller rocker arms are designed for a 3/8-inch-diameter rocker arm stud and are CNC machined from billet-extruded aluminum. They have a precision needle bearing fulcrum and an 8620 steel alloy roller tip, as well as a slotted body for extra stud clearance. The current retail price for a set of 16 is $400, complete with 4140 chrome-moly steel poly-loc nuts and setscrews. The Crane Cams 13750-16 Gold Race 1.70 ratio roller rocker arms for a 7/16-inch-diameter rocker arm stud are also available.

The Scorpion Performance 1041 roller rocker arms are manufactured in the United States and are CNC machined from billet-extruded aluminum. They have a 1.75 ratio and are designed for a 3/8-inch-diameter stud. They also have precision needle bearing fulcrums and tips, a slotted body for extra rocker arm stud clearance, and are blue anodized. The current retail price for a set of 16 is $240, complete with poly-loc nuts and setscrews. They are available at most high-performance parts stores.

The Chevrolet 409-ci V-8 cylinder heads were not equipped with pushrod guide plates. You should consider installing them if 3/8-inch-diameter pushrods will be used with a high lift camshaft. Pushrod guide plates can be modified to fit the 409-ci cylinder heads, and pushrods with hardened tips should be used with them. The pushrod guide plates are mounted under the rocker arm studs. Refer to Chapter 5 for advice about cylinder head assembly.

CYLINDER HEAD BOLTS

The GM 3735721 long cylinder head bolts and 3735722 short cylinder head bolts were installed in the Chevrolet 409-ci V-8 engines. There are 20 long bolts, which are 7/16 inch NC by 3.98 inches long, and there are 16 short cylinder head bolts, which are 7/16 inch NC by 3.32 inches long. Provided they are not badly corroded or have damaged threads, you can glass bead these good-quality Chevrolet cylinder head bolts and paint the exterior bolts, while also coating the bolts inside the valve covers with graphite. The cylinder head bolts in the 409-ci engines are torqued to 65 ft-lbs. General Motors no longer lists these cylinder head bolts.

The ARP 135-3602 high-performance series cylinder head bolt kit is available for 409-ci engines. The bolts are manufactured using heat-treated chrome-moly steel rated at 180,000 psi, and they have 12-point heads. The current retail price for this kit is $85.

A cylinder head stud kit should be installed in a blown engine that will have more than 5 pounds of boost. The ARP 135-4002 cylinder head stud kit consists of 8740 heat-treated alloy steel studs rated at 200,000 psi, hardened-steel hex-head nuts, and parallel-ground washers. The current retail price for this kit is $175. The ARP 235-4202 cylinder head stud kit is the same, except the nuts have 12-point heads. The price for this kit is $150.

VALVE COVERS

The 1961 and 1962 GM 5774089 stamped-steel valve covers were painted silver and installed on the Chevrolet 409-ci V-8 engines with GM 3877670 valve cover hold-down tabs. The valve cover hold-down tabs had a small rubber gasket attached that was positioned against the valve cover lip. If using stock-style valve covers, glass bead them, remove any dents, and paint the underside with Glyptal G-1228A medium-gray gloss enamel (unless they are chrome-plated). This will prevent any rust from forming if there is moisture present.

The valve covers installed on the 409-ci truck engines have large spark plug wire separators located at the top center of each valve cover, unlike passenger car engines where the large spark plug wire separators are located at the rear of the valve covers. The 1963–1965 GM 5732674 left side and 5732676 right side 409-ci valve covers are chrome-plated and have dripper rails installed. The valve covers used on the Canadian 409-ci engines did not have the Chevrolet Bowtie emblem stamped in them, because it was not known at the time of manufacture if the valve covers would be installed on a Chevrolet or a Canadian Pontiac. Refer to Chapter 5 for information about aftermarket valve covers and installation.

B. CAMSHAFT AND CYLINDER HEADS SUMMARY

- New Clevite 77 SH-398S camshaft bearings installed allowing for 0.002-inch camshaft clearance and 0.002-inch end play. No. 1 bearing, SH-398; housing bore diameter: 2.019 to 2.0210 inches. No. 2 bearing, SH-399; housing bore diameter: 2.009 to 2.011 inches. Nos. 3 and 4 bearings, SH-400; housing bore diameter: 1.999 to 2.00 inches. No. 5 bearing, SH-401; housing bore diameter: 2.009 to 2.011 inches. Camshaft journal diameter: 1.870 inches. **$50**
- New Iskenderian Racing Cams 409 (241), grind number 296HYD. Cast-iron alloy hydraulic lifter camshaft with

advertised duration: 296 degrees intake and exhaust; duration at 0.050-inch lift: 234 degrees intake and exhaust; lobe separation angle: 110 degrees; net valve lift (with 1.75 ratio rocker arms): 0.509 inch intake and exhaust; valve lash: zero. Power range: 2,500–6,500 rpm. Camshaft degreed. **$145**

- New Iskenderian Racing Cams 202-HY Superlifters hydraulic valve lifters, 0.842 inch o.d., installed. **$115**
- New Manley Performance Parts 25718-8 intake pushrods, 4130 heat-treated chrome-moly steel—5/16 inch in diameter, 0.080 inch wall, 8.600 inches long overall—with black oxide finish, installed. New Manley Performance Parts 25757-8 exhaust pushrods, 4130 heat-treated chrome-moly steel—5/16 inch in diameter, 0.080 inch wall, 8.950 inches long overall—with black oxide finish, installed. **$105**
- New Cloyes 92101 True Roller timing chain set, three-key-way crankshaft sprocket, installed with new Iskenderian Racing Cams 200-LP camshaft gear locking plate kit and new Manley Performance Parts 42146 aluminum camshaft thrust button. Camshaft gear bolts installed using Loctite and torqued to 20 ft-lbs. GM 3736357 timing gear cover installed with new polished stainless-steel bolts and lockwashers using Loctite and torqued to 15 ft-lbs. Timing gear cover gasket installed using silicone sealant. Inside of timing gear cover painted with Glyptal G-1228A medium-gray gloss enamel, and exterior painted with Plasti-Kote 200 Chevrolet orange high-gloss engine enamel. **$181.92**
- GM 3819333 (casting number) cast-iron cylinder heads, casting date 110 (October 1, 1963). Combustion chamber volume, 7.9 cc; cylinder head weight (bare), 59 pounds each. **$150**
- Cylinder heads hot tanked, Magnafluxed, Redi-Stripped, and pressure tested. Intake and exhaust ports fully ported, polished, and gasket matched; cylinder heads surfaced. New K-Line KL1842STA universal-length 3/8-inch bronze bullet valve guide liners installed; new Enginetech S2890 Viton-material positive-seal valve stem seals, 3/8 inch in diameter, installed. Serdi-machined multi-angle blueprint valve grind performed. Exterior surface painted with Plasti-Kote 200 Chevrolet orange high-gloss engine enamel. Cylinder heads installed with new ARP 135-3602 high-performance series cylinder head bolt kit, heat-treated chrome-moly steel, 180,000 psi, 12-point heads, using Permatex aviation form-a-gasket and torqued to 65 ft-lbs. **$880.83**

- New Manley Performance Parts 11310-8 Race Master NK-842 stainless-steel intake valves—2.200-inch head diameter, 0.3715-inch stem diameter, 5.105 inches long overall—swirl polished, hardened tips, installed. Intake valve weight: 139 grams. New Manley Performance Parts 11311-8 Race Master XH-426 stainless-steel exhaust valves—1.735-inch head diameter, 0.3715-inch stem diameter, 5.105 inches long overall—swirl polished, hardened tips, installed. Exhaust valve weight: 115 grams. Valves installed with Serdi-machined multi-angle blueprint valve grind. **$200**
- New Iskenderian Racing Cams dual valve springs with damper (3105-D outer and 906-AM inner spring), aircraft-quality racing helical coil, oil tempered, shot peened, silicon chrome. Installed height: 135 pounds at 1.750 inches valves closed and 395 pounds at 1.225 inches valves open. Coil bind: 1.160 inches; maximum lift: 0.550 inch; color, natural and blue. New Iskenderian Racing Cams 347-ST heat-treated chrome-moly steel valve spring retainers, 7 degrees, 3/8-inch valve stem, black oxide finish, installed with new Iskenderian Racing Cams VL-3/8 heat-treated 4140 chrome-moly machined-steel valve stem locks, 7 degrees, black oxide finish. **$200**
- New Scorpion Performance 1041 roller rocker arms, 1.75 ratio, CNC-machined billet-extruded aluminum, 3/8-inch-diameter rocker arm stud, precision needle bearing fulcrums and tips, blue anodized, installed with new ARP 134-7101 high-performance series rocker arm stud kit, 170,000 psi, 3/8 inch in diameter. Rocker arm studs installed using Loctite and torqued to 50 ft-lbs. **$270**
- NOS Moon Equipment Company NN-48 No Name polished die-cast finned-aluminum valve covers installed with new polished stainless-steel bolts and lockwashers using Loctite and torqued to 15 ft-lbs. Valve cover gaskets installed using silicone sealant. NOS Moon Equipment Company 166RC polished-aluminum medium upright valve cover breathers, 2-inch width, installed with new polished stainless-steel bolts and lock- washers using anti-seize compound. Valve cover breather gaskets installed using silicone sealant. **$335**

- Camshaft and Cylinder Heads Total: **$2,632.75**

CHAPTER 16
INTAKE SYSTEM

A. INTAKE SYSTEM
INTAKE MANIFOLD

The Chevrolet 409-ci V-8 passenger car engines were equipped with a cast-iron or aluminum single four-barrel carburetor or an aluminum dual four-barrel carburetor intake manifold. The 409-ci Truck engines were equipped with a single four-barrel carburetor cast-iron intake manifold.

The casting numbers for the Chevrolet 409-ci V-8 intake manifolds are:

3767579: 1961, cast iron
3797776: 1961, aluminum (service package)
3814678: 1962–1963, aluminum
3814881: 1962–1964, aluminum (two x four-barrel)
3822929: 1962, aluminum (service package)
3830831: 1963, cast iron
3844463: 1963–1965, aluminum
3844465: 1964–1965, cast iron
3844472: 1962–1965, Truck, cast iron

These are the casting numbers I am aware of, but there may well be others. The 1961 GM 3767579 (casting number) Chevrolet 409-ci V-8 cast-iron single four-barrel carburetor intake manifold has the same casting number as the one used on the 1961 Chevrolet 348-ci V-8 engine. The 409-ci version has larger throttle plate bores for clearance with the primary

Here is the GM 3814880, casting number 3814881, dual four-barrel carburetor aluminum intake manifold for Chevrolet 409-ci V-8 engines.

This is a GM 3844462 aluminum 409-ci intake manifold, casting number 3844463, casting date 1-15-65 (January 15, 1965). A Carter AFB 3783S (GM 3855581) four-barrel carburetor was installed on this intake manifold.

This relic is a GM 3844472 (casting number) cast-iron single four-barrel carburetor intake manifold used on the Chevrolet Truck 409-ci V-8 engines.

throttle plates in the Carter AFB 3270-S (GM 3797698) carburetor. The 1962 GM 3822929 (casting number) open-plenum aluminum intake manifold was a dealer service package, with a Carter AFB 3345-SA or a Rochester 7020028 4GC four-barrel carburetor. It was not installed by the factory on any of the 409-ci passenger car engines. The GM 3814817 oil splash shield was installed on all 409-ci intake manifolds. Refer to Chapter 6 for information about this part.

The 1962 and 1963 GM 3814880, casting number 3814881, Chevrolet 409-ci V-8 aluminum dual four-barrel carburetor intake manifold was equipped with a Carter AFB

Pictured here is the fuel system associated with early 1960s muscle car drag racing, with the GM 3814880 aluminum intake manifold (casting number 3814881), a Carter AFB 3361-S (GM 3815403) four-barrel carburetor on the front, and a Carter AFB 3362-S (GM 3815404) four-barrel carburetor on the rear. The carburetor scoops are vintage Cal Custom 40-40 polished die-cast aluminum.

3361-S (GM 3815403) front carburetor and a Carter AFB 3362-S (GM 3815404) rear carburetor.

In 1963, Chevrolet offered a unique two-piece aluminum intake manifold for the 427-ci RPO Z11 engine. The GM 3830623 (casting number) top section mounted the two x four-barrel carburtors, and the GM 3837733 (casting number) bottom section was the valley cover, similar to the intake setups used on early Chrysler Hemi V-8 engines.

The Mickey Thompson 3746409 Power Ram cast-aluminum dual quad ram-log intake manifold is probably the most sought after intake manifold ever designed for the Chevrolet 409-ci V-8 engine. One was recently sold on eBay for a ridiculous amount. It is a great looking intake manifold and very functional for street use, with a power range from 2,500–7,000 rpm.

Most aftermarket and vintage intake manifolds manufactured for Chevrolet 348-ci V-8 engines were also designed for Chevrolet 409-ci V-8 engines. These intake manifolds are listed in Chapter 6 along with other relevant intake manifold information. The Fel-Pro 9459 intake manifold gaskets, with a port size of 2 1/4 by 1 5/16 inches, are used with the 409-ci standard performance cylinder heads. The Fel-Pro 9788 (GM 3822650) intake manifold gaskets, with

Here is the famous Mickey Thompson 3746409 Power Ram cast-aluminum dual-quad ram-log intake manifold for 409-ci engines. The stainless-steel braided hose at the front is used to equalize the air/fuel mixture in the left and right banks.

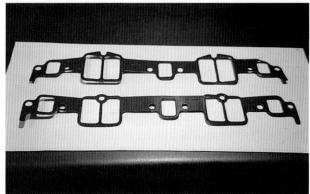

The Fel-Pro 9459 intake manifold gasket (port size of 2 1/4 by 1 5/16 inches) is pictured at the top, and the Fel-Pro 9788 intake manifold gasket (port size of 2 1/2 by 1 3/8 inches) is at the bottom.

This is a rare marine 409-ci V-8 small-port aluminum intake manifold. There is no casting number, casting date, or Winters Foundry snowflake casting mark. The angle of the carburetor pad is very noticeable.

This Offenhauser 5492 low-profile dual-quad intake manifold was modified by Blower Drive Service to accept a GMC 6-71 blower for installation on a 409-ci engine.

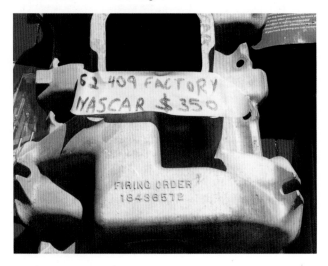

This GM 3822929 (casting number) open-plenum aluminum intake manifold was offered as a service package for Chevrolet 409-ci V-8 engines. Ignore the swap meet labels.

a port size of 2 1/2 inches by 1 3/8 inches, are used with the 409-ci high-performance cylinder heads.

The Blower Drive Service 8036 blower intake manifold is the only off-the-shelf model available today for mounting a GMC 6-71 or GMC 8-71 blower on a Chevrolet 409-ci V-8 engine. This intake manifold is 5 3/4 inches tall, has a pop-off (backfire) valve, and is designed for the standard-performance smaller port size cylinder heads. The current retail price is $750, unpolished. The Blower Drive Service 356-3S1/2 complete blower kit consists of the GMC 6-71 or GMC 8-71 blower, intake manifold, pulleys, brackets, blower belt, and all the necessary gaskets and bolts. The current retail price for this unpolished kit is $2,500.

The owner of the Chevrolet 409-ci V-8 engine described here decided that a lower-profile intake manifold was the order of the day. He sent an Offenhauser 5492 low-profile dual quad aluminum intake manifold to Blower Drive Service to modify it to accept a GMC 6-71 blower. The cost of this service, plus the price of a new Offenhauser 5492 intake manifold and installation of a pop-off valve, was $750.

The GM 3846123 crankcase breather/oil filler tube and 3828373 crankcase breather/oil filler tube cap were installed in the front of the intake manifold on 409-ci engines. The GM 3828373 cap was chrome-plated on 1964–1965 engines.

GMC 6-71 BLOWER

A blower forces a greater volume of the air/fuel mixture into the engine rather than drawing less of the mixture in, which occurs in a normally aspirated engine. The blower creates boost only when it can get enough air, which is usually at wide-open throttle (WOT), when the engine is under load. The boost should only be measured at WOT, and this measurement is in pounds (per square inch). A street performance blown engine will seldom experience boost, provided the driver wants to stay on the local law enforcement officers' good side. The boost effectively raises the engine's compression ratio, but it also raises the cylinder and exhaust temperatures, along with an increase in cylinder pressure. The blower is a very efficient and trouble-free mechanical device when it is properly set up.

A GMC 6-71 blower was installed on the engine described here, so I will give a brief description of this particular model only. The GMC 6-71 blower consists of two of the three-lobe-design helical rotors and gears, a front and rear bearing plate, a front cover, and a blower case. Although this blower has very few parts and is simple in design and construction, the proper clearances and assembly should be left to the services of an expert blower builder. If an amateur starts playing in the expert blower builders' domain, disaster is guaranteed to strike! I have seen blowers so poorly assembled, they produced little or no boost, leaving the owners wondering why their engines did not perform as expected.

The large-bore GMC 6-71 blower cases are the GM 5111715 die-cast model and 5155866 sand-cast model. These two blower cases have a horizontal inside diameter of

This is all there is to a large-bore GMC 6-71 blower: the GM 5111715 die-cast blower case, the two rotors and gears, the GM 5122363 die-cast front and rear bearing plates, and the GM 5114442 die-cast front cover. Notice that the two outer reinforcing ribs in the top opening of the blower case are rounded.

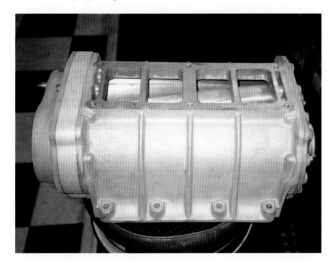

Here is an assembled GM 5138725 6-71 small-bore die-cast blower with a GM 5150219 sand-cast front bearing plate. Notice that the two outer reinforcing ribs in the top opening of the blower case are square.

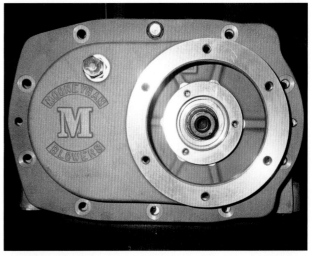

A (Gene) Mooneyham Blowers front blower case cover for a GMC 6-71 blower is pictured here. This cover fits the early sand-cast model bearing plates.

A Mooneyham Blowers rear blower case cover for a GMC 6-71 blower is shown with the bearing support rings.

9 5/8 inches, and the two outer reinforcing ribs in the top opening of the case are rounded. The small-bore GMC 6-71 die-cast blower case is the GM 5138725, with a horizontal inside diameter of 9 3/8 inches. The two outer reinforcing ribs in the top opening of the case are square. The performance difference between the big-bore and small-bore GMC 6-71 blowers is minimal.

There are two different front covers and bearing plates for the GMC 6-71 blowers. The GM 5150233 front cover is the early sand-cast model, has smooth sides, and requires 5/16-inch-NC by 3 1/2-inch-long bolts to secure it to the blower case. The Blower Drive Service 671-1SG, or the Mr. Gasket 770 front cover gasket, and the GM 5150219 sand-cast bearing plates are used with this cover. The GM 5114442 front cover is the later die-cast model, has ribbed sides, and requires 5/16-inch-NC by 2 1/4-inch-long bolts to secure it to the blower case. The Blower Drive Service 671-1DG front cover gasket and GM 5122363 die-cast bearing plates are used with this cover. The bearing plates for both models are interchangeable with the front and rear.

Luke's Custom Machine & Design (see Resources) builds complete GMC 4-71 and 6-71 blower setups. The blower is completely disassembled, and all the parts are carefully inspected for cracks, score marks, wear, or other damage. The blower case, rotors, front and rear bearing plates, and front cover are

This is a (Mert) Littlefield front blower case cover for a GMC 6-71 blower shown with the snout drive. This cover fits the later-model die-cast bearing plates.

Here is a Mooneyham Blowers front bearing plate for a GMC 6-71 blower. It is designed for the early sand-cast front cover.

thoroughly cleaned and glass beaded. The front and rear bearing plates are machined to accept bearing support rings. "Tim the polishing guy" carts off the blower case, front and rear bearing plates, and front cover for his artistic treatment.

All new front and rear bearings and seals, gaskets, and stainless-steel socket-head bolts are installed. A pressure-relief valve, oil-sight gauge, and stainless-steel oil filler and oil drain plugs are installed in the front cover. The rotors are double-pinned, and the blower is accurately clearanced. A Luke's Custom Machine & Design GMC 6-71 small-bore blower was installed on the engine described here.

Anodized-aluminum blower studs kits, consisting of the studs, parallel-ground flat washers, and 12-point nuts are used to secure the blower case to the intake manifold. The

studs should be installed in the intake manifold using anti-seize compound. The (Gene) Mooneyham Blowers 10884 or Blower Drive Service 671-8C anodized-aluminum blower stud kits cost about $42.

BLOWER SNOUT

A Luke's Custom Machine & Design LS3000 medium blower snout was installed on the blower described here. This blower snout is machined from 6061 aircraft-quality aluminum, which is T-6 heat treated, and it measures 5.00 inches from the front of the blower case front cover to the front of the flange for mounting the snout drive pulley. The Luke's Custom Machine & Design LS3300 medium shaft and LS4100 gear coupler were used with this blower snout.

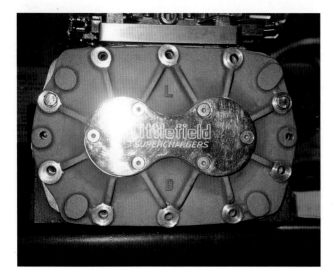

Here is a Littlefield rear blower case cover with the bearing support rings and cover for a GMC 6-71 blower.

This is a Luke's Custom Machine & Design LS3000 polished medium blower snout, complete with the LS3300 medium shaft and LS4100 gear coupler.

The shaft and gear coupler are machined from 4140 chrome-moly heat-treated steel and incorporate the deepest splines currently offered in the industry. The current retail price for the LS3000 polished medium blower snout, LS3300 medium shaft, and LS4100 gear coupler is $390.

IDLER PULLEY AND BRACKET

Luke's Custom Machine & Design machines the 5-inch-o.d. blower belt idler pulley from 6061 T-6 aluminum. The idler pulley has a slight crown on the belt surface to keep the blower belt centered. The idler pulley bracket is milled from 1/2-inch-thick aluminum and is bolted to the front cover of the blower, with or without stainless-steel spacers, depending on the application. This compact design permits the installation of the generator (or alternator), power steering pump, and air conditioning compressor (if equipped) in the stock positions on the engine.

BLOWER DRIVE PULLEYS

The boost for the engine described here was in the 4–5-pound range. The blower drive ratio is adjusted by changing the size of the blower drive pulleys. A crankshaft blower drive pulley with a larger diameter than the snout drive pulley will result in an overdrive ratio. Conversely, a crankshaft blower drive pulley with a smaller diameter than the snout drive pulley will result in an underdrive ratio. A 476-ci V-8 engine with an 8.00:1 compression ratio actually has a final compression ratio of approximately 10.5:1 when the engine experiences 4.5 pounds of boost. Anything higher than a 12.4:1 compression ratio (with boost) for street use is not advisable, particularly when using today's highest octane, unleaded gasoline.

Blower Drive Service offers blower drive pulleys and blower belts in 1/2-inch pitch (Gilmer), 8-millimeter pitch, 13.9-millimeter pitch, and 14-millimeter pitch. The 1/2-inch pitch (Gilmer) blower belts are available in a wide range of lengths, and a multitude of diameters are offered for all the blower drive pulleys. The Blower Drive Service catalog contains some very good blower information, including the tables required for calculating the blower drive ratios and final compression ratio.

The pistons installed in the engine described here were cus-tom manufactured by Ross Racing Pistons. Building a blown 409-ci engine with an 8.00:1 compression ratio is a fairly simple process for places like Ross Racing Pistons, as long as you provide them with all the relevant technical information. This should include the bore and stroke, connecting rod length, camshaft specifications, valve sizes, cylinder head volume, cylinder head gasket volume, blower type, and fuel system. Ross Racing Pistons will then be able to provide pistons with the desired compression ratio.

A Blower Drive Service 6333 crankshaft blower drive billet-aluminum pulley—33 teeth by 3 1/2 inches wide by 1/2-inch pitch (Gilmer)—and a 6330 snout drive billet-aluminum pulley—30 teeth by 3 1/2 inches wide by 1/2-inch pitch (Gilmer)—were installed on the engine described here. A Blower Drive Service 560H300 blower belt, with 1/2-inch pitch (Gilmer) by 3 inches wide by 56 inches long, was also installed. This combination of blower drive pulleys with a small-bore GMC 6-71 blower results in an overdrive of 10 percent and an estimated boost of 4.5 pounds.

CARBURETOR

I do not intend to list every carburetor ever installed on a Chevrolet 409-ci V-8 engine, for there are many good books containing information on casting and part numbers for people looking for numbers-matching carburetors. The Carter AFB and Rochester 4GC four-barrel carburetors were used on 409-ci engines. Refer to Chapter 6 for information about different carburetors. The GM 5650815 glass bowl fuel filter was installed on 409-ci engines. A pair of Holley 0-1850S 4160 nonemission four-barrel carburetors—with silver finish, vacuum secondaries, 600 cfm (each), manual chokes—was installed on the engine described here.

The Blower Drive Service 24B6, Weiand (Holley) 7163, and Weiand 7164 aluminum carburetor adapters mount two Carter AFB or Edelbrock Performer Series four-barrel carburetors inline, or side-mount two Holley four-barrel carburetors. The Blower Drive Service 24B6 adapter is polished, 1 inch tall, and includes the 24B6G blower inlet safety screen and gasket. The Weiand 7163 adapter is unpolished and 1 inch tall, and the Weiand 7164 adapter is unpolished and 2 inches tall. The

A Blower Drive Service 6735 hard-anodized black 14-millimeter pulley with 35 teeth is on the left, and a Blower Drive Service 6852 polished 8-millimeter pulley with 52 teeth is on the right.

There are two Carter AFB 9605 four-barrel carburetors, 600 cfm (each), manual chokes, on top of this GMC 6-71 blower. The really interesting piece in this picture is the autographed scoop cover. Tony Nancy, the legendary upholsterer, engine builder, and drag racer, stitched and signed the cover.

current retail price for one of these adapters is $90.

The Weiand 7166 supercharger carburetor linkage kit is designed for two side-mount four-barrel carburetors. This is a premium quality carburetor linkage kit with ball bearing shaft supports and heim joints. The current retail price for the Weiand 7166 linkage kit is $130. The Weiand 4000 supercharger carburetor linkage is designed for two inline four-barrel carburetors and has a retail price of $39.

Two Holley 0-4781 four-barrel double-pumper carburetors, 850 cfm (each), are installed with a Weiand 7164 carburetor adapter on the GMC 6-71 blower. A Mr. Gasket 5233 Rodware scoop tops off the whole show.

FUEL PUMP

The AC 4657 (GM 6415616) mechanical fuel pump produces 5 1/4- to 6 1/2-psi fuel pressure and was installed on the standard-performance 409-ci engines. This fuel pump is available today for $45. The AC 6842 (GM 5621631) mechanical fuel pump produces 7 1/4- to 8 3/4-psi fuel pressure and was installed on the high-performance 409-ci V-8 engines. This fuel pump costs $85. Refer to Chapter 6 for further mechanical and electric fuel pump information, as well as fuel pump pushrod specifications.

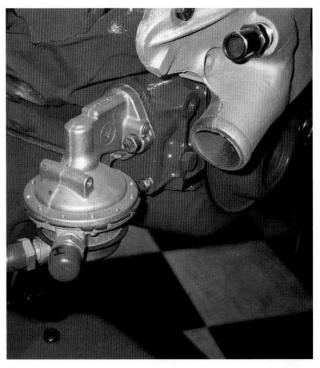

This Carter (Federal-Mogul) M-4891 mechanical fuel pump produces 7 1/4 to 8 3/4 psi and delivers 120 gallons per hour of fuel.

FUEL PRESSURE REGULATOR AND GAUGE

> Refer to Chapter 6 for information about fuel pressure regulators, fuel pressure gauges, and fuel filters.

AIR CLEANER

The GM 5648090 air cleaner was equipped with a polyurethane air filter. In 1963, the GM 3418629 air cleaner assembly was installed on engines rated at 340 horsepower; the GM 5649859 chrome-plated dual-snorkel air cleaner assembly was introduced to engines rated at 400 horsepower; and the GM 6418224 chrome-plated air cleaner assembly was installed on engines rated at 425 horsepower. Refer to Chapter 6 for information about air cleaners and air filters. The GM 3846125 crankcase breather tube was connected to the air cleaner base on the 409-ci engines with a single four-barrel carburetor. The GM 3846136 crankcase breather tube was connected to the rear air cleaner base on 409-ci engines with two x four-barrel carburetors.

This is a rare Mickey Thompson 4599021 cast-aluminum marine flame arrestor, which was often used with Mickey Thompson Power Ram intake manifolds.

B. INTAKE SYSTEM SUMMARY

- New Offenhauser 5492 low-profile dual quad aluminum intake manifold modified by Blower Drive Service to accept a GMC 6-71 blower. Intake manifold installed with new polished stainless-steel hex-head bolts and AN flat washers using Loctite and torqued to 25 ft-lbs. Intake manifold gaskets installed using silicone sealant. New Blower Drive Service 671-8C anodized-aluminum blower studs installed using anti-seize compound and torqued to 25 ft-lbs. GM 3846123 crankcase breather/oil filler tube and GM 3828373 chrome crankcase breather/oil filler tube cap installed. **$822**

- GM 5138725 6-71 aluminum small-bore die-cast supercharger case; GM 5150233 sand-cast front bearing plate with bearing support rings; new (Gene) Mooneyham rear bearing plate/cover; new Blower Drive Service 671SL1 bearing seals; new MRC 5205 front bearings; new MRC 6205 rear bearings; and new Mooneyham front cover assembled with new stainless-steel socket-head bolts, lockwashers, and AN flat washers installed using anti-seize compound. New Blower Drive Service 671GK gasket kit installed using Permatex aviation form-a-gasket. New Blower Drive Service 555 pressure relief valve and 556 oil level sight gauge installed. New stainless-steel oil filler and oil drain plugs, 3/8 inch NPT, installed using pipe thread sealant. Rotors double-pinned, clearanced, and assembled by Luke's Custom Machine & Design. Blower gears lubricated with Castrol Syntec 75W-90 gear oil. **$1,464.27**

- Luke's Custom Machine & Design new LS3000 medium blower drive snout, 6061 T-6 aluminum; new LS3300 medium blower drive snout shaft, 4140 chrome-moly heat-treated steel; and new LS4100 blower drive snout coupler, 4140 chrome-moly heat-treated steel installed with new stainless-steel socket-head bolts using anti-seize compound and torqued to 25 ft-lbs. **$390**

- New Blower Drive Service 6333 crankshaft blower drive pulley, billet 6061 T-6 aluminum—33 teeth by 3 1/2 inches wide by 1/2-inch pitch (Gilmer)—installed with new stainless-steel socket-head bolts, lockwashers, and AN flat washers using Loctite and torqued to 25 ft-lbs. New Blower Drive Service 6330 snout drive pulley, billet 6061 T-6 aluminum—30 teeth by 3 1/2 inches wide by 1/2-inch pitch (Gilmer)—installed with new stainless-steel socket-head bolts, lockwashers, and AN flat washers using Loctite and torqued to 25 ft-lbs. New Blower Drive Service 560H300 blower belt, 1/2-inch pitch (Gilmer) by 3 inches wide by 56 inches long, installed. **$235**

- Luke's Custom Machine & Design new 6061 T-6 aluminum idler pulley, 5 inches o.d., with stand-off, and new aluminum idler pulley bracket, 1/2-inch thick, installed with new stainless-steel hex-head bolts, lockwashers, and AN flat washers using Loctite and torqued to 20 ft-lbs. **$416.67**

- Custom billet-aluminum dual four-barrel carburetor adapter installed with new stainless-steel socket bolts and AN flat washers using anti-seize compound and torqued to 20 ft-lbs. New Blower Drive Service 24B6G blower inlet safety screen and gasket installed using silicone sealant. **$110**

- New Holley 0-1850S, silver-finish four-barrel carburetors, 600 cfm each, vacuum secondaries, manual chokes, installed with new ARP 400-2401 polished stainless-steel carburetor stud kits using anti-seize compound. New Weiand 4000 inline supercharger linkage kit installed. New Mr. Gasket 5233 Rodware polished cast-aluminum dual four-barrel carburetor Hilborn-style scoop installed. **$718**

- New Edelbrock 8090 carburetor fittings, 3/8-inch tube inverted flare, installed. New Holley 12-803 fuel pressure regulators, adjustable from 4 1/2 to 9 psi, installed with new Summit Racing Equipment SUM-220228 polished stainless-steel double-annealed tubing, 3/8 inch o.d. by 0.028 inch wall by 2 feet long; new Weatherhead 100-6 polished-brass inverted flare nuts, 3/8 inch tube; new Weatherhead 402-6-6 polished-brass 90-degree elbows, 3/8 inch tube to 3/8 inch NPT; new Weatherhead 3152-6 polished-brass pipe plug, 3/8 inch NPT; new Weatherhead 2020-6-6 polished-brass adapter, 3/8 inch tube to 3/8 inch NPT (outlet lines); new Weatherhead 3220-6-4 polished-brass adapter, 1/4 inch NPT to 3/8 inch NPT; new Weatherhead 1069-6 polished-brass 90-degree elbow, 3/8 inch i.d. hose to 1/4 inch NPT (inlet line); and new Weatherhead 3220-6-2 polished-brass adapter, 1/8 inch NPT to 3/8 inch NPT (fuel pressure gauge). New Holley 26-500 fuel pressure gauge, 0–15 psi and 1 1/2-inch-diameter face, installed. All fittings installed using pipe thread sealant. **$165.64**

- Intake System Total: $4,321.58

CHAPTER 17
IGNITION SYSTEM

A. IGNITION SYSTEM
DISTRIBUTOR

The GM 1110919 dual-point distributor with mechanical (centrifugal) advance was used in 1961 and 1962 Chevrolet 409-ci V-8 engines. The GM 1111023 single-point distributor with vacuum advance was installed in 409-ci engines from 1962 to 1965. Refer to Chapter 7 for information about aftermarket distributors and electronic conversion kits.

A Mallory YL 461 mechanical (centrifugal) advance distributor with a tachometer drive was installed in the engine

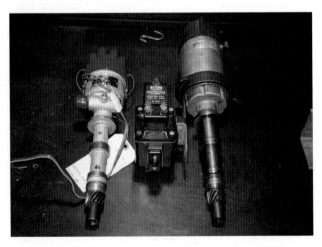

The Chevrolet 409-ci V-8 distributor with mechanical (centrifugal) advance on the left is for a truck. The taller main body section houses a governor. The GM 1111023 single-point distributor with vacuum advance is on the right.

Lamar Walden (Doraville, Georgia) machined the aluminum distributor sleeve and spacer, which permit the installation of small- or big-block Chevrolet distributors in 409-ci engines. A Mallory 2549301 dual-point distributor with centrifugal (mechanical) advance is an older model for a small-block Chevrolet V-8 engine.

A Mallory YL 461 mechanical (centrifugal) advance distributor with a tachometer drive is on the left. A Mallory 503 Unilite self-contained photo-optic infrared LED system conversion kit has been installed. A vintage Mallory 28675 Voltmaster 12-volt ignition coil is in the center. A Joe Hunt magneto, used in the 1960s, is on the right side.

described here. A Mallory 503 Unilite self-contained photo-optic infrared LED system conversion kit was also installed. The owner of the engine wanted the look of a 1960s distributor, rather than the billet look of modern distributors.

Lamar Walden (of Doraville, Georgia) machines a combined aluminum sleeve and spacer that permits the installation of a small- or big-block Chevrolet V-8 distributor in a Chevrolet 348-ci or 409-ci V-8 engine.

COIL AND IGNITION CONTROL

The GM 1110587 ignition coil was installed on 1961–1965 Chevrolet 409-ci V-8 engines using the GM 1929496 ignition coil bracket. The GM 1931614 ballast resistor was used on the 409-ci engines. Refer to Chapter 7 for information about aftermarket ignition coils and ignition control boxes.

A Mallory 29440 Promaster 12-volt ignition coil was installed on the engine described here. This is an excellent ignition coil for street/strip use, and when it is used in conjunction with a Mallory Unilite distributor and Mallory

This is a Mallory 29440 Promaster ignition coil with the ballast resistor, and it is an excellent ignition coil for street/strip use.

This is a set of Taylor/Vertex 73055 Pro Series black 8-millimeter high-performance spark plug wires with a Spiro Pro resistor core and 180-degree (straight) boots, with a set of Spectre 4245 chrome/plastic professional spark plug wire separators.

Hyfire ignition control, it is effective up to 8,000 rpm. The Mallory Promaster ignition coil is larger than most ignition coils; however, the rugged case can withstand a lot of abuse. The current retail price for the Mallory 29440 Promaster ignition coil, which was installed in the engine described here, is $75. A Mallory 6853M Hyfire VI-AL multi-spark ignition system with adjustable rev limiter was also installed.

SPARK PLUG WIRES AND SPARK PLUGS

General Motors started to date code the spark plug wires in January 1961 for every quarter of the year. For example: 1-Q-63 means they were for a January to March 1963 engine. The Chevrolet 409-ci V-8 engines were equipped with black 7-millimeter spark plugs wires, which had black 135-degree boots with the words "Packard Radio LR TVRS" on them and the date code quarter "3-Q-62" (for example) on the wires. Lectric Limited replica spark plug wire sets for Chevrolet 409-ci V-8 engines cost $65 per set. The Lectric Limited 1306-631 spark plug wire set is dated 1-Q-63, and the 1306-623 is dated 3-Q-63 (these are examples). The date code on the spark plug wires may be up to 12 months prior to the build date of the vehicle.

Some Chevrolet 409-ci V-8 engine owners prefer to use aftermarket spark plug wires with 180-degree (straight) boots for their street performance engines. A set of Taylor/Vertex 73055 Pro Series 8-millmeter black high-performance spark plug wires, with Spiro Pro Kevlar resistor core and 180-degree (straight) boots, are very good products for this application. This universal set costs $55 and is available at most speed-equipment stores.

The AC-43N spark plugs were installed in all 409-ci engines with a gap of 0.035 inch. Refer to Chapter 7 for information regarding spark plug wires and the cross-reference of spark plugs.

GENERATOR

The GM 1117765 12-volt generator rated at 62 amps was installed on Chevrolet 409-ci V-8 engines, using the GM 3826453 bottom mounting bracket, 3755726 front

Here is a GM 1117765 12-volt generator, rated at 62 amps, with the 3826453 bottom mounting bracket, 3755726 front mounting bracket, and 3826451 brace.

This is a GM 1117765 12-volt alternator, rated at 62 amps, installed on 1962–1965 Chevrolet 409-ci V-8 engines with the 3826453 bottom mounting bracket, 3826452 front mounting bracket, and 3826451 brace.

mounting bracket, and 3826451 brace.

The GM 1117765 12-volt alternator rated at 62 amps was installed on 409-ci engines, using the GM 3826453 bottom mounting bracket, 3826452 front mounting bracket, and 3826451 brace. The GM 3844100 pulley was installed on the alternator.

STARTING MOTOR

The 1961–1962 starting motors were bolted to the bell housing of the Chevrolet 409-ci V-8 engines, and the 1963–1965 starting motors were bolted to the engine block. The GM 1107342 and GM 1108400 12-volt starting motors were installed on 1963–1965 Chevrolet 409-ci engines. The stock

starting motor is bulky, heavy, and will soak up the heat from exhaust headers. Unless a numbers-matching engine is being built, you should install a modern mini-starter. The Powermaster 3631 mini-starter is an original equipment manufacturer (OEM) replacement model for the 1962–1965 Chevrolet 409-ci V-8 engines.

The TCI Automotive 351100 high-torque racing model is designed to work with a Chevrolet 168-tooth flywheel or flexplate. This starting motor draws 25 amps, produces 2.1 horsepower of cranking output, and the exhaust header heat does not affect it, due to its compact size. This mini-starter is available at most speed equipment outlets for the current retail price of $200.

This is a GM 1108400 starting motor used on 1963–1965 Chevrolet 409-ci V-8 engines. This starting motor bolts to the engine block.

Pictured here is a TCI Automotive 351100 high-torque mini-starter, which draws 25 amps, produces 2.1 horsepower of cranking output, and is designed for a Chevrolet 168-tooth flywheel or flexplate.

B. IGNITION SYSTEM SUMMARY

- Mallory YL 461 mechanical (centrifugal) advance distributor, with tachometer drive, and Mallory 503 Unilite self-contained photo-optic infrared LED system conversion kit installed. GM 3770598 distributor clamp installed with new stainless-steel hex-head bolt and lockwashers using anti-seize compound. Distributor clamp painted with Plasti-Kote 203 universal black engine enamel. New Mallory 29440 Promaster 12-volt ignition coil installed. New Mallory 6853M Hyfire VI-AL multi-spark ignition system with adjustable rev limiter installed. **$525**
- New Taylor/Vertex 79253 409 Pro Race Wire, red 10.4-millimeter spark plug wires, 135-degree boots, Spiro Pro Kevlar resistor core, installed with new Taylor/Vertex 42729 red nylon spark plug wire separators. New NGK GR4 V-power resistor-type spark plugs, 18 millimeters, installed with 0.050-inch gap and torqued to 25 ft-lbs using anti-seize compound. **$130**
- Rebuilt GM 1117765 12-volt generator, 62 amps, installed with GM 3826453 bottom mounting bracket, GM 3826452 front mounting bracket, and GM 3826451 brace using new stainless-steel hex-head bolts, flat washers, and nylocks with anti-seize compound. Generator, mounting brackets, and brace painted with Plasti-Kote 203 universal black engine enamel. **$300**
- New TCI Automotive 351100 high-torque mini-starter installed using anti-seize compound with bolts torqued to 25 ft-lbs. **$200**

- Ignition System Total: **$1,155**

CHAPTER 18
COOLING AND EXHAUST SYSTEMS

A. COOLING AND EXHAUST SYSTEMS
WATER PUMP

Chevrolet installed two types of short-style water pumps in its 409-ci V-8 passenger car engines. The GM 3774213 cast-iron water pumps, with casting numbers 3755787 and 3837853, are fitted with a 0.4688-inch-diameter shaft. The GM 3857853 aluminum water pump, casting number 3850145, is fitted with a 0.5020-inch-diameter shaft. Rebuilt 409-ci water pumps are still available at many automotive parts stores, and the current retail price is $150.

The GM 3837223 cast-aluminum water outlet elbow was used on 409-ci engines. Refer to Chapter 8 for information about cooling and antifreeze. The GM 3789562 five-blade fan with GM 3916139 thermal fan clutch was installed. The 409-ci engines with air conditioning used the GM 3838485 air conditioning compressor mounting bracket.

The GM 3840461 and GM 3850971 single-groove water pump pulleys, 7 inches o.d., were installed on 409-ci engines with power steering. The GM 3770245 and GM 3850141 are double-groove water pump pulleys, 7 inches o.d. The GM 3713774 inner single-groove pulley, 5 3/4 inches o.d., and the GM 3724810 outer single-groove pulley, 5 3/4 inches o.d., are combined on the water pump of high-performance 409-ci engines.

The high-performance 409-ci V-8 engines incorporated an idler pulley to ensure constant tension of the crankshaft pulley/water pump pulley/generator (or alternator) pulley V-belt. The 1961 and 1962 GM 3815358 idler pulley is 3 3/4 inches o.d. by 11/16 inch thick, and the 1963–1965 GM 376539 idler pulley is 4 7/8 inches o.d.

EXHAUST MANIFOLDS

The cast-iron exhaust manifolds installed on Chevrolet 409-ci V-8 passenger car engines are the center-dump design. Today, these exhaust manifolds would be referred to as "block huggers," because they were designed to fit almost against the sides of the engine block to clear the frame. Examples of the exhaust manifolds installed on the 1961

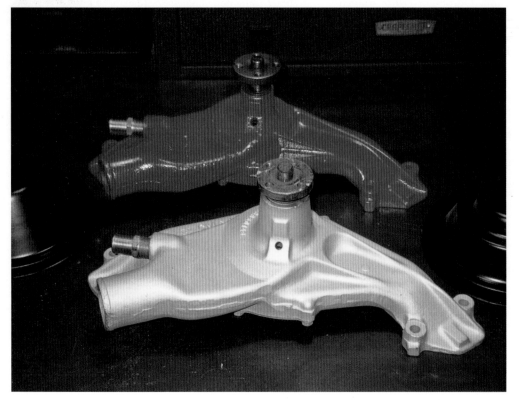

The GM 3774213 cast-iron short-style water pump, casting number 3755787, with a 0.4688-inch-diameter shaft, is in the background. The GM 3857853 aluminum short-style water pump, casting number 3850145, with a 0.5020-inch-diameter shaft, is in the foreground.

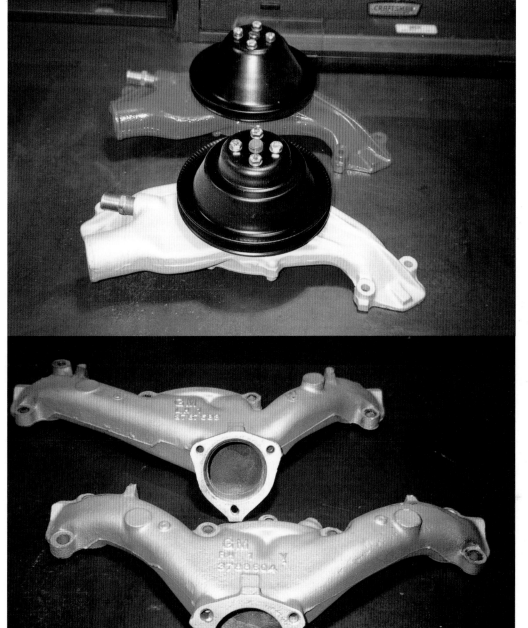

The GM 3840461 single-groove water pump pulley in the background, and the 3850971 single-groove water pump pulley in the foreground, were installed on the 409-ci engines without air conditioning.

The GM 3767583 (casting number) exhaust manifold is at the top, and the 3768804 (casting number) exhaust manifold is at the bottom. These exhaust manifolds were installed on 1961 Chevrolet 409-ci V-8 passenger car engines.

passenger cars are: the left side GM 3767583 (casting number) and the right side GM 3768804 (casting number). Both are similar to the 348-ci cast-iron exhaust manifolds.

The 1962–1965 Chevrolet 409-ci V-8 cast-iron exhaust manifolds are also the center-dump design, although they were longer than the 1961 models, and the collector was swept back. Listed below are some of the more familiar exhaust manifold casting numbers (there may be others):

1961: GM 3767583 left side and
    GM 3767584 right side
1962: GM 3814683 left side and
    GM 3814682 right side

1962–1963: GM 3822923 left side and
    GM 3822924 right side

1962–1964: GM 3822925 left side and
GM 3822926 right side
1963–1964: GM 3814683 left side and
GM 3814682 right side

1965: GM 3855161 left side and
GM 3855162 right side

The Jardine Headers Tri-Y steel tube exhaust headers and Mickey Thompson 3976409 passenger car headers were available for 1961–1965 Chevrolet 409-ci V-8 engines. The Hooker Headers 2171 tubular exhaust headers have a 1 7/8-inch-diameter primary tube and a 3-inch-diameter collector. These uncoated exhaust headers are available today for $400. The Sanderson Headers CC409 block-hugger exhaust headers have a 1 7/8-inch-diameter primary tube and a 3-inch-diameter collector. These uncoated exhaust headers are available today for $350. Refer to Chapter 8 for information about exhaust header installation.

LABOR

The labor costs for checking clearances, gapping piston rings, degreeing the camshaft, painting and detailing, trial assembly of engine, final assembly of engine, blower setup, and the initial startup of the engine have not been included in Section B of the previous chapters on the blown Chevrolet 409-ci V-8 engine. I will include that cost at the end of this chapter.

B. COOLING AND EXHAUST SYSTEMS SUMMARY

- NOS GM 3857853 aluminum short-style water pump, 0.5020-inch-diameter shaft, installed with new stainless-steel hex-head bolts and lockwashers torqued to 25 ft-lbs using Loctite. Water pump gaskets installed using silicone sealant. GM 3840461 single-groove water pump pulley, 7 inches o.d., installed with new stainless-steel hex-head bolts and lockwashers torqued to 25 ft-lbs using Loctite. Water pump pulley painted with Plasti-Kote 203 universal black engine enamel.

New Gates 11A1335 XL crankshaft pulley/water pump pulley/generator pulley V-belt, 7/16 inch by 52 1/2 inches long, installed. New GM 1513321 temperature sending unit installed using pipe thread sealant. GM 3837223 cast-aluminum water outlet elbow and new Gates 33006S Green Stripe Superstat 160-degree (Fahrenheit) superior-performance thermostat installed with bolts torqued to 20 ft-lbs using anti-seize compound. Water outlet elbow gasket installed using silicone sealant. Water outlet elbow painted with Plasti-Kote 203 Chevrolet orange high-gloss engine enamel. **$225**
- New Hooker Headers 2171 tubular exhaust headers, 1-7/8-inch primary tubes, 3-inch-diameter collectors, installed with bolts torqued to 25 ft-lbs using Loctite. Exhaust header gaskets installed using Permatex ultra copper high-temperature silicone sealant. **$400**
- Labor for checking clearances, gapping piston rings, degreeing the camshaft, painting and detailing, trial engine assembly, final engine assembly, blower setup, and initial start-up of engine. **$1,600**

- Cooling and Exhaust Systems Total: **$2,225**

- Engine Grand Total: **$14,702.47**

Note: The estimated output of this engine is 485 horsepower at 5,500 rpm and 551 ft-lbs torque at 3,500 rpm (see Dyno Printouts).

Blown Chevrolet 409-ci V-8 Engine Summary:
$1,001.67 Engine block
$1,270 Crankshaft
$1,556 Connecting rods and pistons
$540.47 Lubrication system
$2,632.75 Camshaft and cylinder heads
$4,321.58 Intake system
$1,155 Ignition system
$2,225 Cooling and exhaust systems
$14,702.47 Total

CHAPTER 19
MISSING PARTS

FLEXPLATE

The GM 3868806 flexplate, 168 teeth by 14 1/8 inches o.d., was installed on Chevrolet 409-ci V-8 engines equipped with an automatic transmission. The 168-tooth flexplate used on small-block Chevrolet V-8 engines will fit 409-ci engines. Refer to Chapter 9 for information about flexplate bolts, the automatic transmission adapter, and the starting motor plate.

The owner of the engine described here installed a 1965 Chrysler Torqueflite three-speed automatic transmission. A Wilcap 350-318 adapter, for small-block Chevrolet V-8 engines, was used along with a Hughes Performance Parts 3992 flexplate, 168 teeth, SFI Specification 29.1.

FLYWHEEL AND BELL HOUSING

The GM 3889694 flywheels, 168 teeth, were installed on Chevrolet 409-ci V-8 engines equipped with a manual (standard) transmission. The 168-tooth small-block Chevrolet V-8 flywheels will fit 409-ci engines. Refer to Chapter 9 for information about flywheel bolts. The 1962 GM 3815758 pearlitic malleable-iron pressure plate was apparently safe for over 10,000 rpm, which is impressive for a factory model. The GM 3785644 aluminum bell housing, casting number 3779553, and the GM 3899621 aluminum bell housing, casting number 3843942, were used on 409-ci engines. The flywheel and bell housings are the same for both 348-ci and 409-ci engines.

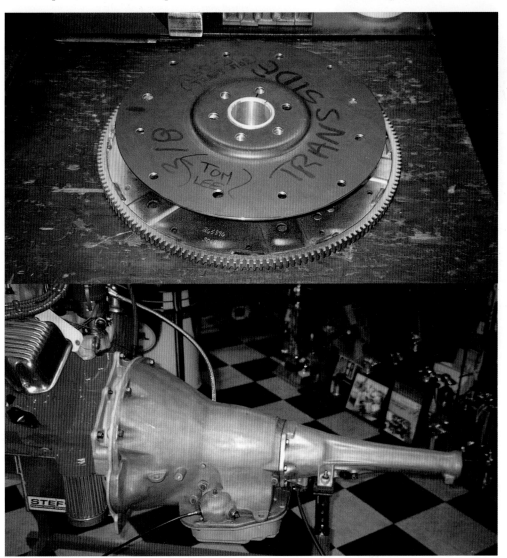

This is a Hughes Performance Parts 3992 flexplate with 168 teeth and a spacer used for adapting a 1962–1968 Chrysler Torqueflite three-speed automatic transmission to a 409-ci engine.

A 1965 Chrysler Torqueflite three-speed automatic transmission has been installed on this Chevrolet 409-ci V-8 engine.

CHAPTER 20
ASSEMBLY

ASSEMBLY

Note: The clearance and torque settings I have indicated in this book are those I use in my own engines, thus I know they work. It is up to the engine builder to ensure the engine is assembled using the proper clearances and torque settings. An experienced engine builder will follow the clearances and torque settings specified by the factory and those recommended by aftermarket equipment manufacturers. Also refer to Chapters 10 and 30.

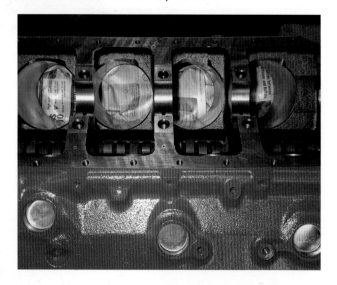

The engine block has been cleaned and painted, and the camshaft has been installed to check the camshaft bearing clearance. Note the notches for the connecting rod nut clearance at the bottom of the cylinders.

The crankshaft is installed, and the main bearing cap stud nuts have been torqued to 100 ft-lbs.

The connecting rod and piston assemblies have been installed with the connecting rod nuts torqued to 45 ft-lbs. The oil pump and pickup is bolted in position.

The gabled-roof (pent-roof) design of the Chevrolet 409-ci V-8 pistons is clearly visible when they are installed.

ENGINE BLOCK
> *Refer to Chapter 10.*

CRANKSHAFT
> *Refer to Chapter 10.*

CONNECTING RODS AND PISTONS
> *Refer to Chapter 10.*

LUBRICATION SYSTEM
> *Refer to Chapter 10.*

CAMSHAFT AND CYLINDER HEADS
> *Refer to Chapter 10. The spark plug gap is 0.050 inch when using a multi-spark ignition system.*

The Cloyes 92101 True Roller timing chain set is installed, and the camshaft has been degreed.

The timing gear cover and Stef's Fabrication Specialties 1085 aluminum pan have been bolted in place.

The hydraulic valve lifters, pushrods, and cylinder heads are installed. The cylinder heads have been torqued to 65 ft-lbs, and the valve lash has been adjusted.

The Moon Equipment Company NN-48 No Name aluminum valve covers and 166RC valve cover breathers look impressive on this engine.

INTAKE SYSTEM

1. Install the intake manifold gaskets using silicone sealant. Place the intake manifold in position on the cylinder heads. Install the intake manifold bolts using Loctite and torque them to 25 ft-lbs. Place the thermostat in the intake manifold. Install the water outlet elbow using silicone sealant. Place the water outlet elbow in position, install the bolts using anti-seize compound, and torque them to 20 ft-lbs.

2. Install the fuel pump block-off plate gasket using silicone sealant. Place the fuel pump block-off plate in position, install the bolts using Loctite, and torque them to 20 ft-lbs.

3. Install the blower mounting studs in the intake manifold

107

using anti-seize compound. Tighten them snugly by hand; do not overtighten them. Install the intake manifold to the blower case gasket using anti-seize compound or wheel bearing grease. Place the blower in position on the intake manifold, and install the stud nuts and flat washers using anti-seize compound. Torque the blower mounting stud nuts to 25 ft-lbs.

4. Install the blower snout gasket using silicone sealant. Place the blower snout in position on the front of the blower case. Install the bolts using anti-seize compound, and torque them to 25 ft-lbs. Position the blower snout pulley on the blower snout, install the bolts using Loctite, and torque them to 25 ft-lbs.

5. Install the water pump gaskets using silicone sealant. Install the water pump using Loctite on the bolts, and torque them to 25 ft-lbs. Place the water pump pulley on the water pump, install the bolts using Loctite, and torque them to 25 ft-lbs.

6. Position the blower belt idler pulley bracket on the front of the blower case, install the bolts using anti-seize compound, and torque them to 20 ft-lbs. Install the blower belt idler pulley on the blower belt idler pulley bracket using anti-seize compound on the stand-off bolt.

7. Install the carburetor adapter to the blower case gasket using silicone sealant. Install the carburetor adapter using anti-seize compound on the bolts, and torque them to 20 ft-lbs. Install the carburetor studs in the carburetor adapter using anti-seize compound. Install the carburetor-to-carburetor-adapter gaskets. Place the carburetors in position on the carburetor adapter, and tighten the stud nuts snugly; do not overtighten them. Install the carburetor fuel lines.

The GMC 6-71 blower is ready for installation on the intake manifold. The Luke's Custom Machine & Design medium blower snout drive has been installed on the front cover.

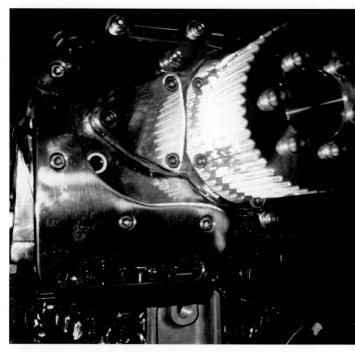

The idler pulley bracket has been installed on the front cover of the blower case.

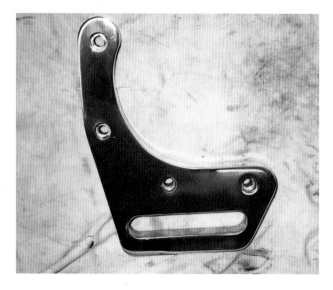

Here is a Luke's Custom Machine & Design polished-aluminum idler pulley bracket.

The GM 3857853 aluminum water pump and 3840461 single-groove water pump pulley are installed.

The idler pulley has been installed on the idler pulley bracket.

The custom billet-aluminum carburetor adapter has been bolted to the GMC 6-71 blower, and dual Holley 0-1850S four-barrel carburetors have been mounted on the adapter.

The Mallory distributor has been installed, and the Taylor/Vertex red 409 spark plug wires are ready to shoot some juice into this 409-ci V-8 engine.

This is the right side of the completed Chevrolet 409-ci V-8 engine. It is now ready for the initial startup.

IGNITION SYSTEM

1. Install the harmonic balancer on the crankshaft snout using a harmonic balancer installation tool (this is a must!). Torque the harmonic balancer bolt and flat washer to 85 ft-lbs using Loctite. Install the crankshaft pulley and blower drive belt pulley on the harmonic balancer, and torque the bolts to 30 ft-lbs using Loctite. Install the blower belt, and adjust the tension with the blower belt idler pulley. There should be 3/4-inch slack in the blower belt when the idler pulley is tightened. Install a boost gauge in the intake manifold below the blower using pipe thread sealant.

2. > Refer to Chapter 10.

3. > Refer to Chapter 10.

4. > Refer to Chapter 10.

5. > Refer to Chapter 10.

6. Install the exhaust header gaskets using Permatex ultra copper high-temperature silicone sealant. Place the exhaust headers in position on the cylinder heads, install the bolts using Loctite, and torque them to 25 ft-lbs.

7. Place the flexplate on the crankshaft flange, install the flexplate bolts using Loctite, and torque them to 60 ft-lbs.

8. Position the starting motor, install the bolts using anti-seize compound, and torque them to 25 ft-lbs.

9. > Refer to Chapter 10.
   This is a very mild blown Chevrolet 409-ci V-8 engine, intended solely for street use. The owner did not want to polish all the aluminum engine components because he wanted to keep the appearance of an early 1960s nonshow-car engine.

SECTION III: LINCOLN 337-CI FLATHEAD V-8 ENGINE

CHAPTER 21
ENGINE BLOCK

This 1951 Lincoln 337-ci flathead V-8 was originally installed in a 1951 Ford F-7 truck. Its most recent owner had it installed in a 1931 Ford two-door sedan. The engine was built by Luke's Custom Machine & Design and completed at the end of September 2005.

A. ENGINE BLOCK
PURCHASE AND MAGNAFLUX
The 1951 Ford Truck (Lincoln) 337-ci V-8 E-Series engine specifications are:
- 336.7-ci (5.5-liter) displacement
- Stock bore: 3.50 inches
- Stock stroke: 4.375 inches
- Stock compression ratio: 6.4:1
- One x two-barrel carburetor
- 145 horsepower at 3,600 rpm and 255 ft-lbs torque at 1,800 rpm

The Ford Motor Company introduced the F-7 and F-8 trucks in 1948. These were Ford's first medium-duty trucks, which were Class 4 through Class 6 with a minimum gross vehicle weight (GVW) of 21,500 pounds. Many of the Ford F-7 and F-8 trucks were used as fire trucks, dump trucks, and tow trucks.

Prior to 1948, the Ford Motor Company was experiencing problems with its flathead V-8 motors installed in commercial trucks. The flathead motors were overheating, and the engine blocks were cracking in the area around the valve seat inserts to the cylinder walls. This might have been the result of truck drivers pushing their right foot down and leaving it there. Zora Arkus-Duntov (1909–1996) and his brother, Yura Arkus-Duntov (1917–1980), designed the Ardun overhead-valve (OHV) hemispherical combustion chamber conversion kit for the Ford flathead V-8 engine in 1947. They had hoped to sell it to the Ford Motor Company as a solution for the flathead truck problems, but that plan never materialized. Instead, Zora Arkus-Duntov went on to fame with the Chevrolet Corvette. The Ardun cylinder heads were forerunners to the legendary early Chrysler Hemi cylinder heads.

The Lincoln 337-ci flathead V-8 engine was installed in the 1948–1953 Ford F-7 and F-8 trucks—to provide the customer with more power—as well as the 1949–1951 Lincoln automobiles. It had a higher compression ratio, resulting in a slight increase in horsepower and torque. The Lincoln flathead V-8 engine has been found in yard and construction equipment. Some of the early 1950s Chris-Craft pleasure boats were powered with the Lincoln 337-ci flathead V-8 engine, and it was also seen at the Bonneville Salt Flats during that era.

The most powerful Lincoln 337-ci flathead V-8 engine was installed in the 1951 Lincoln passenger cars. This engine was rated at 154 horsepower at 3,600 rpm and 275 ft-lbs torque at 1,800 rpm. A hydraulic lifter camshaft, a 7.0:1 compression ratio, and a two-barrel carburetor help the engine achieve that power.

The Lincoln 337-ci flathead V-8 engine block was unchanged from 1948–1953. The only casting number located on the engine block described here was at the middle of the right side (passenger's side) above the oil pan rail. This casting number is F1412. The Lincoln passenger car engine was designated 8EL, and the Ford Truck engine was designated 8EQ.

One of the best sources of technical information for the Lincoln 337-ci flathead V-8 engine is supplied by the Ford Motor Company of Canada with its Master Repair Manual—Engine. Such manuals may still be available from Wilkinson's Automobilia (see Resources).

The Lincoln 337-ci flathead V-8 engine was in this condition when it was delivered to Luke's Custom Machine & Design in mid-February 2005. Remember this when looking at the finished product at the end of this section.

This is the Ford Motor Company of Canada Master Repair Manual—Engine, manual number SE 384A, Section Number Twelve. It was available in the early 1950s for $0.35.

Present-day hot rodders have either ignored the 337-ci flathead due to its large size, or they are not aware of this engine. As a result of this, a complete Lincoln 337-ci flathead V-8 engine can be purchased for a few hundred dollars. The Truck engine block is the most desirable model to purchase because it has solid flat-tappet adjustable valve lifters and factory-installed center-port exhaust baffles. Although a flathead engine, very few of its parts are interchangeable with a Ford flathead V-8. Thus, locating parts for the Lincoln flathead could prove to be troublesome. Many Lincoln flathead engines most likely ended up in overseas scrap yards and were eventually turned into razor blades.

The Lincoln 337-ci flathead V-8 engine block is an absolute monster compared to 1949–1953 Ford flathead V-8 engine blocks. The 1937–1940 Ford flathead V8-60 engine could almost fit in the Lincoln flathead oil pan! The Lincoln flathead engine block is about 2 inches longer and 3 inches wider than a 1949–1953 Ford flathead V-8 engine block, and weighs 280 pounds, compared to 200 pounds for a 1949–1953 Ford flathead V-8 engine block. The Lincoln 337-ci flathead V-8 engine was the biggest flathead V-8 engine the Ford Motor Company produced for passenger cars.

Thoroughly inspect the Lincoln flathead V-8 engine block for any cracks or damage. Commonly, you find cracks around the cylinder head bolt holes between the cylinders, which is probably due to over-torqued cylinder head bolts or a lack of antifreeze during winter months in cold climates. The cracks around the cylinder head bolt holes can be repaired by an expe-

rienced machine shop. Examine all the cylinder head bolt holes to ensure they have not been stripped or drilled off-center by some genius attempting to repair stripped threads. When possible, try to locate an engine block that is not cracked.

The Lincoln 337-ci flathead V-8 engine blocks are notorious for cracks leading from the intake valve seat inserts to the cylinder walls. These cracks can be repaired by stitching using irontite plugs, although new intake valve seat inserts must be installed and the cylinders may have to be sleeved, which is an expensive proposition.

According to the Ford Motor Company of Canada Master Repair Manual—Engine, the maximum size the cylinders in a Lincoln 337-ci flathead V-8 engine block can be safely bored is 0.060 inch oversize, for a final bore of 3.560 inches. The cylinder walls are quite thick, so it may be possible to bore the engine block more than 0.060 inch oversize. Sonic testing the cylinder walls will determine if this is possible. Refer to Chapter 1 for further information about the purchase and Magnaflux of an engine block.

CLEANING

Remove any bolts and fittings, the camshaft bearings, and the rear upper oil seal retainer. The Lincoln 6026 front oil gallery line plug (3/8 inch NPT) is located behind the camshaft gear, and the Lincoln 358132-S rear oil gallery line frost plug (19/32 inch) is located behind the oil pump idler gear cover. There are two 1/4-inch-NPT plugs located at the front of the engine block behind the camshaft timing gear. One plug is located on each side of the main oil gallery line plug, and the plugs block off the valve lifter oil gallery lines. Remove all the pipe plugs. The Lincoln 358099-S freeze plugs are located on each side of the front of the engine block below the water pumps, and on each side of the bottom center of the oil pan rail. Remove all these freeze plugs. Hot tank the engine block after it has been completely stripped down. This should be done prior to having the engine block Magnafluxed to ensure there are no hidden cracks covered up with grease and grime.

Although engine builders commonly grind the OHV engine's valve lifter gallery smooth to assist with oil return to the oil pan, this procedure is not necessary with a flathead engine block. The valve lifter gallery is already quite smooth and it has high-quality casting. You have just been saved from another thankless task.

PORTING AND POLISHING

Port, polish, and gasket match the intake and exhaust ports after the engine block has been hot tanked. Spray or brush some blue machinist's dye around all of the intake and exhaust ports. Position the intake and exhaust manifold gaskets, and scribe around them. Use a high-speed grinder with a carbide bit to gasket match the ports. Remove just enough material to match the gasket openings and clean up any casting flash in the ports. Lightly grind the intake ports all the way to the valve seats, but do not grind the valve seats. Lightly grind the exhaust

A 1952 Ford flathead V-8 engine block is on the left, a 1951 Lincoln flathead V-8 engine block is on the right, and a 1939 Ford flathead V8-60 engine block is at the front.

This picture shows the mild relief the factory provided in the area from the intake valve to the cylinder. The yellow paint shows where it was common for the Lincoln 337-ci flathead V-8 engine blocks to crack.

The 3/8-inch-NPT hole in the center above the camshaft bore is for the main oil gallery line, and the 1/4-inch-NPT holes on each side are for the valve lifter oil gallery lines.

ports as far upward as possible. The intake and exhaust ports in the Lincoln 337-ci flathead V-8 engine block are a superior design to those in the Ford flathead V-8 engine blocks.

DETAILING AND VALVE LIFTER BOSSES
Refer to Chapter 1 for information about detailing the engine block. The Lincoln 8EQ-6500-A solid flat-tappet adjustable valve lifters are the best type to use in a Lincoln 337-ci flathead V-8 engine. These valve lifters can be easily adjusted in the valve lifter gallery without drilling an adjustment hole in the valve lifter bosses, which is necessary in Ford flathead V-8 engine blocks.

FULL-FLOW OILING
The Lincoln 337-ci flathead V-8 engine block should be converted to a full-flow oiling system. The horizontal and vertical holes (for oil line fittings) on the lower left side near the back of the engine block (where the bell housing bolts on) will be used for the drain-back line and an oil pressure gauge. The vertical hole should be drilled and tapped using a 3/8-inch-NPT tap. Drill a hole through the bottom left side of the bell housing flange into the oil pump cavity, and then tap the hole using a 3/8-inch-NPT tap. This hole will be used for the pressure-out line.

RELIEVING THE ENGINE BLOCK
The subject of relieving a flathead engine block will certainly cause a debate when more than one flathead lover is present. Relieving a flathead engine block will lower the compression ratio approximately 0.5 to 0.75 of a point. I have not heard of a situation where lowering the compression ratio in a normally aspirated engine led to an increase in power. The Lincoln 337-ci flathead V-8 engine block has a slight relief at the lower side of the intake valve. Leave this relief alone and press on with more serious matters.

HEAT RISERS
Years ago, engine builders blocked off the heat riser passages in a flathead engine block. Leave the heat riser passages open for street use if your aftermarket intake manifolds have heat

riser passages (many do not). The purpose of the heat riser passages is to warm up the intake manifold as fast as possible when the weather is cold. If the heat riser passages are blocked off and you reside in a colder climate, the engine will run horribly until it reaches normal operating temperature.

RETAP AND CHAMFER BOLT HOLES
Refer to Chapter 1.

REDI-STRIP THE ENGINE BLOCK
> *Refer to Chapter 1.*

GLYPTAL
> *Refer to Chapter 1.*

MACHINING
> *Refer to Chapter 1.*

CYLINDER BORING
The Ford Motor Company of Canada Master Repair Manual—Engine specifies a 0.0015-inch cast-aluminum piston-to-cylinder-bore clearance, as well as 3.560 inches as the maximum cylinder bore size of a Lincoln 337-ci flathead V-8 engine block. This is only 0.060 inch oversize. Remember this when purchasing a used engine block. The engine block described was previously bored 0.040 inch oversize, which meant it was then bored and honed 0.060 inch oversize, for a final cylinder bore of 3.560 inches—the maximum size.

OHV engines should be bored and the cylinders honed and deglazed using a torque plate. The purpose of the torque plate is to simulate the distortion caused to the engine block when the cylinder heads are torqued. On a flathead engine block, the cylinder head bolts (or studs) are not evenly spaced around each cylinder, particularly where the valves are located, and the cylinder bore is relatively small. Thus using a torque plate is not mandatory. If you choose to use it, ensure that the cylinder head bolts (or studs) that will be installed in the engine block are used with the torque plate. Even if these two different types of fasteners are torqued to the same setting, the distortion caused to the engine block is different for bolts and studs. Refer to Chapter 1 for more information about cylinder boring and honing.

ALIGN HONE
All critical measurements are taken from the centerline of the crankshaft. The centerline is used to ensure the engine

block main bearing housing bores, with the main bearing caps attached, are exactly parallel to it. The crankshaft centerline in the Lincoln 337-ci flathead V-8 engine block is offset 0.265 inch to the right, the cylinder banks are exactly 45 degrees to each other, and the main bearing cap bolts are torqued to 125 ft-lbs. The diameter of the main bearing housing bores is 3.067 inches. The engine block described here did not require align honing. Refer to Chapter 1 for further information regarding align honing and align boring.

PARALLEL DECK

The engine block being described was parallel decked. Refer to Chapter 1 for information about parallel decking.

SHOT PEEN

The main bearing caps and bolts for the engine described were shot peened. The Lincoln 6346 main bearing cap bolts were not equipped with lockwashers at the factory. The mating flange of the Lincoln 337-ci flathead V-8 main bearing caps is square to the engine block, which is unlike the curved mating flange of the Ford flathead V-8 main bearing caps. The square mating flange will prevent the main bearing caps from walking when they are torqued, especially if lockwashers are used.

This Sunnen CH-100 horizontal hone, with a Sunnen PLB-100 align bore attachment, is align boring a 1952 Ford flathead V-8 engine block. Luke's Custom Machine & Design fabricated the custom main bearing caps and oil pan rails.

VALVE SEAT INSERTS

If the Lincoln 6057 intake and exhaust valve seat inserts are badly pitted or cracked, you will have to replace them. If there are any cracks leading from the intake valve seat inserts, remove them to repair the cracks. The Clevite 77 218-7697 intake valve seat inserts have a 1.937-inch counterbore diameter, 1.625 inches i.d., and a depth of 0.281 inch. These 7000-series inserts are iron-based high-chrome alloy for use with unleaded gasoline, and they are easily machined. Valve seat inserts should only be removed and installed by a competent machine shop. The Clevite 77 218-7697 valve seat inserts currently cost $9.50 each, and installation costs about $35 for each. Refer to Chapter 5 for information about hardened exhaust valve seat inserts.

VALVE GRIND

High Performance Engines has designed two different jigs for centering purposes when performing Serdi-machined multi-angle blueprint valve grinds in a flathead engine block. This permits the valve seat inserts in a flathead engine block to be ground with or without the valve guides in place. It will cost approximately $250 for a Serdi-machined multi-angle blueprint valve grind of a flathead engine block. Unfortunately, the Lincoln flathead V-8 engine block will not fit on the Serdi 60 automatic centering by spherical and flat air cushion valve seat grinding machine due to its massive size, so a standard-type valve grind must be performed. Refer to Chapter 5 for information about Serdi-machined valve grinds.

DEGLAZE
> *Refer to Chapter 1.*

CLEANING AND PAINTING
> *Refer to Chapter 1.*

B. ENGINE BLOCK SUMMARY

- 1951 Ford Truck (Lincoln) 336.7-ci (5.5-liter) L-head V-8 E-series engine block, casting number F1412; two-bolt main bearing caps; 27-stud block; stock bore: 3.500 inches; stock stroke: 4.375 inches; stock compression ratio: 6.4:1; 145 horsepower at 3,600 rpm and 255 ft-lbs torque at 1,800 rpm. Engine block weight (bare): 280 pounds. **$200**
- Engine block hot tanked and Redi-Stripped. Engine block, main bearing caps, and main bearing cap bolts Magnafluxed. **$225**
- Main bearing caps and bolts shot peened; all threads retapped; cylinder head bolt holes chamfered; valve lifter bosses deglazed allowing for 0.0015-inch valve lifter clearance; new stainless-steel water jacket drain plugs, 1/4 inch NPT, installed using pipe thread sealant, and four new water jacket freeze plugs installed using Permatex aviation form-a-gasket. Valve lifter gallery and front of engine block (behind camshaft gear) painted with Glyptal G-1228A medium-gray gloss enamel. Exterior surface of engine block sanded, detailed, and painted with PPG 74000 red high-gloss polyurethane. **$615.57**
- Engine block converted to full-flow oil system. **$66.67**
- Engine block bored 0.060 inch oversize, and cylinders honed and deglazed using Sunnen 600-series 280-grit stones; final bore: 3.560 inches. Piston-to-bore clearance of 0.0015 inch measured below bottom of wrist pin perpendicular to wrist pin. **$125**
- Engine block parallel decked to 0.010-inch average below deck. **$120**
- New Clevite 77 218-7697 intake valve seat inserts installed and multi-angle blueprint valve grind performed. **$410**
- Intake and exhaust ports fully ported, polished, and gasket matched. **$133.33**

- Engine Block Total: **$1,895.57**

CHAPTER 22
CRANKSHAFT

A. CRANKSHAFT
PURCHASE

The crankshaft installed in the Lincoln 337-ci flathead V-8 engine was a quality forged-steel unit with a stroke of 4.375 (4 3/8) inches. The Lincoln 8EL-6303 crankshaft is big and heavy, weighing 105 pounds. This crankshaft has two oil holes in each connecting rod journal for lubricating

This Lincoln 8EL-6303 forged-steel crankshaft was used in 1948–1953 Ford F-7 and F-8 trucks and 1949–1951 Lincoln automobiles.

a pair of nonfloating connecting rod bearings. The Ford Motor Company of Canada Master Repair Manual—Engine specifies the out-of-round service limit at 0.0015 inch, the taper service limit at 0.001 inch, and the maximum runout at 0.002 inch.

When purchasing a Lincoln 337-ci flathead V-8 crankshaft, remember the main bearings are only available up to 0.040 inch oversize, and the same goes for the connecting rod bearings. If the crankshaft needs to be ground in excess of that size, there are no bearings currently available. The only solution would be to have the crankshaft journals built up. This process is explained in Chapter 2. It will cost approximately $150 for a Lincoln 337-ci V-8 flathead crankshaft in good condition.

MAGNAFLUX
> *Refer to Chapter 2.*

SHOT PEEN AND PLUG REMOVAL

The Lincoln flathead crankshaft has four plugs, 1/2 inch NPT, installed in the ends of the connecting rod journals.

The oil gallery line in the connecting rod journals acts as a sludge trap; therefore these plugs must be removed to properly clean the crankshaft. Refer to Chapter 2 for information about shot peening the crankshaft.

STRAIGHTEN, CHAMFER, AND POLISH
Refer to Chapter 2.

REGRINDING AND CLEANING

The main bearing journals and connecting rod journals of the Lincoln 6303 crankshaft described here were ground 0.020 inch undersize. Refer to Chapter 2 for further information about crankshaft regrinding and cleaning.

This Lincoln 8EL-6303 forged-steel crankshaft has been shot peened, Magnafluxed, and aligned. Also, the journals have been ground, oil holes chamfered, and journals polished.

MAIN BEARINGS

Clevite 77 (Dana Corporation) and Federal-Mogul do not currently list main bearings for the Lincoln 337-ci flathead V-8 engine. Main bearings can be purchased from Egge Parts House. The Egge Parts House MS1184 main bearings are available in standard size, 0.001 inch oversize, 0.002 inch oversize, 0.010 inch oversize, 0.020 inch oversize, 0.030 inch oversize, and 0.040 inch oversize. The current retail price for a set of Egge Parts House main bearings is $320. NOS Globe Motor Bearings 1501-CA-20 (No. 1 bearings), 1502-CA-20 (No. 2 bearings), and Ford 8EQ-6331-C (No. 3 bearings) main bearings, 0.020 inch oversize, were installed in the engine described in this section. The Ford Motor Company of Canada Master Repair Manual—Engine spec-

NOS Ford 8EQ-6331-C (No. 3 bearings), Globe Motor Bearings 1502-CA-20 (No. 2 bearings), 1501-CA-20 (No. 1 bearings) main bearings, 0.020 inch oversize, for the Lincoln 337-ci flathead V-8 engine are shown here.

ified the main bearing clearance to be 0.0004 to 0.0029 inch and the crankshaft end play to be 0.004 to 0.008 inch. Refer to Chapter 2 for information on checking main bearing clearance and crankshaft end play.

CRANKSHAFT GEAR AND PULLEY

The stock Lincoln 6306 cast-iron crankshaft gear has 24 teeth and is entirely suitable for use in a street performance engine. If the crankshaft gear is damaged or missing, the Egge Parts House TG2716 replacement gear is available for the current retail price of $33. Hold the crankshaft gear in position with the Lincoln 356658-S crankshaft gear woodruff key. Position the Lincoln 6310 oil slinger in front of the crankshaft gear. Glass bead the oil slinger, and paint it with Glyptal G-1228A medium-gray gloss enamel.

The Lincoln 6316 crankshaft pulley is a combination of a damper and a double-groove pulley, which is positioned using the Lincoln 356658-S crankshaft pulley woodruff key. The Lincoln 6316 crankshaft damper and pulley is 8 inches o.d. and not an attractive part to install on a street performance engine. The Lincoln 8EL-6303 crankshaft snout is the same 1.320-inch diameter as a 1949–1953 Ford or Mercury 6303 crankshaft snout, which means the 1949–1953 Ford Truck GAUB241815 double-groove crankshaft pulley can be installed on the Lincoln crankshaft. The Ford Truck pulley is 7 inches o.d. and will certainly improve the appearance of the Lincoln engine. The crankshaft pulley is held in position with the Lincoln

Here is the Lincoln 6306 crankshaft gear and 6310 oil slinger. The oil slinger has been painted with Glyptal G-1228A medium-gray gloss enamel.

This is a Lincoln 6316 crankshaft pulley, 8 inches o.d., that is a combination of a damper and pulley.

Here is a 1949–1953 Ford truck GAUB241815 double-groove crankshaft pulley, 7 inches o.d. This pulley fits the Lincoln 8EL-6303 crankshaft snout.

20747-S crankshaft pulley bolt and Lincoln 6378 crankshaft pulley bolt flat washer.

The Fluidampr 690201 internally balanced harmonic balancer was recently introduced for 1949–1953 Ford flathead V-8 passenger car engines. This double-groove, narrow (7/16-inch) V-belt harmonic balancer is 6.00 inches o.d., weighs 6.09 pounds, and the current retail price is $349.

B. CRANKSHAFT SUMMARY

- 1951 Lincoln 8EL-6303 forged-steel crankshaft, casting number C12; Nos. 1 and 2 main bearing journal diameter: 2.8729 to 2.8740 inches; No. 3 main bearing journal diameter: 2.8724 to 2.8735 inches. Connecting rod journal diameter: 2.3991 to 2.4000 inches; nonfloating connecting rod bearings; stock stroke: 4.375 (4 3/8) inches. Crankshaft weight: 105 pounds. **$150**
- Crankshaft hot tanked, Magnafluxed, shot peened, aligned. Main bearing journals ground 0.020 inch undersize, connecting rod journals ground 0.020 inch undersize, oil holes chamfered, journals polished, and crankshaft balanced. New stainless-steel connecting rod journal oil line plugs, 1/2 inch NPT, installed using Loctite. **$285**
- NOS Globe Motor Bearings 1501-CA-20 (No. 1 bearings), 1502-CA-20 (No. 2 bearings), and Ford 8EQ-6331-C (No. 3 bearings) main bearings, 0.020 inch oversize, installed allowing for 0.002-inch crankshaft clearance and 0.005-inch end play. The 1951 Lincoln 6346 main bearing cap bolts torqued to 125 ft-lbs using Molykote. **$320**
- Lincoln 6306 cast-iron helical crankshaft gear, 24 teeth, and Lincoln 6310 oil slinger installed with Lincoln 356658-S crankshaft gear woodruff key. Luke's Custom Machine & Design new crankshaft oil seal sleeve installed. The 1949–1953 Ford Truck GAUB241815 double-groove crankshaft pulley, 7 inches o.d., installed with Lincoln 356658-S crankshaft pulley woodruff key, Lincoln 20747-S crankshaft pulley bolt, and Lincoln 6378 crankshaft pulley bolt flat washer, using Loctite and torqued to 125 ft-lbs. Oil slinger painted with Glyptal G-1228A medium-gray gloss enamel. Crankshaft pulley painted with PPG DGHS 9000 black high-gloss polyurethane. **$192.14**

- Crankshaft Total: **$947.14**

CHAPTER 23
CONNECTING RODS AND PISTONS

This set of Lincoln 8EL-6200 forged-steel I-beam connecting rods, casting number 8EL-6205, has been shot peened.

A. CONNECTING RODS AND PISTONS PURCHASE

The Lincoln 8EL-6200 forged-steel I-beam connecting rods, casting number 8EL-6205, have an average weight of 749 grams and are designed for full-floating pistons. They have a length (center to center) of 8.00 inches, and the diameter of the crankshaft end (big end) is 2.5520 inches. The connecting rod bolts are integral with the connecting rod (they cannot be removed), and they use the Lincoln 6212 connecting rod nuts, which are thin locknuts that are 7/16 inch NF. If the Lincoln 6212 connecting rod nuts are missing or damaged, big-block Chevrolet 7/16-inch-NF connecting rod nuts can be used. It will cost approximately $40 for a set of Lincoln 8EL-6200 connecting rods in decent condition.

The Lincoln 8EL-6200 connecting rods have an oil squirt hole on both faces above the crankshaft end to increase piston lubrication. Oil passes through the hole in the connecting rod bearings into the connecting rod oil squirt holes and then onto the cylinder walls.

MAGNAFLUX AND SHOT PEEN
> *Refer to Chapter 3.*

ALIGN, RESIZE, AND REBUSH
Refer to Chapter 3 for information regarding connecting rod alignment and resizing. The Lincoln 337-ci flathead V-8 connecting rods were fitted with a wrist pin bushing for use with full-floating pistons. After more than 50 years of faithful service,

This is a set of Egge Parts House PB775 wrist pin bushings for the Lincoln 337-ci flathead V-8 connecting rods.

the wrist pin bushings should be replaced. The Egge Parts House PB775 (Federal-Mogul WB-1981) wrist pin bushings are available for the current retail price of $51 for a set of eight. The inside diameter of the wrist pin bushing is 0.8506 inch. The Ford Motor Company of Canada Master Repair Manual—Engine specifies the wrist-pin-to-wrist-pin-bushing clearance to be 0.0002 to 0.0005 inch.

DEBEAM
Debeaming the Lincoln flathead V-8 connecting rods is not recommended for street performance use. These connecting rods don't have a lot of material to play with and sometimes things are best left alone.

Here is a set of Egge Parts House CB-14-020 connecting rod bearings, 0.020 inch oversize, for the Lincoln 337-ci flathead V-8 engine.

Here is an Egge Parts House L946-060 cast-aluminum piston, 0.060 inch oversize, for a Lincoln 337-ci flathead V-8 engine. The piston weighs 595 grams, and the wrist pin weighs 143 grams.

CONNECTING ROD BEARINGS

Clevite 77 (Dana Corporation) and Federal-Mogul do not currently list connecting rod bearings for the Lincoln 337-ci flathead V-8 engine. The Egge Parts House CB-14 connecting rod bearings are available in standard size, 0.001 inch oversize, 0.002 inch oversize, 0.010 inch oversize, 0.020 inch oversize, 0.030 inch oversize, and 0.040 inch oversize. The current retail price for a set of these connecting rod bearings is $170, and the 0.020 inch oversize bearings were installed in the engine described here.

The Ford Motor Company of Canada Master Repair

Here is a 1951 Lincoln 6108 cast-aluminum flat-top piston of the three-ring, solid-skirt design with a weight of 593 grams. The Lincoln 6135 taper-wall wrist pin weighs 114 grams.

Manual—Engine specifies the connecting-rod-bearing-to-crankshaft-journal clearance to be 0.0005 to 0.0025 inch and the side clearance for a pair of connecting rods to be 0.006 to 0.014 inch.

PISTONS

The Lincoln 337-ci flathead V-8 engines were fitted with cast-aluminum flat-top pistons. The pistons in the 1948 to early 1950 engines had a four-ring, split-skirt design. The late 1950 to 1953 pistons had a three-ring, solid-skirt design. The average weight of a 1951 Lincoln 6108 piston is 593 grams.

The Lincoln 6135 taper wall wrist pins are 3.105 inches long overall, 0.850 inch o.d., and weigh 114 grams each. Lincoln 6140 wire clip retainers secure the wrist pins in the piston. Lincoln flathead V-8 pistons and wrist pins are no longer available from the Ford Motor Company. The Ford Motor Company of Canada Master Repair Manual—Engine specifies the wrist-pin-to-piston clearance to be 0.0001 to 0.0004 inch.

The Egge Parts House L946 cast-aluminum flat-top pistons of the three-ring, solid-skirt design are available in standard size, 0.010 inch oversize, 0.020 inch oversize, 0.030 inch oversize, 0.040 inch oversize, 0.060 inch oversize, and 0.080 inch oversize. The current retail price for a set of these pistons, complete with wrist pins and wire clip retainers, is $345, and a set of the 0.060 oversize pistons was installed in the engine described here. These pistons weigh 595 grams each. The wrist pins are 3.109 inches long overall, 0.850 inch o.d., and weigh 143 grams each.

A serious street performance or blown Lincoln 337-ci flathead V-8 engine should be fitted with forged-aluminum pistons. I am not aware of any piston manufacturer currently offering off-the-shelf forged-aluminum pistons for the Lincoln flathead engine. Ross Racing Pistons would certain-

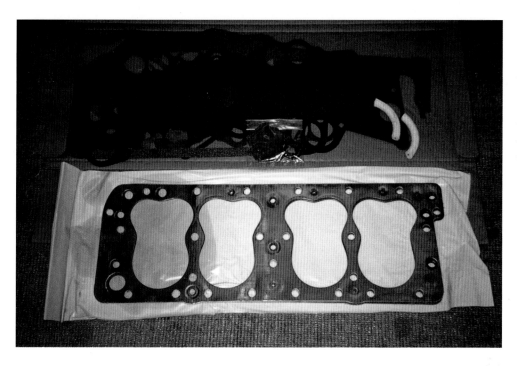

This is the Best Gasket of California RS726 complete gasket set for the Lincoln 337-ci V-8 engine. The Fitzgerald 0505 copper sandwiched cylinder head gaskets are included in the gasket set.

ly be able to supply custom pistons for this application.

The Egge Parts House SRH-562 cast-iron piston ring set is available for the current retail price of $87. The Ford Motor Company of Canada Master Repair Manual—Engine specifies the compression ring gap and oil ring gap to be 0.007 to 0.047 inch for the 1948 to early 1950 Lincoln 337-ci V-8 engines, and 0.047 inch for the late 1950 to 1953 engines. Refer to Chapter 3 for information about piston rings and valve-to-piston clearance. Checking the valve-to-cylinder-head clearance in a flathead engine is similar to checking the valve-to-piston clearance in an OHV engine.

BALANCING
Refer to Chapter 3.

GASKETS
The Fel-Pro FS7694-B complete gasket set is available for the Lincoln 337-ci flathead V-8 engine. The Best Gasket of California RS726 and Egge Parts House RS726SA complete gasket sets are similar. The current retail price for a complete gasket set is $229.

B. CONNECTING RODS AND PISTONS SUMMARY
- 1951 Lincoln 8EL-6200 forged-steel I-beam connecting rods, casting number 8EL-6205. Nonfloating connecting rod bearings. Connecting rod length: 8.00 inches (center to center). Connecting rod weight: 749 grams each. Connecting rod ratio: 1.83 (with 4.375-inch stroke). **$40**

- Connecting rods shot peened, aligned, Magnafluxed, resized, and balanced. New Egge Parts House PB775 wrist pin bushings, 0.8506 inch i.d., installed allowing for 0.0015-inch wrist pin clearance. Lincoln 6212 connecting rod nuts installed using Loctite and torqued to 55 ft-lbs. **$317.71**

- New Egge Parts House CB-14-020 connecting rod bearings, 0.020 inch oversize, installed allowing for 0.002-inch crankshaft clearance and 0.012-inch side clearance per pair of connecting rods. **$170**

- New Egge Parts House L946-060 cast-aluminum flat-top pistons: 0.060 inch oversize, three-ring, solid-skirt design, 9.5:1 compression ratio. Piston weight: 595 grams. Piston ring grooves: top compression ring, 3/32 inch; second compression ring, 3/32 inch; and oil ring, 5/32 inch. New Egge Parts House full-floating heat-treated chrome-moly steel straight-wall wrist pins installed with wire clip retainers. Wrist pin length: 3.109 inches; wrist pin diameter: 0.850 inch; and wrist pin weight: 143 grams. New Grant Piston Rings P3102.060 cast-iron piston ring set, 0.060 inch oversize, installed within manufacturer's recommended arc. Top compression ring gap: 0.014 inch; second compression ring gap: 0.014 inch; and oil ring gap: 0.014 inch. New displacement: 348.4 ci (5.7 liter). **$432**

- Complete V-8 engine balance. New Best Gasket of California 1039 complete gasket set installed. **$466.50**

- Connecting Rods and Pistons Total: **$1,426.21**

CHAPTER 24
LUBRICATION SYSTEM

A. LUBRICATION SYSTEM
OIL PUMP AND PICKUP

The Lincoln 6603 oil pump is a high-volume model that many hot rodders installed in Ford flathead V-8 engines during the 1950s, prior to the advent of aftermarket high-volume oil pumps. An oil pressure relief valve is installed in the oil pump body. The oil pressure relief valve spring tension should be 12.42 pounds (plus or minus 2 ounces) at 2.18 inches. The Egge Parts House R-311 oil pump is a replacement model available for the current retail price of $149, plus a core charge of $125 if a used oil pump is not exchanged.

The Lincoln 6615 oil pump pickup tube is used with the Lincoln 6603 oil pump. This oil pump pickup tube requires four bolts to secure it to the oil pump. The Lincoln 6623 oil pump pickup tube screen is held in position with the Lincoln 6628 retainer.

Located in the front of the valve lifter gallery is the oil pressure relief valve, which is designed to open at 15 psi to provide a constant oil flow within the Lincoln 337-ci flathead V-8 engines equipped with hydraulic valve lifters. This oil pressure relief valve should be left in place, even if solid valve lifters are installed. The oil pressure relief valve consists of the Lincoln 6666 nut, 6654 spring, and 353082-S ball. The Lincoln 358132-S rear oil gallery line plug has a 3/32-inch (0.09375-inch) hole in the center to feed oil at the rear of the engine block to the valve lifter oil gallery lines.

OIL PAN

The Lincoln 337-ci V-8 oil pan is a two-piece unit consisting of the Lincoln 6676 oil pan and Lincoln 6695 sump, which is secured to the oil pan with 16 pieces: 5/16-inch-NF nylocks and 5/16-inch AN flat washers. Although not the best-looking oil pan for a street performance engine, it is desirable for its 7-quart oil capacity (8 quarts with the oil filter) and internal baffle. The Lincoln 6683 baffle is secured to the oil pan section with four clips. The Lincoln 6750 dipstick and 6754 dipstick tube are located on the left side of the oil pan. The oil pan should be bolted to the engine block using 18 pieces: 5/16-inch NC by 3/4-inch-long hex-head bolts, lockwashers, and AN flat washers.

The Lincoln 6751 dipstick tube boss is secured to the oil

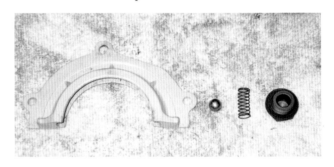

Shown here are a Lincoln 8EL-6335 upper rear oil seal retainer and the valve lifter oil pressure relief valve consisting of the Lincoln 353082-S ball, 6654 spring, and 6666 nut.

Here is a Lincoln 6603 high-volume oil pump with the Lincoln 6615 oil pump pickup tube and Lincoln 6623 screen installed.

The Lincoln 6676 oil pan is on the left, and the 6695 sump is on the right.

pan using the Lincoln 63359-S rivets. Prior to hot tanking and Redi-Stripping the oil pan, grind the heads off the four rivets, and remove the dipstick tube boss. Prior to painting the oil pan, reinstall the dipstick tube boss with four pieces: 10-32 by 3/4-inch-long pan head screws and nuts using Loctite. A new gasket will have to be fabricated from good quality gasket material and installed using silicone sealant. Grind any excess material off the ends of the screws, and stake them with a center punch.

Bolt the Lincoln 8EL-6335 aluminum upper-rear oil seal retainer to the back of the engine block using four pieces: 5/16-inch NC by 3/4-inch-long hex-head bolts and lockwashers. Install a gasket between the engine block and oil seal retainer. Install the Lincoln 6701 cord material rear oil seal in the retainer.

Immediately after the gasket set is purchased, place the cord material rear oil seals in a can of motor oil, and let them soak in the oil for at least a week to become thoroughly saturated. These oil seals are extremely tough when they are new and dry, making installation a difficult proposition. After the oil seals have been soaked in oil, they become more pliable.

OIL PUMP IDLER GEAR

Install the Lincoln 6655 oil pump idler gear in the rear of the engine block—next to the rear camshaft gear—with the Lincoln 6657 oil pump idler gear bushing and Lincoln 6656 oil pump idler gear shaft. Insert a 1 1/2-inch-long bolt with a thick flat washer into the 3/8-inch NC threaded hole in the face of the oil pump idler gear shaft. Attach the jaws of a slide hammer to the bolt and washer, and pull the oil pump idler gear out of the engine block. The Lincoln OEL-6658 oil

Here is the Lincoln OEL-6658 oil pump idler gear cover and 6655 oil pump idler gear. The Lincoln 6657 oil pump idler gear bushing and 6656 oil pump idler gear shaft are installed in the oil pump idler gear. The inside of the cover has been painted with Glyptal G-1228A medium-gray gloss enamel.

pump idler gear cover is manufactured using cast steel and secured in position with six pieces: 5/16-inch NC by 3/4-inch-long hex-head bolts and lockwashers.

FUEL PUMP PUSHROD BUSHING AND PUSHROD

If you remove the fuel pump pushrod when using an electric fuel pump, there will be a loss of oil pressure. To prevent this

situation from occurring, plug the 1/8-inch (0.125-inch) hole located at the rear of the engine block in the center of the upper gasket surface for the oil pump idler gear cover. Drill and tap this hole for a 10-32 setscrew, and install the setscrew using Loctite. The fuel pump pushrod used in the Lincoln 337-ci flathead V-8 engines is 0.440 inch o.d. by 11.682–11.688 inches long, and there is no fuel pump pushrod bushing.

A small screwdriver is inserted in the hole that must be plugged if the fuel pump pushrod will not be installed.

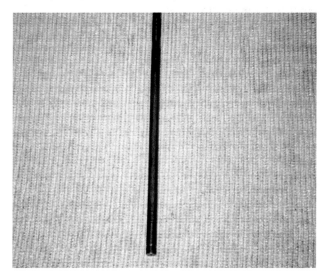

This is a Lincoln 337-ci flathead V-8 fuel pump pushrod that is 0.440 inch o.d. by 11.682 inches long.

VALVE LIFTER GALLERY BAFFLE

The Lincoln 6524 valve lifter gallery oil return hole baffle is secured in position with two spring clips. Glass bead this item, and paint it with Glyptal G-1228A medium-gray gloss enamel.

OIL FILTER

You can install an oil filter on a Lincoln flathead engine—utilizing a full-flow oil system—by mounting it on the cylinder head with a remote oil filter bracket. Luke's Custom Machine & Design fabricates a polished-aluminum, or polished stainless-steel, mounting bracket for the left cylinder head. Mount

Pictured here is the Lincoln 6524 valve lifter gallery oil return hole baffle. It has been painted with Glyptal G-1228A medium-gray gloss enamel.

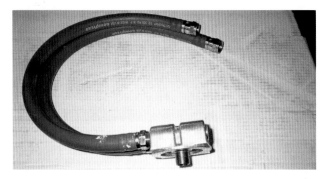

A Trans-Dapt 1045 remote oil filter adapter with the Trans-Dapt 1032 neoprene rubber oil filter hose kit is pictured here.

the remote oil filter bracket with the oil filter using a mounting bracket. A Trans-Dapt 1045 aluminum remote oil filter adapter, with horizontal inlets and outlets, can also be mounted to the firewall, or under the floorboards, if you wish to keep the oil filter out of sight. The oil filter adapter has a silver finish, but it can be buffed for a true show appearance. The Trans-Dapt 1032 neoprene rubber hose kit, 24 inches long by 1/2 inch NPT, is used with the remote oil filter bracket. Connect the inlet side of the remote oil filter bracket to the pressure-out fitting in the engine block. Then connect the outlet side of the remote oil filter bracket to the drain-back fitting in the engine block.

The Trans-Dapt 1045 remote oil filter adapter accepts the Fram PH8A (Ford) oil filter. If mounting the remote oil filter bracket on the cylinder head, a Mr. Gasket 9759 chrome oil filter cover or a Moroso 22400 chrome oil filter should be installed.

B. LUBRICATION SYSTEM SUMMARY

- New front oil gallery line plug, 3/8 inch NPT; new rear oil gallery line frost plug, 19/32 inch; and new valve lifter oil gallery line plugs, 1/4 inch NPT—installed using Permatex aviation form-a-gasket. Fuel pump pushrod oil hole blocked-off with 10-32 setscrew using Loctite. Lincoln 6655 oil pump idler gear installed with Lincoln 6657 oil pump idler gear bushing, and Lincoln 6656 oil pump idler gear shaft allowing for 0.002-inch clearance. Lincoln OEL-6658 oil pump idler gear cover installed with new stainless-steel hex-head bolts and lockwashers using Loctite and torqued to 15 ft-lbs. Oil pump idler gear cover gasket installed using silicone sealant. Inside of oil pump idler gear cover and Lincoln 6524 valve lifter gallery oil return hole baffle painted with Glyptal G-1228A medium-gray gloss enamel. Valve lifter gallery oil pressure relief valve (Lincoln 353082-S ball, 6654 spring, and 6666 nut) installed using Permatex aviation form-a-gasket. **$105.83**

- NOS Lincoln 6603 high-volume oil pump installed with Lincoln 6615 oil pump cover and inlet tube, Lincoln 6623 oil pump cover screen, and Lincoln 6628 oil pump cover screen retainer. Oil pump end clearance: 0.00025 inch. Oil pump cover and inlet tube gasket installed using silicone sealant with bolts torqued to 80 in-lbs using Loctite. Lincoln 8EL-6335 upper rear oil seal retainer installed with new stainless-steel hex-head bolts and lockwashers using Loctite and torqued to 15 ft-lbs. Upper rear oil seal retainer gasket installed using silicone sealant. Rear oil seal packings (Lincoln 6701) soaked in SAE 30-weight motor oil and installed. New Speedway Motors 912-S12853 front one-piece oil seal installed using silicone sealant. **$228.95**

- Lincoln 6676 oil pan, 7-quart capacity, installed with new stainless-steel hex-head bolts, lockwashers, and AN flat washers using Loctite and torqued to 15 ft-lbs. Lincoln 6683 oil pan baffle installed. Lincoln 6695 oil pan sump installed with new stainless-steel nylocks and AN flat washers using Loctite and torqued to 15 ft-lbs. Oil pan and sump gaskets installed using silicone sealant. Lincoln 6751 dipstick tube boss installed with new stainless-steel pan-head screws, star washers, and nuts using Loctite. Dipstick tube boss gasket installed using silicone sealant. Lincoln 6750 dipstick and 6754 dipstick tube installed. Oil pan, sump, dipstick tube, and dipstick painted with PPG 7400 red high-gloss polyurethane. Engine lubricated with 8 quarts of Pennzoil HD-30 weight motor oil. **$314.07**

- New Trans-Dapt 1045 silver-finish remote oil filter bracket with horizontal inlet/outlets, new Moroso 22400 chrome oil filter, and new Trans-Dapt 1032 neoprene rubber oil filter hoses, 24 inches long by 1/2 inch NPT, installed. New Weatherhead 48-8 polished-brass compression fittings, 1/2 inch tube to 3/8 inch NPT; new Weatherhead 3400-6 polished-brass 90-degree street elbows, 3/8 inch NPT; new Weatherhead 3300-6 brass long nipple, 3/8 inch NPT by 3 inches long; and new Weatherhead 3400-2 polished-brass reducer, 3/8 to 1/8 inch NPT, installed using pipe thread sealant. **$140.73**

- Lubrication System Total: **$789.58**

CHAPTER 25
CAMSHAFT AND CYLINDER HEADS

A. CAMSHAFT AND CYLINDER HEADS
CAMSHAFT BEARINGS

Clevite 77 and Federal-Mogul (1097M) do not currently list camshaft bearings for the Lincoln 337-ci V-8 flathead engine. A set of Egge Parts House F-6 camshaft bearings is available for $47. The Ford Motor Company of Canada Master Repair Manual—Engine specifies a camshaft bearing clearance of 0.0013 to 0.0023 inch and camshaft end play of 0.003 to 0.006 inch. The camshaft journal diameter is 1.925 inches. The Lincoln 6287 fuel pump driveshaft eccentric sleeve is installed on the rear of the camshaft. The sleeve must be removed before the camshaft can be removed from the engine block.

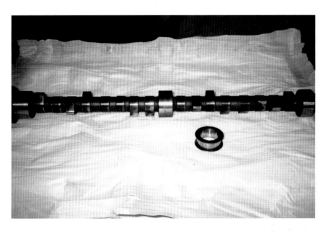

This is a 1951 Lincoln 8EQ-6250 solid lifter camshaft and the Lincoln 6287 fuel pump driveshaft eccentric sleeve.

This is a NOS set of Bohnalite 1133-CK camshaft bearings for the Lincoln 337-ci flathead V-8 engine.

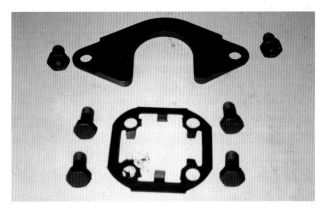

At the top are the Lincoln 6269 camshaft thrust plate and 42592-S camshaft thrust plate bolts. At the bottom are the Lincoln 6258 camshaft gear lockwasher plate and 350400-S camshaft gear bolts.

CAMSHAFT

The 1948–1953 Ford Truck engines were equipped with the Lincoln 8EQ-6250 solid lifter camshaft, and the 1949–1951 Lincoln passenger car engines were equipped with the Lincoln 8EL-6250 hydraulic lifter camshaft. The early 1949 Canadian Ford Truck engines were equipped with the Lincoln 8EL-6250 hydraulic lifter camshaft, and the late 1949–1953 Canadian Ford Truck engines were equipped with the Lincoln 8EQ-6250 solid lifter camshaft. The Egge Parts House VML1 flat-tappet camshaft is available for the current retail price of $64, plus a $150 core charge if an exchange camshaft is not provided.

The Lincoln 337-ci flathead V-8 camshaft is secured in position with the Lincoln 6269 thrust plate, which is bolted to the front of the engine block (behind the camshaft gear) using the two Lincoln 42592-S thrust plate bolts. The camshaft end play is measured between the front of the camshaft thrust plate and the rear of the camshaft gear flange on the front of the camshaft. The camshaft is installed first, then the thrust plate, and finally the camshaft gear.

The Iskenderian Racing Cams 44 three-quarter race camshaft was available in the 1950s. It had an advertised duration of 248 degrees intake and 250 degrees exhaust, and a lobe separation angle of 111 degrees. The net valve lift was

123

0.365 inch intake and 0.363 inch exhaust, and valve lash (hot) was 0.010 inch intake and 0.012 inch exhaust. The Iskenderian Racing Cams 1021 track-grind camshaft was also available in the 1950s. It had an advertised duration of 259 degrees intake and 260 degrees exhaust, and a lobe separation angle of 111 degrees. The net valve lift was 0.363 inch intake and 0.361 inch exhaust, and valve lash (hot) was 0.012 inch intake and 0.014 inch exhaust. Crower Cams & Equipment reground the Lincoln 8EQ-6250 solid lifter camshaft for the engine described here. Its advertised duration is 262 degrees intake and exhaust, and its duration at 0.050-inch lift is 212 degrees intake and exhaust. The lobe separation angle is 112 degrees, net valve lift is 0.340 inch intake and exhaust, and the valve lash (hot) is 0.012 inch intake and exhaust. This is a very good street performance camshaft for a naturally aspirated Lincoln 337-ci flathead V-8 engine.

DEGREE CAMSHAFT

> Refer to Chapter 5.

VALVE LIFTERS

The valve lifters used in the Lincoln 337-ci flathead V-8 engines are the flat-tappet mushroom type. Thus the diameter of the face is wider than the diameter of the main body, so they must be installed from the underside of the engine block prior to installing the camshaft. When a valve lifter or camshaft has to be replaced, the engine has to be removed from the vehicle and almost completely disassembled to replace these parts. This procedure applied to Ford trucks and Lincoln passenger cars. The chance of having problems with solid lifters is less likely than encountering problems with hydraulic lifters.

The Lincoln 8EL-6500 hydraulic mushroom valve lifter consists of the Lincoln 6502 body and Lincoln 6508 plunger

This is a NOS set of Lincoln 8EQ-6500-A solid flat-tappet adjustable mushroom valve lifters for the Lincoln 337-ci flathead V-8 engines.

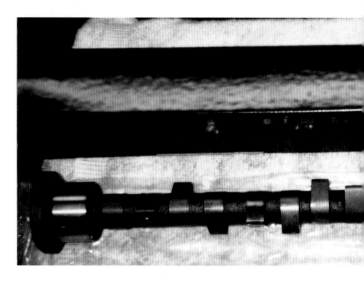

This Lincoln 8EQ-6250 solid lifter camshaft was reground by Crower Cams & Equipment. The advertised duration is 262 degrees intake and exhaust; duration at 0.050-inch lift is 212 degrees intake and exhaust; lobe separation angle is 112 degrees; net valve lift is 0.340 inch intake and exhaust; and valve lash (hot) is 0.012 inch intake and exhaust.

and cylinder assembly. To check the valve clearance when using hydraulic lifters, rotate the camshaft until the valve lifter is on the base circle of the camshaft lobe. Then depress the valve lifter plunger; the valve-stem-to-plunger clearance should be 0.040 to 0.090 inch. The Lincoln 8EL-6500 hydraulic mushroom valve lifters are no longer available from the Ford Motor Company. The Egge Parts House VL337 hydraulic mushroom valve lifters are available for the current retail price of $891 for a set of 16.

The Lincoln 8EQ-6500-A solid flat-tappet adjustable mushroom valve lifters are the most desirable type to install in a Lincoln 337-ci flathead V-8 engine. Each lifter consists of the Lincoln 6500 body and Lincoln 6549 adjusting screw. The diameter of the face is 1.165 inches, the diameter of the body is 0.720 inch, and each one weighs 90 grams. These valve lifters are no longer available from the Ford Motor Company and they rarely appear on eBay or in Hemmings Motor News. The owner of the engine described here managed to locate a NOS set of Lincoln 8EQ-6500-A valve lifters for the bargain basement price of $225.

VALVES

The Lincoln 6507 intake valves have a 1.795-inch head diameter, 11/32-inch stem diameter, and are 5.715 inches long overall. Each intake valve weighs 119 grams. The Egge Parts House V1836 intake valves are replacement models, and the current retail price for a set of eight is $123. The Lincoln 6505 exhaust valves have a 1.505-inch head diameter, 11/32-inch stem diameter, and are 5.615 inches long overall. Each exhaust valve weighs 102 grams. The Egge Parts House S1835 exhaust valves are replacement models, and the

current retail price for a set of eight is $123. The intake and exhaust valves in the engine described here were all in such good condition, they appeared almost new after they were glass beaded and polished in a lathe.

Exhaust (free) valves were installed in Lincoln 337-ci flathead V-8 engines in early 1949. Exhaust (free) valves means they are rotating exhaust valves and have a lash cap. In mid-1950, a new design of exhaust (free) valve was introduced with a shorter lash cap. The Ford Motor Company of Canada Master Repair Manual—Engine specifies the clearance between the bottom inside of the lash cap and the tip of the exhaust (free) valve to be 0.0002 to 0.004 inch with the valve stem locks in place. The Lincoln 8EQ-6534 exhaust valve locking kit eliminated the rotating exhaust valves by replacing the valve stem locks, lash cap, and lower valve spring retainer.

VALVE GUIDE BUSHINGS

The Lincoln 6510 intake and exhaust valve guide bushings used in the Lincoln flathead engine block are the pressed-in type, unlike those in Ford flathead engines, which are installed and removed with a valve spring compressor bar. The Ford Motor Company of Canada Master Repair Manual—Engine specified the valve-stem-to-valve-guide-bushing clearance to be 0.0022 to 0.0037 inch. The top of the intake and exhaust valve guides are installed 1.28 inches below the deck surface of the engine block. If the valve guide bushings are cracked or excessively worn, the Egge Parts House G627 valve guide bushings are good replacements and are available for $7 each, or $112 for a set of 16. The valve guide bushings in the engine described here were all in good condition.

VALVE SPRINGS

A NOS set of Lincoln 8EL-6513 single helical coil valve springs was measured at High Performance Engines and installed in the engine described in this section. The installed height is 70 pounds at 1.6875 (1 11/16) inches valves closed, and 150 pounds at 1.3275 inches valves open (0.360-inch

This is a set of 1951 Lincoln 6507 intake valves with a 1.795-inch head diameter, 11/32-inch stem diameter, and an overall length of 5.715 inches. The weight of one of these valves is 119 grams.

This is a set of 1951 Lincoln 6505 exhaust valves with a 1.505-inch head diameter, 11/32-inch stem diameter, an overall length of 5.615 inches, and each weighs 102 grams.

Here is a set of original 1951 Lincoln 8EL-6513 single helical coil valve springs used in the Lincoln 337-ci flathead V-8 engines.

lift). It is 1.515 inches o.d., 1.130 inches i.d., and 2.045 inches long overall, and the coil bind is 1.200 inches. A naturally aspirated Lincoln 337-ci flathead V-8 engine does not require a lot of valve spring tension. A set of Egge Parts House VS581 replacement valve springs is available for the current retail price of $102.

VALVE SPRING RETAINERS, LOCKS, AND LASH CAPS

The Lincoln 337-ci flathead V-8 engines were equipped with upper and lower valve spring retainers. The Lincoln 6516 upper valve spring retainers fit over the stem of the valve guide bushings against the engine block. The Lincoln 6507 intake valves are designed for Lincoln 6514 lower valve spring retainers

This set of Lincoln 6516 upper valve spring retainers has been glass beaded and sprayed with graphite.

The Lincoln 6518 valve stem locks are at the top, and the 6514 valve spring retainers and sleeves are in the middle and at the bottom. These parts are used with Lincoln 6507 intake valves.

and sleeves, along with Lincoln 6518 valve stem locks. This setup is similar in design to the 1952–1953 Ford flathead V-8 valve spring retainers and sleeves. If the intake valve stem locks are worn or damaged, the Manley Performance Parts 13127-16 stamped-steel valve stem locks can be used.

The Lincoln 6505 exhaust valves are designed for the Lincoln 6534 nonrotating exhaust valve locking kit, which consists of the 6514 lower valve spring retainer, 6518 valve stem locks, and 6550 lash caps. Lincoln 337-ci flathead V-8 valve spring retainers, sleeves, lash caps, and valve stem locks are no longer available from the Ford Motor Company. It might prove difficult to locate these parts today.

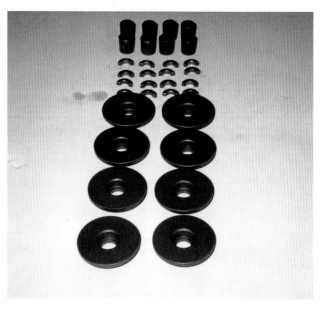

The Lincoln 6534 nonrotating exhaust valve locking kit is pictured here. The lash caps are at the top, the valve stem locks are in the middle, and the lower valve spring retainers are at the bottom.

CAMSHAFT GEAR AND TIMING COVER

The Lincoln 6256 aluminum helical camshaft gear is suitable for a street performance Lincoln 337-ci flathead V-8 engine, including a blown one. If the camshaft gear is damaged or missing, the Egge Parts House TG2715 aluminum camshaft gear is a replacement model available for the current retail price of $37. The Lincoln 6256 camshaft gear has 48 teeth, and the Ford Motor Company used to offer these aluminum camshaft gears in 0.006 and 0.012 inch oversize.

The Lincoln 6256 aluminum camshaft gear is secured to the camshaft with four of the Lincoln 350400-S camshaft gear bolts and the Lincoln 6258 lockwasher plate. The bolt holes in the camshaft gear and camshaft are not symmetrical; the camshaft gear can only be installed in one position to prevent a novice from incorrectly degreeing the camshaft.

The Lincoln 8EL-6059-A2 polished-aluminum timing gear cover is installed on Lincoln 337-ci flathead V-8 engines. This item buffs up nicely when someone like "Tim the polishing guy" attacks it. Install the timing gear with six

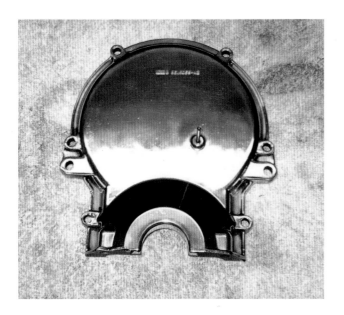

This is a Lincoln 8EL-6059-A2 polished-aluminum timing gear cover for Lincoln 337-ci flathead V-8 engines. "Tim the polishing guy" has tuned this baby up!

pieces: 5/16-inch NC by 1-inch-long polished stainless-steel hex-head bolts and lockwashers.

ONE-PIECE OIL SEAL AND SLEEVE

The Speedway Motors 912-S12853 one-piece front oil seal is manufactured for all 1928–1953 Ford four-cylinder and V-8 engines, except the V8-60. This excellent item should have been introduced decades ago, and the current retail price for one is $20. The sleeve of the Lincoln 337-ci flathead V-8 crankshaft damper and pulley has spiral grooves in it that are designed to work with the original two-piece cord material front oil seal. The spiral grooves will eventually destroy the one-piece front oil seal. Luke's Custom Machine & Design

Here is a Speedway Motors 912-S12853 one-piece front oil seal and a Luke's Custom Machine & Design crankshaft sleeve. These parts will fit a Lincoln 337-ci flathead V-8 engine.

fabricates a crankshaft sleeve designed to work with the Speedway Motors 912-S12853 one-piece front oil seal, and both the oil seal and sleeve will fit the Lincoln 337-ci flathead V-8 crankshaft snout and timing gear cover. This crankshaft sleeve is available for the current retail price of $25.

CYLINDER HEADS

The Lincoln 337-ci flathead V-8 engines were all equipped with cast-iron cylinder heads, except the cylinder heads installed on the late 1950–1953 Truck engines had external water pump bypass tubes attached beneath the water outlet elbows. These are definitely not high-performance cylinder

This is a pair of late-1950 and 1951 truck cylinder heads with a casting number of 8EO-B and casting dates of D17-1 (April 17, 1951) and F7-1 (June 7, 1951). The external water pump bypass tubes are bolted to the front of the water pumps.

heads. The Lincoln passenger car cylinder head on the left side has casting number 8EL-60508, and the Lincoln passenger car cylinder head on the right side has casting number

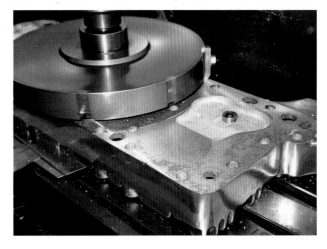

This Edelbrock cast-aluminum cylinder head for a Lincoln 337-ci flathead V-8 engine is being surfaced at High Performance Engines.

This is a pair of polished Edelbrock aluminum cylinder heads for the Lincoln 337-ci flathead V-8 engine. These cylinder heads have a 55-cc combustion chamber volume and a 9.5:1 compression ratio.

8EL-60498. The late 1950–1953 Truck cylinder heads, left and right, have casting number 8EO-B.

The only aftermarket aluminum cylinder heads produced in the 1950s for the Lincoln flathead engines (that I am aware of) were manufactured by Edelbrock and Edmunds. The Edelbrock cast finned-aluminum cylinder heads were available with an 8.0:1, 8.5:1, or 9.5:1 compression ratio when using the standard flat-top pistons. The 9.5:1 compression ratio cylinder heads have a 55-cc combustion chamber volume. Most speed-equipment manufacturers did not list a part number in the 1950s, as was the case with the Edelbrock aluminum cylinder heads. The purchase of used cylinder heads is risky business; they should be Magnafluxed and will most likely have to be surfaced. The owner of the engine described here managed to purchase a pair of Edelbrock aluminum cylinder heads in almost-new condition at the Portland, Oregon, swap meet a year ago for $800.

Ken Austin (see Resources) manufactures superb-quality cast-aluminum intake manifolds for Ardun OHV conversion engines and Ford flathead V-8 engines. He has recently introduced cast finned-aluminum cylinder heads for Lincoln 337-ci flathead V-8 engines. The Austin cylinder heads are available for the current retail price of $950 for a pair.

CYLINDER HEAD GASKETS AND BOLTS

Edelbrock recommends the use of copper sandwiched cylinder head gaskets with its aluminum cylinder heads. The Fitzgerald 0505 can be purchased from Best Gasket of California as part of its RS726 complete gasket set for Lincoln 337-ci flathead V-8 engines.

The Lincoln 6066 cylinder head bolts are 7/16 inch NC by 2 3/4 inches long, which are the same dimensions as the 1949–1953 Ford 6066 long cylinder head bolts. Each cylinder head requires 27 bolts; provided they are not badly corroded and the threads are not stripped, they can be glass beaded, painted, and reused. The Speedway Motors 910-10115 chrome acorn nut covers for an 11/16-inch head will fit the Lincoln 6066 cylinder head bolts. Hardened-steel flat washers, such as the Manley Performance Parts 42102 heat-treated head bolt washers, must be used when installing aluminum cylinder heads to prevent damage.

WATER OUTLET ELBOWS

The Lincoln 8592 and 8593 cast-iron water outlet elbows, which aren't the classiest looking parts, are bolted to the top front of the cylinder heads. Luke's Custom Machine & Design fabricates a flat polished-aluminum plate to adapt a 1949–1953 Ford 8592 cast-iron water outlet elbow to each cylinder head. The Speedway Motors 910-15852 cast-aluminum stock-style water outlet elbows are also available for the current retail price of $12.95 each. Have them buffed.

Thermostats should be installed in any engine that is being used on the street. Removing the thermostats will cause the coolant in the engine to move too fast for the heat to be dissipated. Small-block Chevrolet V-8 thermostats, or Speedway Motors 910-15802 thermostats, will fit the 1949–1953 Ford 8592 water outlet elbows.

EXHAUST BAFFLES

Install exhaust port baffles in a Lincoln 337-ci flathead V-8 engine to keep the exhaust gases from the two center cylinders on each side of the engine block from mixing with each other. Without the exhaust port baffles, the exhaust gases from the two center cylinders will collide with each other before they exit the engine block. The Lincoln flathead engine block used in the Ford trucks have an exhaust port baffle cast into the engine block. The Speedway Motors 916-15201 exhaust port baffles can be adapted to fit the Lincoln 337-ci flathead V-8 passenger car engine block.

B. CAMSHAFT AND CYLINDER HEADS SUMMARY

- NOS Bohnalite 1133-CK camshaft bearings installed allowing for 0.002-inch camshaft clearance and 0.005-inch camshaft end play. Nos. 1 and 2 bearings: 6241 with housing bore of 2.0605 to 2.0615 inches. No. 3 bearing: 6242 with housing bore of 2.0605 to 2.0615 inches. Camshaft journal diameter: 1.925 inches. **$47**
- Lincoln 8EQ-6250 solid flat-tappet camshaft reground by Crower Cams & Equipment. Street grind with 262 degrees intake and exhaust; duration at 0.050-inch lift of 212 degrees intake and exhaust; and lobe separation angle of 112 degrees. Net valve lift, 0.340 inch intake and exhaust; and valve lash (hot), 0.012 inch intake and exhaust. Camshaft degreed. Lincoln 6269 camshaft thrust plate installed with Lincoln 42592-S bolts using Loctite and torqued to 20 ft-lbs. Lincoln 6287 fuel pump driveshaft eccentric sleeve installed. **$250**
- New Ford 8EQ-6500-A solid flat-tappet adjustable mushroom valve lifters installed. Solid body lifter weight: 90 grams each. **$225**
- Lincoln 6510 intake and exhaust pressed-in valve guide bushings installed. New Egge Parts House VS581 single helical coil valve springs with installed height: 70 pounds at 1.6875 inches valves closed, and 150 pounds at 1.3275 inches valves open (0.360-inch lift); 1.515 inches o.d., 1.130 inches i.d., 2.045 inches long; and coil bind of 1.200 inches. Lincoln 6516 upper valve spring retainers installed. Lincoln 6514 intake valve spring retainers and sleeves and Lincoln 6518 valve stem locks installed. Lincoln 6534 nonrotating exhaust valve locking kit installed. **$214**
- Lincoln 6507 intake valves—11/32-inch stem diameter, 1.795-inch head diameter, and 5.715 inches long overall—installed. Intake valve weight: 119 grams. Lincoln 6505 nonrotating exhaust valves—11/32-inch stem diameter, 1.505-inch head diameter, and 5.615 inches long overall—installed. Exhaust valve weight: 102 grams. Valves installed with multi-angle blueprint valve grind. **$123**
- NOS Lincoln 6256 aluminum camshaft helical timing gear, 48 teeth, installed with Lincoln 6258 lockwasher plate and Lincoln 350400-S camshaft gear bolts using Loctite and torqued to 20 ft-lbs. Lincoln 8EL-6059-A2 polished-aluminum timing gear cover installed with new polished stainless-steel hex-head bolts and lockwashers using Loctite and torqued to 15 ft-lbs. Timing gear cover gasket installed using silicone sealant. **$110.33**
- New Fitzgerald 0505 copper sandwiched cylinder head gaskets installed using Permatex copper spray-a-gasket. Edelbrock cast finned-aluminum cylinder heads, 9.5:1 compression ratio, 55-cc combustion chamber volume, installed with Lincoln 6066 cylinder head bolts and new Manley Performance Parts 42102 heat-treated steel head bolt washers, 7/16 inch i.d., using Permatex aviation form-a-gasket and torqued to 40 ft-lbs. New Speedway Motors 910-10115 chrome acorn nut covers, 11/16-inch head size, installed. **$895.95**
- Luke's Custom Machine & Design new, polished-aluminum water outlet elbow adapters installed with 1949–1950 Ford 8BA-8592-A2 cast-iron water outlet elbows, using new, polished stainless-steel hex-head bolts and lockwashers with anti-seize compound and torqued to 20 ft-lbs. Water outlet elbows and adapter plate gaskets installed using silicone sealant. New Speedway Motors 910-15802 thermostats, 180 degrees (Fahrenheit), installed. Water outlet elbows painted with PPG 74000 red high-gloss polyurethane. **$108.47**

- **Camshaft and Cylinder Heads Total: $1,973.75**

CHAPTER 26
INTAKE SYSTEM

A. INTAKE SYSTEM
INTAKE MANIFOLD

The Lincoln 337-ci flathead V-8 engines were equipped with a single two-barrel carburetor intake manifold designed to accept a four-bolt carburetor. The well-designed Lincoln OEL-6520 cast-iron intake manifold functions nicely on stock engines. A street performance engine will require more carburetion than a stock single two-barrel carburetor. A limited number of aftermarket intake manifolds were available in the 1950s for the Lincoln flathead. Vic Edelbrock Sr., Eddie Edmunds, Nicson (Nick and son Chuck Glaviano), and Tommy Thickstun all manufactured dual two-barrel carburetor aluminum intake manifolds designed to accept three-bolt carburetors. These intake manifolds occasionally appear at swap meets or on eBay.

Dual two-barrel carburetor intake manifolds are the most popular among flathead owners, although I have my doubts about this setup's ability to deliver fuel economy and low emissions. One of the best intake manifolds for a street performance flathead engine is a triple two-barrel carburetor model. Installing a progressive linkage with the three carburetors will result in fuel economy, lower emissions, and excellent throttle response.

Ken Austin manufactures premium-quality cast-aluminum intake manifolds for the Lincoln 337-ci flathead V-8 engine. The Austin LT triple two-barrel carburetor intake manifold, designed to accept three-bolt carburetors, and the Austin LB blower intake manifold, for mounting a GMC 4-71 blower,

The Lincoln OEL-6520 single two-barrel carburetor cast-iron intake manifold was used on the 1951 Ford Truck engines. It is designed to accept a four-bolt carburetor.

Here is an Austin LT triple two-barrel-carburetor intake manifold for the Lincoln 337-ci flathead V-8 engine. This model permits the generator to be mounted in the stock position. The gleaming elegance was provided by "Tim the polishing guy."

This is a piece of real hot rod history, a polished Nicson (Nick and his son, Chuck, Glaviano) F8 super dual two-barrel-carburetor cast-aluminum intake manifold.

are available today for the current retail price of $600 each. There are two types of Austin LT intake manifolds. One is designed to mount the generator in the stock position at the front, and the other is designed to mount the generator on the cylinder head. This intake manifold, with the generator mounted in the stock position, was installed on the engine described here.

CARBURETOR

The Lincoln 337-ci flathead V-8 engines were fitted with a two-barrel carburetor. The engines used in Ford trucks (rated at 4 and 5 tons) came equipped with the Holley (Lincoln 8EQ) dual concentric, side-draft two-barrel carburetor fitted with the Holley centri-vac governor. This vacuum governor worked in conjunction with the governor on the distributor. This carburetor is definitely not a high-performance model.

The Holley 94 and Stromberg 97 carburetors are the most popular two-barrel carburetors installed on flathead engines; both are the three-bolt design. I prefer the Holley 94 carburetor because of its simplicity; it is easy to work on and does not have any delicate parts (emulsion tubes). The main jets and power valves are available from any Holley parts outlet and the tune-up kits can be purchased from most automotive supply stores. The best tune-up kit I have found for the Holley 94 carburetor is the Niehoff CK-302A. Speedway Motors and Vintage Speed sell tune-up kits for the Stromberg 97. Refer to Chapter 6 for further information about carburetors.

The Stromberg 97 carburetor was used on larger Ford flathead V-8 engines from 1936 to 1938. In 1938, Chandler-Groves introduced a carburetor to replace the Stromberg 97, due to problems the Ford Motor Company was having with it. In 1939, Holley started producing the Chandler-Groves carburetor, and thereafter, it was named the Holley 94 due to the 94/100-inch venturi. The Holley 94 carburetor is rated at approximately 160 cfm, and the Stromberg 97 carburetor is rated at approximately 155 cfm. Holley produced all the two-barrel carburetors for the Ford Motor Company from 1939 to 1957. Stromberg Carburetor Limited of England is now reproducing the Stromberg 97, and it is available from speed-equipment outlets, such as Jitney Auto Parts, at the current retail price of $400.

When the Holley 94 is used for multi-carb setups, you may encounter a problem with the power valve. A single power valve is designed to work with engines up to about 250 ci. If two, three, or four Holley 94 carburetors with power valves are installed on a 337-ci engine, obviously the spark plugs will

This little gem is a Holley (Lincoln 8EQ) dual concentric side-draft two-barrel carburetor used on the 1948–1953 Ford Truck (4- and 5-ton) engines. The Holley centri-vac governor is attached to the base.

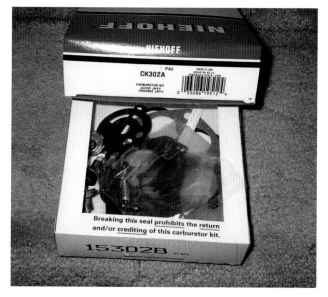

Here is a Niehoff CK-302A complete tune-up kit for the Holley 94 carburetor.

This pair of vintage Stromberg 97 carburetors has been buffed by "Tim the polishing guy."

"Tim the polishing guy" provided the luster for this Holley 94 carburetor that I built.

be easily fouled. One of the reasons I prefer to run a three-carburetor setup with the Holley 94 is that the power valve in the end carburetors can be blocked off using the Holley 26-36 power valve plug.

If the power valve in the end carburetors is blocked off when using a three-carburetor setup, replace the idle adjustment screws in the end carburetors with polished stainless-steel button-head socket screws, 10-32 by 3/8 inch length. Only the center carburetor will now operate at idle, and the two end carburetors will start to function at 50 percent, 60 percent, or whatever part-throttle position desired, which is the beauty of using progressive linkage with a three-carburetor setup.

I have built dozens of Holley 94 carburetors over the past few years—to the point that I fall asleep counting the little rascals. I now try and convince people to install a four-barrel carburetor on a flathead engine rather than have me build Holley 94s. The best idea is to call Charley Price at Vintage Speed and order a container load of Holley 94s. I start the Holley 94 romance with the complete disassembly of the carburetor, all the parts are cold tanked, the body and base are glass beaded, and all the gasket mating areas are resurfaced. I employ the services of "Tim the polishing guy" for all my buffing work. After the carburetor body has been buffed, spray it with Eastwood Company 10200Z Diamond Clear gloss finish or VHT SP-115 clear high-temperature coating to prevent the carburetor body from tarnishing.

The base of the carburetor can be painted with Plasti-Kote 203 universal black engine enamel, or the same color (within reason) as the engine block. Fit a Vintage Speed H-39C extended throttle shaft, 0.005 inch oversize, allowing for 0.002-inch clearance, and install a Vintage Speed CL-35 torsion base spring. Install a Niehoff CK-302A complete tune-up kit, and assemble the carburetor with polished stainless-steel fasteners using anti-seize compound. Do not remove the choke assembly from the carburetor, as it aids with the direction of the airflow. Install stock (at sea level) Holley 0.051-inch main jets, although they may have to be changed a few sizes up or down depending on the particular engine application and altitude. Set the float level at 1 11/32 inches and the float drop at 1 7/16 inches. The completed Holley 94 looks great and it works.

FUEL PRESSURE REGULATOR AND FUEL BLOCK

The Lincoln 9350 fuel pump is designed to provide sufficient fuel for a single two-barrel carburetor. If installing multiple carburetors on a Lincoln 337-ci flathead V-8 engine, then install an electric fuel pump. Mount the electric fuel pump as close to the gas tank as possible to push the fuel and not pull it.

The Austin LT intake manifold does not have the crankcase breather/road-draft tube or the crankcase breather/oil filler tube openings at the left front. A 1939–1948 Ford 9415 crankcase breather/fuel pump stand with an Offenhauser 5265 fuel pump block-off plate can be mounted at the rear of the intake manifold. Have the crankcase breather/fuel pump stand and the fuel pump block-off plate buffed, and finish up with the addition of a Speedway Motors 910-15195 chrome crankcase breather/oil filler cap.

A fuel pressure regulator should be used in conjunction with an electric fuel pump. The Holley 12-804 fuel pressure regulator is adjustable from 1 to 4 psi, which is usually preset at 3 psi at the factory. This unit has a silver finish, and the current retail price is $22. The maximum fuel pressure a Holley 94 carburetor should be operated with is 2 1/2 to 3 psi, and for a Stromberg 97 carburetor, it is 2 to 2 1/2 psi. Refer to Chapter 6 for information on fuel pressure gauges.

A few companies manufacture fuel blocks for three-carburetor setups, and they are inexpensive items. The Mooneyes USA MP1011 is a polished cast finned-aluminum fuel block, the Mr. Gasket 6151 is a chrome fuel block, and the Offenhauser 1081 is a cast-aluminum fuel block. Luke's

Custom Machine & Design fabricates a polished stainless-steel bracket for mounting the fuel block and fuel pressure regulator as a unit. The unit is mounted on the left side of the intake manifold, next to the cylinder head.

Fuel Lines and Progressive Linkage

I have always liked the look of the old-style red vinyl fuel lines on any flathead engine. Fuel lines available today are manufactured using high-quality vinyl, which does not harden, crack, or discolor with age. The Speedway Motors 910-11450 ruby red fuel line is available in 3/8 inch i.d. only. The Vintage Speed FL-H-R fuel line is available in red, green, blue, yellow, or clear, and with a 3/8 or 5/16 inch i.d. The Mooneyes USA AF4215 red fuel line is 5/16 inch i.d., and the AF4216 red fuel line is 3/8 inch i.d. Vintage Speed is the only source today I am aware of for the original Eelco fuel line fittings.

The Offenhauser 6271 progressive linkage is designed for a three-carburetor setup. Have someone like "Tim the polishing guy" buff up the linkage arms, and purchase stainless-steel cotter pins, washers, and linkage rods to complete the detailing. The Offenhauser 6271 progressive linkage is available from most speed-equipment outlets for the current retail price of $50.

AIR CLEANERS

Air cleaners used on Holley 94 or Stromberg 97 carburetors are commonly the velocity stack, scoop, louvered, and helmet designs. A popular new addition is the (Ron) Greenfield cast-aluminum air cleaner top, which is similar in design to the original Stelling and Hellings bonnet-style. However, the Greenfield model is slightly oval, permitting a greater flow of air. The Greenfield air cleaner tops will fit most of the aftermarket air cleaner bases. Jitney Auto Parts sells a very nice cast-aluminum air cleaner base, and the Speedway Motors 910-11005 base is a stamped-steel

chrome air cleaner base. Air cleaner bases are not expensive.

Regardless of what type of air cleaners are used, a decent air filter must be installed in each air cleaner. The K & N E-3120 air filters (3.875 inches in diameter by 2 inches tall) will fit most of the popular two-barrel carburetor air cleaners, as well as provide an unrestricted airflow. The current retail price is $30.

BOLTS

The Lincoln 21533-S intake manifold bolts can be reused if they are not badly corroded, the threads are not stripped, and they are glass beaded and painted. The alternative is to use new Grade 8 or stainless-steel 3/8-inch NC by 1 1/2-inch-long hex-head bolts, and AN flat washers. The Austin LT intake manifold requires 17 pieces of 3/8-inch NC by 1-inch-long hex-head bolts. To keep the traditional flathead appearance, install the Speedway Motors 910-10125 chrome acorn nut covers (for 9/16-inch head size).

PCV VALVE

In cooler climates, all flathead engines are subject to some serious condensation inside the engine block, particularly the valve lifter gallery. The water vapor condensation will lead to sludge forming inside the engine. The Lincoln 337-ci flathead V-8 intake manifolds were equipped with the Lincoln 6762 crankcase breather/road-draft tube, which did little to solve the condensation problem. Installing a positive crankcase ventilation valve (PCV valve) will result in a direct-flow sealed crankcase ventilation system.

Drill and tap a 1/8-inch-NPT hole approximately 2 inches from the right side front of the intake manifold. This hole will protrude into the valve lifter gallery. Install a Weatherhead 3400-2 polished-brass 90-degree elbow, 1/8

A Jitney Auto Parts cast-aluminum air cleaner base and a (Ron) Greenfield polished cast-aluminum air cleaner top are pictured here.

inch NPT. Install a Mopar Performance Parts (Chrysler) BU-1412 PCV valve (one end is threaded for 1/8 inch NPT) in the 90-degree elbow. Drill and tap a 1/8-inch-NPT hole on the right side of the intake manifold approximately 1 1/2 inches below the top (not the top of the carburetor mounting flange) at the center. This hole will protrude into the center carburetor intake runner. Install a Weatherhead 3400-2 polished-brass 90-degree elbow, 1/8 inch NPT. Install a Weatherhead 1068-4 polished-brass male connector, 1/4 inch i.d. hose to 1/8 inch NPT, in the 90-degree elbow. Connect the PCV valve and hose fitting using an appropriate length of 1/4 inch i.d. PCV hose with stainless-steel line clamps. Fresh air will now be drawn through the crankcase breather/oil filler tube cap, and the crankcase will be vented through the PCV valve. Aluminum plugs must be fabricated to block off the crankcase breather/road-draft tube opening and the crankcase breather/oil filler tube at the front of the intake manifold, if so equipped.

B. INTAKE SYSTEM SUMMARY

- New Ken Austin LT triple two-barrel carburetor polished cast-aluminum intake manifold installed, with new stainless-steel hex-head bolts and AN flat washers using Loctite and torqued to 25 ft-lbs. Intake manifold gasket installed using silicone sealant. New Speedway Motors 910-10125 chrome acorn nut covers (for 9/16-inch head size) installed. 1939–1948 Ford 9415 polished crankcase breather/fuel pump stand installed with new polished stainless-steel acorn nuts, lockwashers, and AN flat washers using anti-seize compound. New Offenhauser 5265 polished-aluminum fuel pump block-off plate installed with new polished stainless-steel hex-head bolts and AN flat washers using anti-seize compound. Crankcase breather/fuel pump stand and fuel pump block-off plate gaskets installed using silicone sealant. New Speedway Motors 910-15195 chrome crankcase breather/oil filler cap installed. New Mopar Performance Parts BU-1412 PCV valve installed with new Weatherhead 3400-2 polished-brass 90-degree male elbows, 1/8 inch NPT; new Weatherhead 1068-4 polished-brass male connector, 1/4 inch i.d. hose to 1/8 inch NPT; and new PCV hose, 1/4 inch i.d. by 1 inch long. **$565**

- Three x two-barrel Holley 94 polished carburetors— 94/100-inch (15/16-inch) venturi, 480 cfm (approximate total)—installed with new Papco 264-016 engine studs, 5/16 inch by 1 3/4 inches long (reduced to 1 1/2 inches long), and new polished stainless-steel acorn nuts and lockwashers using anti-seize compound. New Offenhauser 6271 polished progressive linkage installed using anti-seize compound. New Speedway Motors 910-11005 louvered air cleaner tops; new K & N E-3120 air filters, 3.875 inches in diameter by 2 inches tall; and new Jitney Auto Parts polished cast-aluminum air cleaner bases assembled with new, polished stainless-steel acorn nuts, AN flat washers, and nylocks using anti-seize compound. **$1,269.17**

- New Mr. Gasket 6151 chrome fuel block with new Weatherhead 1068-4-4 polished brass male connectors, 5/16 inch i.d. hose to 1/4 inch NPT, installed with new Mooneyes USA AF4215 red vinyl fuel lines, 5/16 inch i.d., using new stainless-steel line clamps. New Holley 12-804 silver-finish fuel pressure regulator, adjustable from 1 to 4 psi, installed with new Weatherhead 3220-6-4 polished-brass bushing, 3/8 inch NPT to 1/4 inch NPT; new Weatherhead 1069-6 polished-brass 90-degree male elbow, 3/8 inch i.d. hose to 1/4 inch NPT (inlet line); new Weatherhead 3700-6 polished-brass T-fitting, 3/8 inch NPT; new Weatherhead 3326-6 brass close nipples, 3/8 inch NPT; new Weatherhead 3152-6 polished-brass hex-head plug, 3/8 inch NPT (outlet line); and new Weatherhead 3220-6-2 polished-brass bushing, 3/8 inch NPT to 1/8 inch NPT (fuel pressure gauge). New Holley 26-500 fuel pressure gauge, 1–15 psi, 1 1/2-inch-diameter face, installed. All fittings installed using pipe thread sealant. Fuel block and fuel pressure regulator mounted with Luke's Custom Machine & Design new polished-aluminum mounting bracket. **$180.44**

- Intake System Total: **$2,014.61**

CHAPTER 27
IGNITION SYSTEM

A. IGNITION SYSTEM
DISTRIBUTOR

The distributor is located at the rear of the Lincoln 337-ci flathead V-8 engine, unlike Ford flathead V-8 engines where the distributor is located at the front of the engine. The 1949 Lincoln 8EL-12127 distributor operated with a combination of centrifugal (mechanical) and vacuum advance. The 1950–1951 Lincoln OEL-12127 distributors operated with vacuum advance only. The Lincoln 8EQ-12127 distributors installed in 1948–1953 Ford trucks operated with vacuum advance only and were equipped with a vacuum governor assembly used in conjunction with a Holley (Lincoln 8EQ) dual concentric, side-draft two-barrel carburetor fitted with a centri-vac governor. All Lincoln 337-ci flathead V-8 distributors have single points and a skinny distributor shaft with a tiny drive gear attached. The ignition system in 1949–1951 Lincoln passenger cars and 1948–1953 Ford trucks functioned on 6 volts.

Mallory dual-point distributors and Joe Hunt magneto drives were available for Lincoln flatheads in the 1950s. At the present time, no company manufactures a distributor for these engines. Lincoln 337-ci flathead V-8 distributors should be brought into the modern era by installing an electronic conversion kit. The Pertronix Performance Products 1283

This vintage Mallory YCM Magspark polished distributor has been converted using a Mallory 609 magnetic breakerless module. The 4215C rotor and 4001 distributor cap are also new.

Ignitor solid-state ignition system replaces the factory distributor points with an electronic high-energy ignition (HEI) style trigger. This is an easy conversion, and the current retail price for this kit is $75.

A vintage Mallory YCM Magspark dual-point centrifugal (mechanical) advance distributor was discovered at the Portland, Oregon, swap meet and was installed in the engine described here. This distributor was converted using a Mallory 609 magnetic breakerless module, and a new Mallory 4215C rotor with the Mallory 4001 distributor cap was installed. As a final touch, "Tim the polishing guy" gave some gleam to the distributor housing.

COIL AND IGNITION CONTROL
> *Refer to Chapter 7.*

SPARK PLUG WIRES AND SPARK PLUGS

The Pertronix Performance Products 808290 Flame Thrower high-performance 8-millimeter black spark plug wires with 90-degree boots are well suited for a Lincoln flathead. These spark plug wire boots have a similar design to the original flathead spark plug wire boots and are not the massive type commonly found on OHV spark plug wires. The whole set is available for the current retail price of $45. The Spectre

This fine-looking piece of equipment is a Lincoln 8EQ-12127 distributor equipped with a vacuum governor for use on 1948–1953 Ford trucks.

This is a set Pertronix Performance Parts 808290 Flame Thrower 8-millimeter high-performance spark plug wires with 90-degree boots.

4245 chrome/plastic spark plug wire separators are a nice addition and cost $10.

The most common 18-millimeter spark plugs used in Lincoln 337-ci flatheads are the Autolite 216, Champion H10, and NGK B-6L. Always coat the threads on the spark plugs with anti-seize compound when installing in aluminum cylinder heads to prevent the threads from galling. You can coat the spark plugs threads with anti-seize compound when they are installed in cast-iron cylinder heads.

GENERATOR

The Lincoln 10002 generator, 6 volts, is not suitable for most of today's hot rods that utilize a 12-volt electrical system. The owner of the engine described in this section wanted to keep

A 1956 Ford B6A-10002-A chrome generator was installed on the Lincoln flathead V-8 engine described here.

the classic look of his engine by using a generator rather than an alternator. The 1956 Ford B6A-10002-A generator, rated at 30 amps and 15 volts, was installed on the front of the intake manifold using a 1949–1953 Ford 8BA-10153-C generator mounting bracket. A polished-aluminum generator pulley was produced by Luke's Custom Machine & Design and installed in his engine. The generator body was chrome-plated, and a new Koyo K62002RS03 front bearing and Koyo 62032RSC3 rear bearing were installed. The engine also had a Super Sunny S8867 polished-aluminum generator fan installed, which added a nice detailing touch.

The Powermaster 282011 polished 12-volt alternator is a new product for the 1938–1946 Ford flathead V-8 engines. This alternator looks the same as a flathead generator, but it has an output of 75 amps. The current retail price is $400. The Powermaster 82011 black-finish alternator has a 75-amp output and is available for $350.

STARTING MOTOR

The Lincoln 11002 starting motor, 6 volts, is designed to function with Lincoln 6384 flywheel ring gear, which is 15 1/4 inches o.d. and has 120 teeth. A 1949–1953 Ford 6384 flywheel ring gear was adapted to the Lincoln 6375 flywheel installed in the engine described here. The Lincoln 11002 starting motor will not function with the Ford 6384 flywheel ring gear, which is 14.20 inches o.d. and has 112 teeth.

The 12-volt Powermaster 9507 XS torque mini-starter is a starting motor that is compatible with the 1949–1953 Ford 6384 flywheel ring gear. This starting motor's compact size will also simplify the fabrication and installation of custom exhaust headers. The Powermaster 9507 mini-starter is available at most speed-equipment outlets for the current retail price of $189.95.

A Powermaster 9507 XS torque starting motor for Ford flathead V-8 engines is pictured here.

B. IGNITION SYSTEM SUMMARY

- Mallory YCM Magspark polished dual-point centrifugal (mechanical) advance distributor converted using new Mallory 609 magnetic breakerless module. New Mallory 4001 distributor cap and new 4215C rotor installed. Total advance: 34 degrees at 3,000 rpm. New MSD 6A 6200 multiple spark discharge ignition control and new MSD 8200 Blaster 2 chrome ignition coil, 45,000 volts, installed. New Mr. Gasket 6777 chrome ignition coil bracket installed. **$485.23**

- New Pertronix Performance Products 808290 Flame Thrower high-performance 8-millimeter black spark plug wires, 90-degree boots, installed with new Spectre 4245 chrome/plastic professional wire separators. New NGK B-6L spark plugs, resistor-type 18 millimeters, installed with 0.050-inch gap and torqued to 15 ft-lbs using anti-seize compound. **$75**

- Rebuilt 1956 Ford B6A-10002-A chrome generator, rated at 30 amps and 15 volts, installed with 1949–1953 Ford 8BA-10153-C generator mounting bracket using Lincoln 352740-S stud, new stainless-steel lockwasher, and Lincoln 356075-S stud nut with anti-seize compound. Luke's Custom Machine & Design new polished-aluminum generator pulley, new Super Sunny 8867 polished-aluminum generator fan, new Koyo K62002RS03 front bearing, and new Koyo 62032RSC3 rear bearing installed. Generator mounting bracket painted with PPG 74000 red high-gloss polyurethane. **$408**

- New Powermaster 9507 XS torque starting motor installed with new, polished stainless-steel hex-head bolts and lockwashers using anti-seize compound. **$189.95**

- Ignition System Total: **$1,158.18**

CHAPTER 28
COOLING SYSTEM AND MISCELLANEOUS

A. COOLING SYSTEM AND MISCELLANEOUS
WATER PUMPS

The water pumps used on Lincoln 337-ci flathead V-8 engines are completely different from the water pumps used on Ford flathead V-8 engines. The late 1950–1953 Lincoln 8EQ-8505 and 8EQ-8506 wide (5/8-inch) V-belt water pumps, installed on the Ford trucks, were fitted with

The bypass tube that connects the Lincoln 8EQ-8505 right-side (passenger-side) water pump to the cylinder head on the 1951 Ford Truck engine is shown here.

an external bypass tube that was connected to the cylinder head below the water outlet elbow. The 1948 to early 1950 Ford truck and 1949–1951 Lincoln water pumps did not have the external bypass tube. All the water pumps used on Lincoln 337-ci flathead V-8 engines have a horizontal motor mount flange.

The external bypass tubes will have to be blocked off on Lincoln 8EQ-8505 and 8EQ-8506 water pumps if installing aftermarket cylinder heads. There is no provision for an external bypass tube on aftermarket cylinder heads. Fabricate the block-off plates with 1/8-inch-thick steel using the bypass tube gasket as a template. Bolt the block-off plates to the water pumps prior to painting them.

The Ford A8C-8591 water pump rebuild kit can be used for the Lincoln 337-ci flathead V-8 water pumps. However, the bearing shaft that comes with this kit must be reduced in length. The long end of the Ford bearing shaft must be reduced from 2 1/2 to 1 3/4 inches, and the short end from 1 to 3/4 inches. This is a simple procedure for any competent machine shop. Jitney Auto Parts (see Resources) is a good source for flathead water pump rebuild kits.

LABOR

The labor costs for checking clearances, gapping piston rings, degreeing camshaft, painting and detailing, trial assembly of

The Lincoln 8EQ-8505 and 8EQ-8506 water pumps are shown here with the bypass tube block-off plates installed.

The bearing shaft included with the Ford A8C-8591 water pump rebuild kit is pictured at the top, and the Lincoln 8578 bearing shaft is pictured at the bottom. The Ford bearing shaft must be reduced in length to fit the Lincoln water pumps.

the engine, final assembly of the engine, and initial startup of the engine have not been included in Section B of the previous chapters on the Lincoln 337-ci flathead V-8 engine. I will include that cost at the end of this chapter.

B. COOLING
SYSTEM AND MISCELLANEOUS TOTAL

- The 1951 Lincoln 8EQ-8505 and 8EQ-8506 water pumps rebuilt with NOS Ford A8C-8591 water pump rebuild kits and installed with new polished stainless-steel hex-head bolts and lockwashers using Loctite and torqued to 25 ft-lbs. Water pump gaskets installed using silicone sealant. New Gates 15A1495 high-performance crankshaft pulley/water pump pulleys/generator pulley V-belt (11/16 inch by 59 inches long) installed. Water pumps painted with PPG 74000 red high-gloss polyurethane. **$283.33**
- Labor for checking clearances, gapping piston rings, degreeing camshaft, painting and detailing, trial assembly of engine, final assembly of engine, and initial startup of engine. **$1,200**

- Cooling System and Miscellaneous Total: **$1,483.33**

Note: The estimated output of this engine is 223 horsepower at 3,500 rpm and 373 ft-lbs torque at 2,000 rpm (see Dyno Printouts).

Lincoln 337-ci Flathead V-8 Engine Total:
$1,895.57 Engine block total
$947.14 Crankshaft total
$1,426.21 Connecting rods and pistons total
$789.58 Lubrication system total
$1,973.75 Camshaft and cylinder heads total
$2,014.61 Intake system total
$1,158.18 Ignition system total
$1,483.33 Cooling system and miscellaneous total
$11,688.37 Total

CHAPTER 29

MISSING PARTS

EXHAUST MANIFOLDS

The Ford truck 8EQ-9430 right side and 8EQ-9431 left side cast-iron exhaust manifolds were installed on Lincoln 337-ci flathead V-8 engines. A street performance engine should be equipped with exhaust headers, although no major exhaust header manufacturers currently offer a model for the Lincoln 337-ci flathead V-8 engine. This means custom exhaust headers will have to be fabricated. The exhaust manifolds or exhaust headers should be installed with 12 pieces: 3/8-inch-

This picture shows the top half of the Lincoln 7009 bell housing adapter welded to the back of a 1949–1953 Ford 6392 passenger car bell housing.

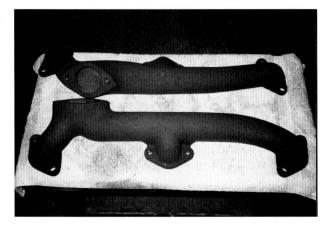

The Ford truck 8EQ-9430 and 8EQ-9431 cast-iron exhaust manifolds are pictured here. They have been painted with Tremclad high-temperature (1,200 degrees Fahrenheit) flat black enamel.

NC by 1 1/4-inch-long stainless-steel hex-head bolts and lockwashers using Loctite and torqued to 25 ft-lbs. The exhaust manifold gaskets should be installed using Permatex ultra copper high-temperature silicone sealant.

FLYWHEEL AND BELL HOUSING

The Lincoln 6392 bell housing was bolted to the Lincoln 7009 bell housing adapter plate, which was bolted to the rear of the engine block. The Lincoln 337-ci flathead V-8 engines' bell housing is not the most desirable type for adapting later-model transmissions. The Lincoln 6375 flywheel is 15 1/4 inches in diameter and weighs 50 pounds. The Lincoln 6384 flywheel ring gear has 120 teeth and is designed to work with the Lincoln 11002 starting motor.

The owner of the engine described in this section wanted to adapt a Borg-Warner T-5 manual (standard) five-speed transmission to his engine. The Borg-Warner T-5 transmission has been used in the Ford Mustangs equipped with a V-8 engine since 1983 and is currently used in the Ford Mustangs

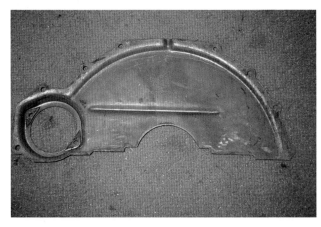

This 1949–1953 Ford 8BA-6366 starting motor plate is used with the 1949–1953 Ford 6392 bell housing.

equipped with a V-6 engine. The best Borg-Warner T-5 transmission is the T-5Z model used in the 1993 Mustang Cobra. This transmission is apparently capable of handling 450 horsepower and 330 ft-lbs torque, although it should not be used for drag racing. Luke's Custom Machine & Design adapted the transmission installed in the engine described here by cutting the Lincoln 7009 bell housing adapter in half horizontally. Then, using a dial indicator, the top section of the Lincoln 7009 bell housing adapter was centered on the top section of a 1949–1953 Ford 6392 passenger car bell housing. Finally, the top section of the Lincoln 7009 bell housing adapter was welded to the top section of the Ford

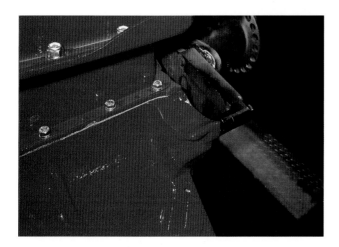

The bottom of the ear on the right side of the engine block has a concave shape after grinding, which has to be performed to provide clearance for the starting motor.

6392 bell housing. The Ford 8BA-6366 starting motor plate is used with the 1949–1953 Ford 6375 bell housing.

The bottom of the ear on the right side of the engine block, where the bell housing bolts on, must be curved up slightly to afford clearance for the starting motor. Use a high-speed grinder with a carbide bit to perform this job.

The next step involves the flywheel modification. Reduce the outside diameter of the Lincoln 6375 flywheel to fit a 1949–1953 Ford 6384 flywheel ring gear to it. Reduce the thickness of the rear face of the flywheel mounting flange (where it bolts to the crankshaft flange) by 0.065 inch to provide the correct starting motor engagement. Use a lathe to machine 0.150 inch off the clutch face and the front of the flywheel mounting flange to provide adequate pressure-plate-to-bell-housing clearance. The length of the six flywheel bolts must be reduced by 0.150 inch so you do not bottom out the rear of the engine block. Machine material from the

rear face of the flywheel (the side facing the engine) to reduce the weight of the Lincoln 6375 flywheel from 50 to 35 pounds. Finally, have the clutch face surfaced.

The Lincoln 6387 crankshaft dowels and 350627-S flywheel bolts with the 7609 flywheel bolt washer plate are installed using Loctite and torqued to 80 ft-lbs. A Centerforce 280700 clutch disc (1968–1970 Ford Mustang), 11 inches in diameter by 1 1/16 inches in shaft diameter by 10 splines (coarse), is installed with a 1949–1951 Ford 7563 long-style pressure plate, 11 inches diameter. ARP 150-2201 high-performance series hex-head pressure plate bolts, 170,000 psi, are installed using Loctite and torqued to 35 ft-lbs. A bronze pilot bearing—2.050 inches o.d. by 0.640 inches i.d.—must be fabricated. The flywheel, clutch disc, and pressure plate assembly should be balanced. A McLeod hydraulic throwout bearing is used due to the limited clearance between the 11-inch-diameter pressure plate and the 1949–1953 Ford 6392 bell housing.

Refer to *How to Build a Flathead Ford V-8* and *How to Build Ford Flathead V-8 Horsepower* for information on how to adapt other transmissions to flathead engines.

A 1949–1951 Ford 7563 long-style pressure plate and a Centerforce 280700 clutch disc, 11 inches in diameter by 1 1/16 inches in shaft diameter by 10 splines (coarse), are pictured here.

The rear face of this Lincoln 6375 flywheel has been machined to reduce the weight from 50 to 35 pounds. A 1949–1953 Ford 6384 flywheel ring gear has been installed.

The Ford 7563 long-style pressure plate and the Centerforce 280700 clutch disc have been installed on the Lincoln 6375 flywheel.

CHAPTER 30
ASSEMBLY

ASSEMBLY

Note: The stages of assembly I am about to list can be followed, or some of the later steps can be combined with some of the earlier steps. The sequence of assembly is entirely up to the party assembling the engine. The only important part of the assembly is not to have any leftover pieces. Also refer to Chapters 10, 20, and 40.

ENGINE BLOCK

1. Clean the camshaft bearings with clean solvent using a clean, lint-free cloth. Install the camshaft bearings (dry) in the engine block using a camshaft bearing installation tool (this is a must!). Take special care to line up the oil holes in the camshaft bearings with the oil holes in the engine

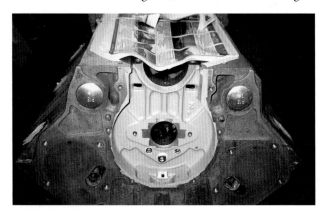

The engine block has been cleaned and masked prior to painting. The two frost plugs in the front of the engine block have been installed.

block. Do not lubricate the camshaft bearing bosses.

2. Install a new stainless-steel 3/8-inch-NPT plug in the oil gallery line at the front of the engine block (behind the camshaft gear) using pipe thread sealant. Install a new 19/32-inch frost plug in the oil gallery line at the rear of the engine block (above the oil pump idler gear cover) using Permatex aviation form-a-gasket. Install new stainless-steel 1/4-inch-NPT plugs in the valve lifter oil gallery lines at the front of the engine block (behind the camshaft gear) using pipe thread sealant. Install a new 10-32 setscrew in the fuel pump pushrod lubrication hole at the rear of the engine block (behind the oil pump idler gear cover) using Loctite. Install new stainless-steel 1/4-inch-NPT plugs in the water jacket drain holes using pipe thread sealant. Install the two freeze plugs in the bottom of the engine block (in the center of the

The Lincoln 8EQ-6500-A solid flat-tappet adjustable mushroom valve lifters have been installed through the bottom of the engine block.

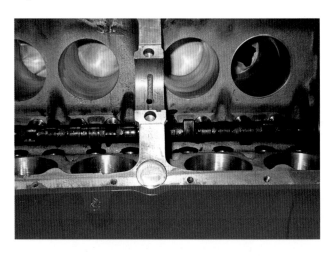

The camshaft has been installed using a liberal amount of Crower 86094 assembly prelube on the camshaft lobes.

oil pan rails) and the two freeze plugs in the front of the engine block (behind the water pumps) using Permatex aviation form-a-gasket.

3. Apply motor oil to the body of the valve lifters and camshaft assembly lubricant (provided by the camshaft manufacturer) to the base of the valve lifters. Install the valve lifters from the underside of the engine block.

4. Lubricate the camshaft bearings using Clevite 77 Bearing Guard, and generously apply the camshaft assembly lubri-

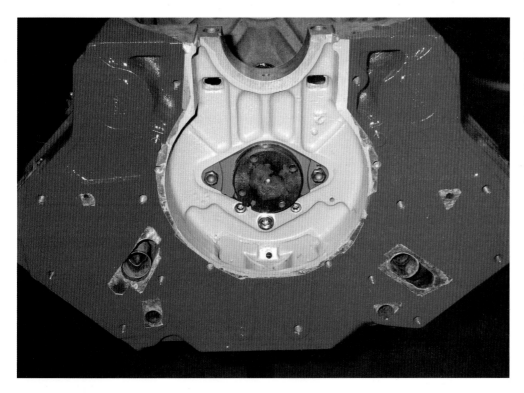

The Lincoln 6269 thrust plate is installed along with a new stainless-steel oil gallery line plug (center) and two valve lifter gallery oil line plugs.

cant to the lobes of the camshaft. Gently slide the camshaft into the engine block, taking care not to nick the camshaft bearings. Install the camshaft thrust plate using Loctite on the bolts, and torque them to 20 ft-lbs. Apply some motor oil to the fuel pump driveshaft eccentric sleeve, and slide it over the rear end of the camshaft.

5. Install the camshaft gear on the camshaft using Loctite on the bolts, and torque them to 20 ft-lbs. Bend the camshaft locking plate tabs over the heads of the camshaft gear bolts.

6. Lubricate the oil pump idler gear shaft with motor oil, and slide the oil pump idler gear on it. Place the oil pump idler gear shaft in position at the rear of the engine block, and tap it into the engine block using a rubber mallet. Install the oil pump idler gear cover gasket using silicone sealant. Place the oil pump idler gear cover in position, install the bolts and lockwashers using Loctite, and torque them to 25 ft-lbs.

CRANKSHAFT

1. Install the rear main bearing upper oil seal retainer gasket at the rear of the engine block using silicone sealant. Place the retainer in position, and install the bolts and lockwashers using Loctite and torque them to 20 ft-lbs. Install the rear upper cord material oil seal in the retainer, either by rolling it into place with a large socket or using the head of a large ball peen hammer and tapping the head of the hammer with another hammer.

2. Clean the main bearings with clean solvent using a clean, lint-free cloth. Line up the locking tang (tab) on the main

bearings with the notch in the main bearing saddles, and install the main bearings in the engine block (dry). Do not lubricate the main bearing saddles in the engine block. Use Clevite 77 Bearing Guard to lubricate the face of the main bearings after installing them in the engine block. Line up the locking tang on the main bearings with the notch in the main bearing caps, and install the main bearings in the main bearing caps (dry). Do not lubricate the main bearing caps. Use Clevite 77 Bearing Guard to lubricate the face of the main bearings after installing them in the main bearing caps.

3. Install the stainless-steel connecting rod journal oil line plugs in the crankshaft using Loctite. Place the crankshaft

The crankshaft has been installed with the main bearing cap bolts torqued to 125 ft-lbs.

143

gear woodruff key in the crankshaft using anti-seize compound, and gently tap the woodruff key into position with a hammer. Apply anti-seize compound to the snout of the crankshaft, and slide the crankshaft gear onto the snout as far as it will go by hand. The crankshaft gear side with a dot, or a line, faces outward. Line up the crankshaft gear with the crankshaft gear woodruff key, and gently tap the crankshaft gear into position using a piece of pipe that is a little larger than the diameter of the crankshaft snout.

4. Gently lower the crankshaft into the main bearing saddles, taking special care not to nick the crankshaft bearings. Make certain to line up the timing marks on the crankshaft and camshaft gears. The crankshaft gear has a dot, or a line, marking, and so does the camshaft gear. These marks should be vertically in line with each other. Place the main bearing caps in the correct order in the engine block, with the tang in the engine block and the tang in the main bearing caps on the same side. Lubricate the main bearing cap bolts with Molykote, and torque them to 125 ft-lbs. The crankshaft should now turn freely in the engine block. Slide the oil slinger onto the crankshaft snout.

CONNECTING RODS AND PISTONS

1. Remove the wrist pin from the pistons. Coat the wrist pin bushings in the connecting rods and the wrist pins with motor oil. Some cast pistons have an arrow marking on the piston head, or an "F" cast into the side, to indicate which side faces the front of the engine block. The cylinder numbers stamped in the connecting rods are on the same side as the bearing notch in the connecting rods, and these always face outward from the crankshaft. Assemble the connecting rods and pistons, and install the wrist pin retainers.

2. Gap all the piston rings for all the cylinders. Install the piston rings on the pistons using a piston ring expander tool, and rotate each of the piston rings on the pistons so they are within the manufacturer's recommended arc, also known as "preferred ring gap location".

3. Clean the connecting rod bearings with clean solvent using a clean, lint-free cloth. Install the connecting rod bearings (dry) in the connecting rods and connecting rod caps. Do not lubricate the connecting rods or the connecting rod caps. Line up the locking tang on the connecting rod bearings with the notch in the connecting rods and connecting rod caps. Apply Clevite 77 Bearing Guard to the face of the connecting rod bearings. Place plastic connecting rod bolt protectors on the connecting rod studs.

4. Apply motor oil to the inside of the piston ring compressor, and place the piston ring compressor around the piston. Tighten the piston ring compressor, and insert the connecting rod into the cylinder (with the connecting rod bearing locking tang facing outward from the crankshaft), and gen-

This pressure-out line fitting passes through the bell housing flange on the right side of the engine block and into the oil pump cavity.

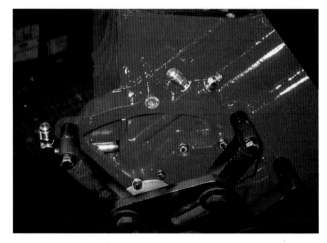

The 90-degree fitting on the lower left side of the photo is for the pressure-out line, the center fitting is for the drain-back line, and the right fitting is for the oil pressure gauge.

The connecting rods and piston assemblies have been installed with the connecting rod nuts torqued to 55 ft-lbs.

The Lincoln 6603 high-volume oil pump and the 6615 oil pump cover and inlet tube are installed.

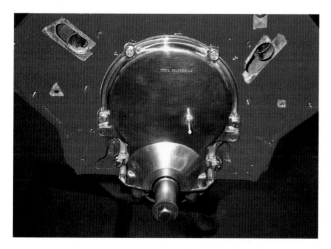

The Lincoln 8EL-6059-A2 polished-aluminum timing gear cover is installed. The two water passage tubes at the front of the engine block direct water to the rear of the engine block to aid with cooling.

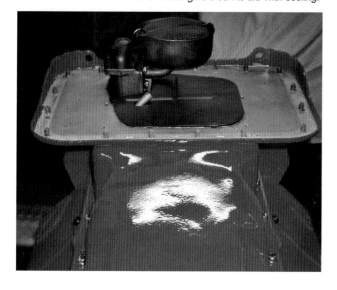

The oil pan is installed using stainless-steel hex-head bolts.

tly tap the piston down into the cylinder using the handle of a rubber mallet or a piece of wood. Guide the connecting rod studs around the crankshaft journal as the piston is being pushed downward. After the connecting rod is on the connecting rod journal, install the connecting rod cap with the locking tang on the same side as the locking tang in the connecting rod. Install the connecting rod nuts using Loctite, and torque them to 55 ft-lbs. Repeat this procedure for the rest of the connecting rod and piston assemblies.

5. Install the crankshaft bolt in the crankshaft, and turn the crankshaft. The rotating assembly should turn over smoothly. Use a feeler gauge to check the side clearance for each pair of connecting rods.

LUBRICATION SYSTEM

1. Install the new stainless-steel 1/4-inch-NPT plug inside the vertical drain-back oil line hole in the engine block using pipe thread sealant. Install the oil line fittings for the pressure-out oil line and drain-back oil line using pipe thread sealant.

2. Install neoprene rubber O-rings around the neck of the oil pump body. Install the oil pump cover and inlet tube gasket using silicone sealant. Place the oil pump cover and inlet tube in position on the oil pump, and install the bolts and lockwashers using Loctite and torque them to 80 in-lbs. Lubricate the oil pump drive gear with motor oil, and install the oil pump assembly in the engine block. Install the oil pump bolt and lockwasher using Loctite, and torque it to 15 ft-lbs.

3. Slide the crankshaft sleeve onto the crankshaft snout, and gently tap it into position using a piece of pipe and a hammer. Slide the one-piece oil seal over the crankshaft sleeve.

The oil pan baffle is snapped into position after the oil pan has been installed and prior to installing the oil pan sump.

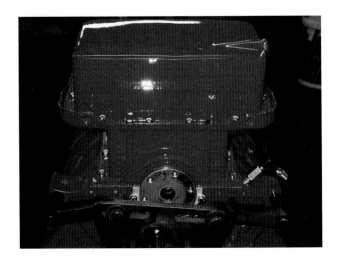

The oil pan sump has been bolted in place with stainless-steel nylocks. This is one weird-looking oil pan assembly!

Install the timing gear cover gasket using silicone sealant, and apply silicone sealant to the inside of the timing gear cover where the oil seal is located. Place the timing gear cover in position on the engine block, and install the bolts and lockwashers using Loctite and torque them to 15 ft-lbs.

4. Install the oil pan cord material rear oil seal by either rolling it into place with a large socket or using the head of a large ball peen hammer and tapping the head of the hammer with another hammer. Install the oil pan gaskets using silicone sealant. Place the oil pan in position on the engine block, and install the bolts, lockwashers, and AN flat washers using Loctite and torque them to 15 ft-lbs. Install the oil pan baffle by snapping it into position. Place some putty on the oil pump pickup screen and position the oil pan sump. Push down firmly on the oil pan sump, and then remove it. Measure the compressed thickness of the putty. The proper oil-pan-sump-to-oil-pump-pickup-screen clearance should be 3/4 to 1 inch. If the clearance is correct, carry on. If not, adjust the oil pump pickup screen arm until obtaining the correct clearance. Install the oil pan sump gasket using silicone sealant. Place the oil pan sump in position, and install the nylocks and AN flat washers using Loctite and torque them to 15 ft-lbs. Screw the dipstick tube into the oil pan using silicone sealant, and install the dipstick.

5. Install the oil line from the pressure-out fitting in the engine block to the inlet side of the oil filter adapter using pipe thread sealant. Install the oil line from the drain-back fitting in the engine block to the outlet side of the oil filter adapter using pipe thread sealant. Fill the oil filter with motor oil and install it on the oil filter adapter.

CAMSHAFT AND CYLINDER HEADS
Refer to Chapter 10 for information on how to degree the camshaft.

All the intake and exhaust valves—along with the valve springs, valve spring retainers, and valve stem locks—have been installed.

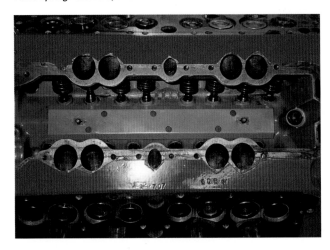

The Lincoln 6524 valve lifter gallery oil return hole baffle is painted with Glyptal G-1228A medium-gray gloss enamel.

1. Install all the upper valve spring retainers on the valve guide bushings. Lubricate all the valve springs, valve spring retainers, and valves with motor oil, and install them. Install the sleeves on the tips of the intake valves. Use a valve spring compressor to install all the valve stem locks. Adjust all the valves according the camshaft manufacturer's specifications. Refer to Chapter 10 for information about valve adjustment. Press the valve lifter gallery baffle in position. Install the valve lifter gallery oil pressure relief valve using Permatex aviation form-a-gasket.

2. Place some putty on any intake or exhaust valve for the same cylinder, and then place the cylinder head in position on the engine block. Lightly tighten the cylinder head down using two cylinder head bolts (one at each end). Do not use a cylinder head gasket. Turn the crankshaft through 360 degrees at least twice. Remove the cylinder head, and measure the thickness of the compressed putty. The absolute minimum valve-to-cylinder-head clearance is 0.040 inch.

The Edelbrock aluminum cylinder head is installed and torqued to 40 ft-lbs. The water outlet elbow adapter and water outlet elbow have been bolted in position.

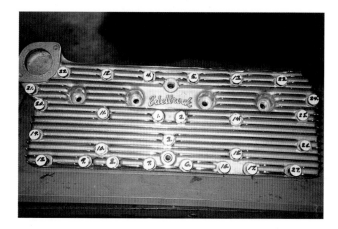

The numbers on the cylinder head bolts indicate the torque pattern specified by the Ford Motor Company for the Lincoln 337-ci flathead V-8 engine.

The Luke's Custom Machine & Design polished-aluminum water outlet elbow adapter has been bolted to the Edelbrock cylinder head.

3. Spray the copper sandwiched cylinder head gaskets with Permatex copper spray-a-gasket and install them. Place the cylinder heads in position on the engine block, and install the cylinder head bolts with hardened flat washers using Permatex aviation form-a-gasket. Torque the cylinder head bolts to 40 ft-lbs (for aluminum cylinder heads) using the factory-approved torque pattern. Do not install the chrome acorn nut covers until the engine has been started for the first time and the cylinder heads have been retorqued.

4. Install the water outlet elbow adapter gaskets using silicone sealant. Place the water outlet elbow adapters in position, and install the bolts using anti-seize compound and torque them to 15 ft-lbs. Install the water outlet elbow gaskets using silicone sealant, and install the thermostats. Place the water outlet elbows in position, and install the bolts and lockwashers using anti-seize compound and torque them to 15 ft-lbs.

INTAKE SYSTEM

1. Install the carburetor studs in the intake manifold using anti-seize compound. Install the crankcase breather/fuel pump stand gasket using silicone sealant. Install the crankcase breather/fuel pump stand using anti-seize compound on the studs, and torque the acorn nuts to 15 ft-lbs. Install the fuel pump block-off plate gasket using silicone sealant. Install the fuel pump block-off plate using anti-

The Holley 94 carburetors and Offenhauser 6271 progressive linkage have been installed on the (Ken) Austin LT intake manifold.

seize compound on the bolts, and torque them to 15 ft-lbs. Install the crankcase breather/fuel pump stand breather cap. Place the carburetor gaskets in position on the intake manifold. Install the carburetors on the intake manifold using anti-seize compound on the studs. Tighten the acorn nuts and lockwashers snugly; do not overtighten these nuts. Install and adjust the progressive carburetor linkage using anti-seize compound on the linkage arm setscrews.

2. Trace the intake manifold outline on the intake manifold gasket, and trim the gasket accordingly. Install the intake

The polished-aluminum fuel block mounting bracket was fabricated by Luke's Custom and Design.

The Mallory distributor and MSD 8200 ignition coil with ballast resistor have been installed.

manifold gasket using silicone sealant. Place the intake manifold in position on the engine block, and install the bolts and AN flat washers using Loctite and torque them to 25 ft-lbs. Torque the intake manifold bolts using the factory-approved torque pattern. Install the chrome acorn nut covers on the intake manifold bolts. Install the PCV valve fittings in the intake manifold, and install the PCV valve using pipe thread sealant. Connect the PCV valve hose, and tighten the hose clamps. Install the air cleaners.

3. Install the fuel pressure regulator in the fuel block and the fuel pressure gauge in the fuel pressure regulator using pipe thread sealant. Mount the fuel pressure regulator with the fuel block on the mounting bracket, and install the assembly on the engine. Connect the fuel lines from the fuel block to the carburetors, and tighten the fuel line clamps.

IGNITION SYSTEM

1. Place the crankshaft pulley woodruff key in the crankshaft slot using anti-seize compound, and gently tap the woodruff key into position with a hammer. Apply some anti-seize compound to the snout of the crankshaft, and install the crankshaft pulley. The pulley should have a snug fit, but it should not require the use of a harmonic balancer installation tool. Gently tap the crankshaft pulley onto the crankshaft snout using a rubber mallet, or a piece of wood and a hammer. Install the crankshaft pulley bolt and washer using Loctite, and torque it to 125 ft-lbs.

2. Rotate the crankshaft until the engine is set with the No. 1 piston at 10 degrees before top dead center (TDC). Insert the distributor in the rear of the intake manifold with the distributor rotor at the No. 1 spark plug lead position. Install the distributor bolt and lockwasher using anti-seize compound and snugly tighten it.

The flywheel has been installed, with the flywheel bolts torqued to 80 ft-lbs.

3. Gap the spark plugs at 0.050 inch, and install them in the cylinder heads using anti-seize compound and torque them to 15 ft-lbs (for aluminum cylinder heads). Lay out the spark plug wires, and cut them to length for each cylinder. The cylinders on the right side are numbered 1, 2, 3, and 4 from the front of the engine block. The cylinders on the left side are numbered 5, 6, 7, and 8 from the front of the engine block. The firing order is: 1, 5, 4, 8, 6, 3, 7, and 2. Install the spark plug wires on the spark plugs and in the distributor cap. Install the ignition coil with the ignition coil bracket and the ballast resistor. Connect the ignition coil wire to the distributor.

4. Install the generator mounting bracket on the front of the intake manifold, and install the generator in the mounting bracket using anti-seize compound on the bolt.

5. Install the pilot bearing in the flywheel using anti-seize

This photo of the rear of the Lincoln flathead V-8 engine shows the 1949–1953 Ford 6392 bell housing installed.

The front view of the Lincoln flathead V-8 engine shows the 1956 Ford B6A-10002-A chrome generator mounted with the 1949–1953 Ford 8BA-10153-C bracket.

The Lincoln 8EQ-8505 and 8EQ-8506 water pumps have been rebuilt and are ready for installation.

What a gruesome sight this is! I am standing behind the Lincoln flathead V-8 engine, and Luke Balogh (wearing a rented T-shirt) is standing behind a blown 1952 Ford flathead V-8 engine destined for the Bonneville Salt Flats. A 1948 Ford model 59 flathead V-8 engine is at the front.

compound. Install the flywheel on the crankshaft flange using Loctite on the bolts, and torque them to 80 ft-lbs. Install the pressure plate with the clutch disc, and torque the pressure plate bolts to 35 ft-lbs using Loctite. Install the bell housing on the rear of the engine block using anti-seize compound on the bolts and lockwashers, and torque them to 25 ft-lbs. Install the starting motor plate on the bell housing using anti-seize compound on the bolts, and torque them to 20 ft-lbs. Install the starting motor using anti-seize compound on the bolts.

6. Install the water pump gaskets using silicone sealant. Place the water pumps in position, and install the bolts and lockwashers using Loctite and torque them to 25 ft-lbs. Install the crankshaft pulley/water pump pulleys/generator pulley V-belt allowing for 3/4- to 1-inch slack.

7. Install the exhaust manifold gaskets using Permatex ultra copper high-temperature silicone sealant. Place the exhaust manifolds in position, and install the bolts and lockwashers using Loctite and torque them to 25 ft-lbs.

8. Mount a radiator with some water in it, connect the ignition system with a starter switch, and hook up a battery. Start the engine, and adjust the timing and carburetors. Allow the engine to run at approximately 2,000 rpm for 30 minutes to break in the camshaft. After the engine is at full operating temperature, shut it off, and allow the engine to cool. Retorque the cylinder heads using the factory-approved torque pattern, and install the chrome acorn nut covers on the cylinder head bolts.

The horsepower and torque for this engine have been increased by approximately 50 percent over a stock Lincoln 337-ci flathead V-8 engine, which is quite an impressive accomplishment for a street performance engine.

SECTION IV: FORD FLATHEAD V8-60 ENGINE

CHAPTER 31
ENGINE BLOCK

The Ford 136-ci flathead V-8 engine was introduced in 1937 as a concept by the Ford Motor Company to achieve better fuel economy for Ford passenger cars and light-duty commercial vehicles. This goal was achieved at low speeds; however, the fuel economy went out the window when the vehicle neared its 55-mile-per-hour maximum speed. Commonly referred to as the "Ford V8-60" due to its 60-horsepower rating, this engine was a dismal failure toward providing adequate power for the vehicles in which it was installed. Its last production year was 1940. The V8-60 engine really achieved fame when it was installed in quarter midget race cars and early small (cracker box) race boats. The smaller Offenhauser engines powered most of the winning quarter midget race cars until 1937, when the Ford V8-60 engine appeared and gave the Offenhauser-powered race cars a run for their money. The Ford V8-60 engine was also installed in Chris Craft pleasure boats. Many hot rod fans have a fondness for the Ford V8-60 engine because of its miniature size and unique flathead sound.

A promoter intending to develop a quarter midget race car series at the Polo Grounds wanted a cheaper alternative to Offenhauser engines. Zora Arkus-Duntov subcontracted the design and foundry work for an overhead-valve (OHV) conversion kit for the Ford V8-60 engine to a company named Veritas, located in what became East Germany. At the time, Veritas was manufacturing engines built to a pre–World War II design of the BMW 328 engine. That hemispherical cylinder head engine had transverse pushrods between the rocker arm shafts on the exhaust side, which is the design used for the Ardun V8-60 conversion kit. Incidentally, the name Ardun is derived from letters within Zora's last name. The quarter midget race car series at the Polo Grounds never materialized; as a result, the promoter did not take delivery of the Ardun OHV conversion kits for the Ford V8-60 engine.

Over the past few years, I have had the pleasure of dealing with a fine gentleman named E. Dean Butler. Dean and his brother, Don, are the owners and managers of Zakira's Garage (www.zakiras.com), located in Cincinnati, Ohio. Their shop restores, maintains, and races vintage automobiles. They also reproduce Ford Model T and Mercer T-head engine blocks and (Harry) Miller carburetors. Dean had many conversations

with Zora over the years, and during one of those conversations, Zora mentioned that only 20 sets of the Ardun V8-60 conversions kits had been manufactured. One of the Ardun V8-60 conversion kits Dean purchased in the United Kingdom came wrapped in East German newspapers! The Ardun V8-60 aluminum cylinder heads were not fitted with valve seat inserts because Zora did not believe they were necessary, as the Ardun V8-60 engine was designed for a short-duration racetrack.

In 1935, Ford Societe Anonyme Francaise (SAF) entered into a joint venture with a French automobile company named Mathis. This partnership was named Matford, and it produced automobiles for the French market. The Ford V8-60 engines initially installed in some of the Matford vehicles were manufactured in the United States, although from 1936 to 1939 they were manufactured in France. The V8-60 engine was also installed in British automobiles from 1936 to 1939. World War II ended production in Britain and France, as well as the Mathis/Ford joint venture. Ford SAF produced the V8-60–powered Vedette automobile from 1949 to 1954, then it sold the business to Societe Industrielle de Mecanique et Carrosserie Automobile (Simca). Simca used a modified version of the V8-60 until 1961. Apparently, a French copy was installed in Simca automobiles in Brazil from 1960 to 1969. Also, Chrysler do Brasil (Chrysler of Brazil) was said to have manufactured this engine in 1969 only for the Brazilian market. French copies of the Ford V8-60 engines have also turned up in Australia. French V8-60 engines have very few parts that are interchangeable with the original Ford V8-60 engines. Recently there has been a renewed interest in the Ford V8-60 engine. One novel case in particular is Honest Charley (see Resources), which installs them in motorcycles. Jitney Auto Parts and Honest Charley are good sources for Ford V8-60 engine components, and parts frequently appear for sale on eBay and in Hemmings Motor News.

A. ENGINE BLOCK

I will document all the parts and modifications, as well as the assembly, of a 1939 Ford flathead V8-60 street performance engine. Some of the procedures in Section B, the summary section of each chapter, have not been carried out with this engine, but I have listed them anyway, because they would have been carried out if the engine had been built and assembled properly.

PURCHASE AND MAGNAFLUX

The 1937–1940 Ford 136-ci L-Head V-8 engine specifications are:

135.9-ci (2.2-liter) displacement
Stock bore: 2.600 inches
Stock stroke: 3.200 inches
Stock compression ratio: 6.6:1
60 horsepower at 3,500 rpm and 94 ft-lbs torque at 2,500 rpm

The Ford V8-60 engine model numbers are:
1937: Model 74
1938: Model 82A
1939: Model 922A
1940: Model 022A

The casting number A-1 is shown in the middle of the bell housing. The oil pressure line hole, in the rear center of the gasket area for the intake manifold, mates with a hole in the intake manifold that exits behind the fuel pump boss.

Here is Luke Balogh attempting to abscond with a Ford V8-60 engine block. The engine block weighs 109 pounds.

The Ford 136-ci flathead V-8 engine block is a smaller version of the early Ford 221-ci flathead V-8 engine block with the integral bell housing. The 1937 Ford V8-60 engine block is unique, as 1937 was the only year that sheetmetal sides were used with a cast-iron engine block. The 1938–1940 Ford V8-60 engine blocks are entirely cast iron and similar to each other. The only casting or serial number visible on the engine block described in this section was located on top of the bell housing, and this was casting number A-1. The Ford V8-60 engine block weighs (bare) 109 pounds. Refer to Chapter 21 for information about engine block inspection and Magnafluxing.

A limited number of Ford V8-60 engines was produced, which means they are becoming harder to find today. It will cost approximately $250 for a Ford V8-60 engine block in good condition.

CLEANING

A 1/8-inch-NPT oil gallery line plug is located in the front of the Ford V8-60 engine block (behind the camshaft gear), and another one is located in the rear of the engine block (above the rear camshaft boss plug). Two 1/4-inch-NPT water jacket drain plugs are located at the bottom front of the engine block (one on each side) behind the water outlet castings. Two 1 1/16-inch-diameter freeze plugs are located (one on each side) at the bottom center of each oil pan rail. The rear camshaft boss plug is 1 3/4 inches in diameter. Remove all

The Ford V8-60 rear camshaft boss plug and rear oil gallery line plug are shown here.

these plugs prior to having the engine block hot tanked. There is one hole on each side of the bottom front of the integral bell housing for attaching frame support rods. There is a 1 1/4-inch-diameter oil filler tube hole in the top left side (driver side) of the bell housing. Also refer to Chapter 21.

PORTING AND POLISHING

There is not a lot of material around the intake and exhaust ports in a Ford V8-60 engine block. This means porting and polishing should be limited to gasket matching the intake and exhaust ports and cleaning up the ports. Do not attempt to enlarge them. Refer to Chapter 21 for more information on this subject.

DETAILING AND VALVE LIFTER BOSSES

Refer to Chapter 1 for information about detailing the engine block. Drill a 3/16-inch (0.1875-inch) hole in the center of each valve lifter boss, approximately 3/4 inch from the top of the boss. The purpose of these holes is to simplify the valve lifter adjustment. Insert a 3/16-inch drill bit (use the chuck end), or a punch, in the hole to prevent the valve lifter (tappet) from turning. The valve lifter is then easily adjusted using a thin tappet wrench. This method is far superior to smashing your knuckles using the Johnson adjustable lifter

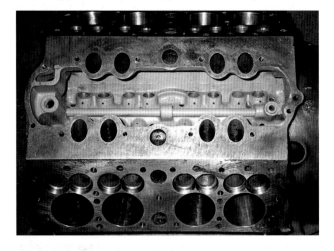

The valve lifter bosses have been drilled with a 3/16-inch adjustment hole, and the valve lifter gallery has been painted with Glyptal G-1228A medium-gray gloss enamel.

wrenches that are usually supplied with the valve lifters, and it takes half the time. This system will not work if the adjustable valve lifters do not have the common oval indents or slots in the sides.

FULL-FLOW OILING

A full-flow oiling system can be installed in a Ford V8-60 engine block, even though there are no external oil filter line fitting holes in the rear of the engine block. Also, the oil pump is part of the No. 1 main bearing cap. There is an internal oil pressure line passage in the rear of the engine block that is vertical and exits in the rear center of the gasket area for the intake manifold. A hole in the rear center of the intake manifold connects with the internal oil pressure line passage and exits behind the fuel pump boss on the intake manifold. An oil pressure gauge line is connected at the rear of the intake manifold.

Drill and tap a 3/8-inch-NPT hole in the internal oil pressure line passage in the rear of the engine block. The hole should be approximately 2 inches down from the gasket area

for the intake manifold. A new Weatherhead 3750-6 polished-brass street tee, 3/8 inch NPT, should be installed in the threaded hole using pipe thread sealant. This will be the pressure-out fitting for the full-flow oiling system, as well as the fitting for connecting an oil pressure gauge line. Drill and tap a 1/8-inch-NPT hole in the internal oil pressure line passage where it exits in the gasket area for the intake manifold. Then install a 1/8-inch-NPT plug in the threaded hole. Install a 1 1/4-inch-diameter polished-aluminum plug in the crankcase breather/oil filler tube hole in the left side of the bell housing. Drill and tap a 3/8-inch-NPT hole in the center of the plug, and install a new Weatherhead 3400-6 polished-brass 90-degree street elbow in the threaded hole using pipe thread sealant. This will be the drain-back line fitting for the full-flow oiling system.

Install new Weatherhead 48-8 polished-brass compression line fittings, 1/2 inch tube to 3/8 inch NPT, in the pressure-out and drain-back oil line fittings in the engine block. Connect the pressure-out line to the inlet side of the oil filter adapter, and connect the drain-back line to the outlet side of the oil filter. Install a new Weatherhead 3220-6-2 polished-brass bushing, 3/8 inch NPT to 1/8 inch NPT, in the pressure-out line fitting to connect the oil pressure gauge line. Install a new Trans-Dapt 1045 silver finish remote oil filter adapter with the Trans-Dapt 1032 oil filter adapter lines, 1/2 inch NPT by 24 inches long. Install all the oil filter lines and fittings using pipe thread sealant. An extra quart of oil will be required with the addition of an oil filter. Refer to Chapter 24 for information about oil filters.

RELIEVING THE ENGINE BLOCK

The factory gave the Ford V8-60 engine blocks a very slight relief from the lower edge of the valve seat inserts to the upper edge of

The freeze plugs in the oil pan rails are visible opposite the center main bearing cap in this Ford V8-60 engine block..

the cylinder bores. Leave this relief alone, and refer to Chapter 21 for information regarding relieving the engine block.

HEAT RISERS

> *Refer to Chapter 21.*

RETAP AND CHAMFER BOLT HOLES
> *Refer to Chapter 1.*

REDI-STRIP THE ENGINE BLOCK
The Ford V8-60 engines came equipped with cylinder head studs. If these studs have been in the engine block for any length of time, leave them in place and send the engine block off to be Redi-Stripped. The studs will be easier (without guarantee) to remove after the Redi-Strip process, and this will limit the possibility of breaking the studs or damaging the engine block threads when removing them. Refer to Chapter 1 for information about Redi-Stripping.

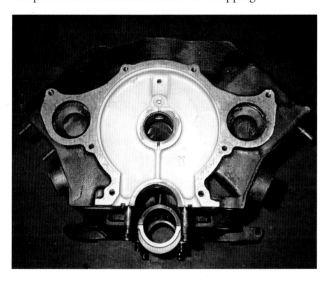

The front of this Ford V8-60 engine block has been painted with Glyptal G-1228A medium-gray gloss enamel. The front oil gallery line plug is just visible above the camshaft bore. The oil drain hole above the oil gallery line plug is functional when the oil pressure relief valve opens.

GLYPTAL
> *Refer to Chapter 1.*

MACHINING
> *Refer to Chapter 1.*

CYLINDER BORING
The cylinders in Ford V8-60 engine blocks apparently have been bored to 0.125 (1/8) inch oversize. Before attempting a bore of that size, the cylinders in a Ford V8-60 engine block should be sonic tested to ensure there will be adequate material left in the cylinder walls. The engine block described here had previously been bored 0.040 inch oversize, and the cylinders honed and deglazed using Sunnen 600-series 280-grit stones (for cast-iron piston rings). The Ford Motor Company specified the piston-to-cylinder-bore clearance to be 0.002 to 0.0025 inch for the factory cast-alloy steel pistons. Cast-aluminum pistons are usually installed in a naturally aspirated street performance engine with 0.0015- to 0.0025-inch

piston-to-cylinder-bore clearance. Always follow the piston manufacturer's recommendation for the piston-to-cylinder-bore clearance. Refer to Chapter 21 for more information on cylinder boring, honing, and deglazing.

ALIGN HONE
The centerline of the crankshaft is the point from which all critical measurements are taken, and it is used to ensure the engine block main bearing housing bores, with the main bearing caps attached, are exactly parallel to it. The Ford V8-60 engine block crankshaft centerline is offset 0.200 inch to the right, the cylinder banks are exactly 45 degrees to each other, and the angle between the valves is 103.5 degrees. The diameter of the main bearing housing bores in 1937–1939 Ford V8-60s is 2.170 inches, and the main bearing cap stud nuts are torqued to 80 ft-lbs. The engine block described here did not require align boring or align honing. Refer to Chapter 21 for information pertaining to this subject.

The main bearing journals and connecting rod journals of the crankshaft used in the 1940 Ford V8-60 engine are 0.100 inch larger in diameter than the journals of the 1937–1939 Ford V8-60 crankshafts, thus making the main bearing housing bores 2.270 inches in diameter.

PARALLEL DECK
> *Refer to Chapter 21.*

SHOT PEEN
There are three main bearing caps in the Ford V8-60 engine block. The front main bearing cap incorporates the oil pump, and the rear main bearing cap accepts the oil pan rear gasket and crankshaft rear oil slinger. The main bearing caps in the Ford V8-60 engine block have a curved flange for mating with the engine block. The main bearing caps are secured in

The Ford V8-60 main bearing caps have been shot peened and sprayed with graphite. The front main bearing cap incorporates the oil pump.

position with the Ford 52-6345 main bearing caps studs, which have 7/16-inch-NC threads on the engine block end and 7/16-inch-NF threads on the main bearing cap end.

The main bearing caps, with studs and nuts, should be shot peened to assist with removing stress from those items. The main bearing cap studs have a hole near the top that permits wire to be passed through the Ford 52-6212 castle nut and stud to prevent the nut from coming loose. If the castle nuts are damaged or missing, the 7/16-inch-NF connecting rod nuts used in big-block Chevrolet engines can substitute them. The best substitutes are the GM 3942410 nuts that were installed with the Boron 10B39 steel bolts (rated at 220,000 psi) in the 1969 L88 and ZL-1 engines. The ARP 200-8605 (single nut) 7/16-inch-NF hex-head nuts, 8740 chrome-moly steel, 190,000 psi, can also be used. There is still sufficient room to pass a stainless-steel safety wire through the end of the stud when the big-block Chevrolet connecting rod nuts are installed.

VALVE SEAT INSERTS
> *Refer to Chapter 5.*

VALVE GRIND
> *Refer to Chapter 5 and Chapter 21.*

CLEANING AND PAINTING
> *Refer to Chapter 1.*

B. ENGINE BLOCK SUMMARY
- A 1939 Ford 135.9-ci (2.2-liter) 922A L-head V-8 engine block, casting number A-1; two-bolt main bearing caps; 17-stud block; stock bore: 2.600 inches; stock stroke: 3.200 inches; stock compression ratio: 6.6:1; 60 horsepower at 3,500 rpm and 94 ft-lbs torque at 2,500 rpm. Engine block weight (bare): 109 pounds. **$250**

- Engine block hot tanked and Redi-Stripped. Engine block, main bearing caps, and main bearing cap studs Magnafluxed. **$225**

- Main bearing caps and studs shot peened; all threads retapped; cylinder head bolt holes chamfered; valve lifter bosses deglazed allowing for 0.0015-inch valve lifter clearance; valve lifter bosses drilled with 3/16-inch (0.1875-inch) hole for valve lifter adjustment; new stainless-steel front and rear oil gallery line plugs, 1/8 inch NPT; and new stainless-steel water jacket drain plugs, 1/4 inch NPT, installed using pipe thread sealant. New engine block freeze plugs, 1 1/16 inches in diameter, and new camshaft rear boss plug, 1 3/4 inches in diameter, installed using Permatex aviation form-a-gasket. New polished-aluminum oil filler tube hole plug, 1 1/4 inches in diameter, installed in bell housing using Permatex aviation form-a-gasket. Valve lifter gallery and front of engine block (behind camshaft gear) painted with Glyptal G-1228A medium-gray gloss enamel. Exterior surface of engine block sanded, detailed, and painted with PPG 74000 red high-gloss polyurethane. **$433.33**

- Engine block bored 0.040 inch oversize, and cylinders honed and deglazed using Sunnen 600-series 280-grit stones. Final bore: 2.640 inches. Piston-to-bore clearance: 0.0025 inches, measured below bottom of wrist pin perpendicular to wrist pin. **$125**

- Engine block parallel decked to 0.007-inch average, below deck. **$120**

- Serdi-machined multi-angle blueprint valve grind performed. **$250**

- Intake and exhaust ports fully ported, polished, and gasket matched. **$133.33**

- Engine Block Total: **$1,536.66**

CHAPTER 32
CRANKSHAFT

A. CRANKSHAFT
PURCHASE

The Ford V8-60 crankshafts were manufactured using cast-alloy steel with a 3.200-inch stroke and are designed for full-floating connecting rod bearings. The main bearing journal diameter of the 1937–1939 Ford 52-6303 crankshaft is 1.9980 to 1.9990 inches, and the connecting rod journal diameter is 1.5980 to 1.5990 inches. The main bearing journal diameter of the 1940 Ford 92-6303 crankshaft is 2.0980 to 2.0990 inches, and the connecting rod journal diameter is 1.6980 to 1.6990 inches. The Ford Motor Company specified the out-of-round service limit to be 0.0015 inch, the taper service limit to be 0.001 inch, and the maximum runout to be 0.002 inch. The crankshaft end play is 0.002 to 0.006 inch with the No. 3 main bearing controlling the thrust. Some hot rodders believe the 1940 Ford V8-60 crankshaft is the best model because of the larger journals, but I am at a loss to see how 0.100-inch larger diameter journals could lead to any major performance gain other than being a good candidate for a stroker crankshaft. The weight of a 1937–1939 Ford 52-6303 crankshaft is 45 pounds. It will cost approximately $150 for a Ford V8-60 crankshaft in decent condition.

This is a 1939 Ford 52-6303 cast-alloy steel crankshaft for the Ford V8-60 engine. The main bearing journals are 1.9980 to 1.9990 inches in diameter, and the connecting rod journals are 1.5980 to 1.5990 inches.

MAGNAFLUX
> Refer to Chapter 2.

SHOT PEEN

There are no connecting rod journal oil line plugs in Ford

Here is a (Henry) Velasco billet 4340 chrome-moly steel crankshaft with a 4.250-inch stroke for a Ford flathead V-8 engine. It is one of the finest crankshafts available today.

This 1939 Ford 52-6303 crankshaft has been shot peened, aligned, and Magnafluxed. The main and connecting rod journals have been ground 0.010 inch undersize, the oil holes chamfered, the journals polished, and the crankshaft balanced. The whole nine yards!

V8-60 crankshafts, unlike the crankshafts in full-size Ford flathead V-8 engines. Refer to Chapter 2 for information about shot peening crankshafts.

STRAIGHTEN, CHAMFER, AND POLISH
> Refer to Chapter 2.

REGRINDING AND CLEANING

The crankshaft main and connecting rod journals were ground 0.010 inch undersize for the engine described here. If the 1937–1939 Ford 52-6303 crankshaft main and connecting rod journals are already 0.030 inch undersize and the crankshaft journals need to be ground, main and connecting rod bearings are not currently available. Nor are they available if

the 1940 Ford 92-6303 crankshaft main and connecting rod journals are already 0.040 inch undersize and the crankshaft journals need to be ground. Refer to Chapter 2 for information about repairing the crankshaft journals.

MAIN BEARINGS

Clevite 77 (Dana Corporation) and Federal-Mogul do not currently offer main bearings for Ford V8-60 engines. Jitney Auto Parts is a good source for new old stock (NOS) main bearings for Ford flathead V-8 engines. The Egge Parts House MS280 main bearings for 1937–1939 Ford V8-60 engines are available in standard size, 0.010 inch oversize, 0.020 inch oversize, and 0.030 inch oversize, and the current retail price for a set is $160. The Egge Parts House MS906 main bearings for the 1940 Ford V8-60 engine are available in standard size, 0.001 inch oversize, 0.002 inch oversize, 0.010 inch oversize, 0.020 inch oversize, 0.030 inch oversize, and 0.040 inch oversize, and the current retail price for a set is $213. The Ford Motor Company specified the main bearing clearance to be 0.0006 to 0.0031 inch. Refer to Chapter 2 for information about the measurement of main bearing clearance and crankshaft end play.

NOS sets of Bohnalite 5339-010 (No. 1 bearings), McQuay-Norris 2891 (No. 2 bearings), and Ford 52-6331-C (No. 3 bearings) main bearings, 0.010 inch oversize, were installed in the engine described here. The thickness of each of these bearings is 0.195 inch.

CRANKSHAFT GEAR AND PULLEY

The stock Ford 52-6306 cast-iron crankshaft gear is entirely suitable for use in a street performance engine. If this gear is damaged or missing, the Egge Parts House TG2710 replacement crankshaft gear is available for the current retail price of $21.25. Jitney Auto Parts also stocks Ford V8-60 crankshaft gears. The Ford 52-6310 oil slinger should be glass beaded and painted with Glyptal G-1228A medium-gray gloss enamel.

The main bearings on the left are Bohnalite 5339-010 (No. 1 bearings), the Ford 52-6331-C main bearings are in the middle (No. 3 bearings), and McQuay-Norris 2891 main bearings are on the right (No. 2 bearings). These are the NOS bearings, 0.010 inch oversize, which was installed in the engine described here.

Pictured here is a 1939 Ford 52-6312 single-groove crankshaft pulley, 4 1/4 inches o.d. by 1-inch snout diameter.

A 1939 Ford 52-6312 single-groove crankshaft pulley, 4 1/4 inches o.d. by 1-inch snout diameter, was installed on the engine described here. This crankshaft pulley requires the use of the wide (5/8-inch) V-belt. The 1940 Ford V8-60 crankshaft pulley has a flange on the front for mounting a fan. The snout of the 1940 Ford V8-60 crankshaft is approximately 2 inches longer than the 1937–1939 Ford V8-60 crankshaft snouts and, therefore, requires a different crankshaft pulley.

The Ford 52-6319 crankshaft pulley bolt has four claws on it and was referred to as the "starting crank ratchet". This bolt is designed for use with a hand crank to start the engine, which is obviously a job for a strong, healthy person.

B. CRANKSHAFT SUMMARY

- A 1939 Ford 52-6303 cast-alloy steel crankshaft, casting number 882; main bearing journal diameter: 1.9980 to 1.9990 inches; connecting rod journal diameter: 1.5980 to 1.5990 inches; full-floating connecting rod bearings; stock stroke: 3.200 inches. Crankshaft weight: 45 pounds. **$150**
- Crankshaft Magnafluxed, aligned, shot peened, main bearing journals ground 0.010 inch undersize, connecting rod journals ground 0.010 inch undersize, oil holes chamfered, journals polished, and crankshaft balanced. **$265**
- NOS Bohnalite 5339-010 (No. 1 bearings), McQuay-Norris 2891 (No. 2 bearings), and Ford 52-6331-C (No. 3 bearings) main bearings, 0.010 inch oversize, installed allowing for 0.002-inch crankshaft clearance and 0.004-inch end play. Ford 52-6345 main bearing cap studs and new GM 3942410 main bearing cap stud nuts installed using Molykote, and torqued to 80 ft-lbs. **$192**
- Ford 52-6306 cast-iron crankshaft gear, 21 teeth, and Ford 52-6310 oil slinger installed with Ford 74152-S crankshaft gear woodruff key. A 1939 Ford 52-6312 single-groove crankshaft pulley, 4 1/4 inches o.d., installed with 52-6332 crankshaft pulley bolt washer and 52-6319 crankshaft pulley bolt. Crankshaft pulley bolt installed using Loctite, and torqued to 50 ft-lbs. Ford 52-6310 oil slinger painted with Glyptal G-1228A medium-gray gloss enamel. Crankshaft pulley painted with PPG DGHS 9000 black high-gloss polyurethane. **$100**

- Crankshaft Total: **$707**

CHAPTER 33
CONNECTING RODS AND PISTONS

A. CONNECTING RODS AND PISTONS
CONNECTING RODS

The 1937–1939 Ford 52A-6200 vanadium steel drop forged I-beam connecting rods have an average weight of 264 grams and are full floating. They do not have any bearing tang (tab) notches. They are 6.125 inches long (center to center), and the diameter of the crankshaft end (the big end) is 1.795 to 1.800 inches. The diameter of the crankshaft end of the 1940 Ford 92A-6200 connecting rods is 1.895 to 1.900 inches. The connecting rod studs have a hole near the end that permits passage of a safety wire through the castle nuts to prevent them from coming loose. Ford V8-60 crankshafts have one hole in each connecting rod journal for the lubrication of the full-floating connecting rod bearings. It will cost approximately $40 for a used set of Ford V8-60 connecting rods in decent condition.

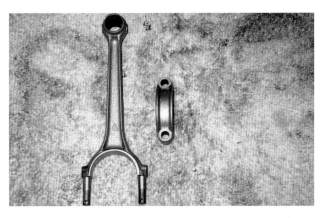

This 1939 Ford 52A-6200 forged-steel I-beam connecting rod assembly has been shot peened. The average weight of one of these connecting rods is 264 grams.

If the 1937–1940 Ford 52-6212 connecting rod stud castle nuts are damaged or missing, the OHV small-block Ford 5/16-inch-NF connecting rod nuts can be substituted. When installing these nuts, there is still sufficient room at the end of the connecting rod stud to insert a stainless-steel safety wire.

MAGNAFLUX AND SHOT PEEN
> *Refer to Chapter 3.*

ALIGN, RESIZE, AND REBUSH
The 1937–1940 Ford 52-6207 wrist pin bushings are 0.6876 to 0.6879 inch i.d. and are no longer available from the Ford

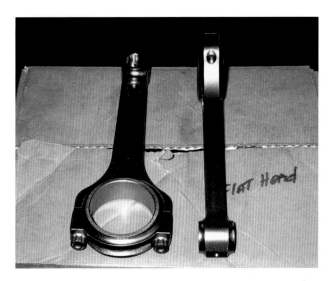

These are Cunningham Rods forged H-I beam 4340 chrome-moly steel connecting rods for a Ford flathead V-8 engine. The bolts are rated at 296,000 psi.

Motor Company. Clevite 77 (Dana Corporation) and Federal-Mogul do not currently list wrist pin bushings for Ford V8-60 engines. The Egge Parts House PB754 wrist pin bushings are available at the retail price of $26 for a set of eight. The Ford Motor Company specified the wrist-pin-to-wrist-pin-bushing clearance to be 0.001 to 0.003 inch and the connecting rod side clearance for a pair of connecting rods to be 0.006 to 0.014 inch. Refer to Chapter 3 for information on connecting rod alignment, resizing, and rebushing.

DEBEAM
The debeaming of the Ford V8-60 connecting rods is not recommended for street use. There is not a lot of material to play with on these connecting rods, and some things are best left alone.

CONNECTING ROD BEARINGS
Clevite 77 (Dana Corporation) and Federal-Mogul do not currently list connecting rod bearings for Ford V8-60 engines. The Egge Parts House CB4 full-floating connecting rod bearings for 1937–1939 Ford V8-60 engines are available in standard size and 0.010 inch oversize only, and one set costs $221. The Egge Parts House CB235 full-floating connecting rod bearings for the 1940 Ford V8-60 engine are

Here is a NOS set of Clawson & Bals S-5388 full-floating connecting rod bearings, 0.010 inch oversize, for a 1937–1939 Ford V8-60 engine.

The spread (end width) of this Ford V8-60 connecting rod bearing is being increased. This is only a demonstration; the bearing should be on a block of wood.

available in standard size, 0.001 inch oversize, 0.002 inch oversize, 0.010 inch oversize, 0.020 inch oversize, 0.030 inch oversize, and 0.040 inch oversize, and one set costs $204. Jitney Auto Parts is a good source for NOS Ford V8-60 connecting rod bearings. A set of NOS Clawson & Bals S-5388 full-floating connecting rod bearings, 0.010 inch oversize, was installed in the engine described here. The thickness of these bearings is 0.210 inch each.

Many NOS Ford flathead V-8 bearings are covered with the factory protective cloth and coated with Cosmoline. Soak the bearings in very hot water for a few minutes to remove this coating. Many thanks to Tom Hood for this helpful tip, especially after I had wasted hours trying to remove the stuff with lacquer thinner, grease remover, and solvent.

The 1937–1939 Ford V8-60 full-floating connecting rod bearings have a flange on the outer edge, while the 1940 Ford V8-60 full-floating connecting rod bearings do not. Installing full-floating connecting rod bearings in a Ford flathead V-8 engine is not as simple as installing nonfloating connecting rod bearings. Three important measurements must be performed to ensure proper bearing clearance. First, the clearance between the bearing and the connecting rod journal should be 0.0015 to 0.0035 inch. The second clearance, between the big end of the connecting rod and the bearing, should also be 0.0015 to 0.0035 inch. The final clearance to check is the bearing side width with the width of the connecting rod journal, and it should be 0.005 to 0.015 inch.

In order to find the spread (end width) of a full-floating connecting rod bearing for a 1937–1939 Ford V8-60 engine, measure the outside diameter of the bearing with a micrometer. The spread should be 1.795 to 1.800 inches. The spread for a 1940 Ford V8-60 full-floating connecting rod bearing should be 1.895 to 1.900 inches. Measuring the spread will also determine if the connecting rod bearing is round and not out of shape.

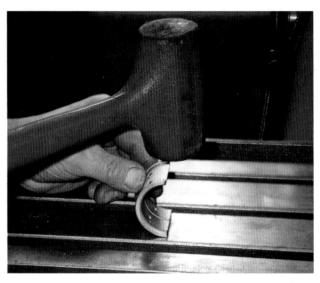

The spread of this Ford V8-60 connecting rod bearing is being reduced. This only a demonstration; the bearing should be on a block of wood.

There is a crude but effective method of adjusting the spread of the connecting rod bearings. If the bearing spread is inadequate, place the bearing with both ends on a block of wood, and tap the center back of the bearing with a rubber mallet. If the bearing spread is excessive, place one end of the bearing on a block of wood, and tap the other end with a rubber mallet. This is definitely Mickey Mouse engine building, but it works.

PISTONS

The factory pistons installed in Ford V8-60 engines were manufactured using cast-alloy steel and were the three-ring, solid-skirt design. The Egge Parts House E121 cast-aluminum pistons are available in standard size, 0.020 inch oversize, 0.030 inch oversize, 0.040 inch oversize, 0.060 inch oversize, 0.080 inch oversize, 0.100 inch oversize, and 0.125 inch oversize. They are the three-ring solid-skirt design, complete with wrist pins and wire clip retainers, and the current retail price for a set is $279. The Egge Parts House SRH123 cast-iron piston rings are available in standard size, 0.020 inch oversize, 0.030 inch oversize, 0.040 inch oversize, 0.060

Pictured here is a set of NOS Ford 82A-6149-H cast-iron piston rings, 0.040 inch oversize, for a Ford V8-60 engine.

inch oversize, and 0.080 inch oversize only. The current retail price for a set of these piston rings is $101. Jitney Auto Parts is a great source for NOS Ford V8-60 pistons and piston rings in most of the popular sizes.

A set of original NOS Silv-O-Lite 310-040 solid-skirt, three-ring, cast-aluminum pistons, 0.040 inch oversize, were installed in the engine described here. Each of these pistons weighs 199 grams. The Silv-O-Lite heat-treated chrome-moly steel straight-wall wrist pins are 2.290 inches long, 0.688 inch in diameter, and weigh 61 grams each. The wrist pins are secured in position with factory-style wire clip retainers. A set of NOS Ford 82A-6149-H cast-iron piston rings, 0.040 inch oversize, was installed with Silv-O-Lite pistons.

If you will be using your engine for all-out racing, then you should use forged-aluminum pistons. Ross Racing Pistons can custom manufacture forged-aluminum pistons for Ford V8-60 engines, complete with wrist pins and moly piston rings.

BALANCING
> *Refer to Chapter 3.*

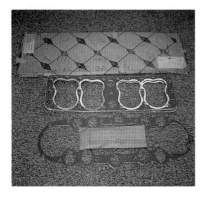

This is the Fel-Pro HSC6018 complete gasket set for 1937–1940 Ford V8-60 engines.

Here is a Silv-O-Lite 310-040 cast-aluminum piston, 0.040 inch oversize, with the wrist pin for a Ford V8-60 engine. The piston weighs 199 grams, and the wrist pin weighs 61 grams.

GASKETS
The Fel-Pro HSC6018 complete gasket set used to be available for Ford V8-60 engines. The Egge Parts House RS520S complete gasket set is available for the current retail price of $131.

B. CONNECTING RODS AND PISTONS SUMMARY

- The 1939 Ford 52A-6200 forged-steel I-beam connecting rods, full-floating connecting rod bearings. Connecting rod length (center to center): 6.125 inches. Connecting rod weight: 264 grams each. Connecting rod ratio: 1.91 (with 3.200 inches stroke). **$40**
- Connecting rods shot peened, aligned, Magnafluxed, resized, and balanced. New Egge Parts House PB754 wrist pin bushings, 0.6880 inch i.d., installed allowing for 0.002-inch wrist pin clearance. New OHV small-block Ford connecting rod nuts, 5/16 inch NF, installed using Loctite and torqued to 40 ft-lbs. **$372.67**
- NOS Clawson & Bals S-5388 full-floating connecting rod bearings, 0.010 inch oversize, installed allowing for 0.002-inch connecting rod journal clearance, 0.002-inch connecting rod big-end clearance, and 0.009-inch connecting rod bearing side clearance. Connecting rod side clearance (per pair): 0.012 inch. **$221**
- NOS Silv-O-Lite 310-040 cast-aluminum three-ring, solid-skirt pistons: 0.040 inch oversize, 9.0:1 compression ratio. Piston weight: 199 grams each. Piston grooves: top compression ring, 3/32 inch; second compression ring, 3/32 inch; and oil ring, 5/32 inch. New Silv-O-Lite heat-treated and case-hardened full-floating wrist pins installed with new wire clip retainers. Wrist pin length: 2.290 inches; wrist pin diameter: 0.688 inch; and wrist pin weight: 61 grams. NOS Ford 82A-6149-H cast-iron piston rings, 0.040 inch oversize, installed within manufacturer's recommended arc. Top compression ring gap, 0.012 inch; second compression ring gap, 0.012 inch; and oil ring gap, 0.010 inch. New displacement: 140.1 ci (2.3 liter). **$380**
- Complete V-8 engine balance. NOS Fel-Pro HSC6018 complete gasket set installed. **$381**

- Connecting Rods and Pistons Total: **$1,394.67**

CHAPTER 34
LUBRICATION SYSTEM

A. LUBRICATION SYSTEM
OIL PUMP

The oil pump installed in Ford V8-60 engines is unique, as it is an integral part of the No. 1 main bearing cap. The crankshaft gear engages the Ford 52-6608 large gear and shaft assembly on the front of the main bearing cap, which is connected to the Ford 52-6610 and 52-6614 smaller set of gears

The Ford 52-6603 oil pump is an integral part of the No. 1 main bearing cap in 1937–1940 Ford V8-60 engines.

The Ford 6663 valve plunger is on the left, the 6654 spring is in the middle, and the 6666 nut is on the right. These parts make up the later-model Ford flathead V-8 oil pressure relief valve, although they can be used in Ford V8-60 engines.

in the rear of the oil pump. If the gears in the Ford 52-6603 oil pump are worn out or damaged, you may have trouble finding NOS gears, as no one today appears to be manufacturing them. The Ford 52-6603 oil pump is said to produce 30 psi of oil pressure at 3,200 rpm.

The oil pressure relief valve for the oil pump is located in the front of the valve lifter gallery in Ford V8-60 engines. The earliest Ford flathead V-8 engines were equipped with an oil pressure relief valve consisting of a ball bearing, spring, and adjustable valve nut. Around 1940, this assembly

was replaced with the Ford 6663 oil pressure relief valve plunger, the 6654 oil pressure relief valve spring, and the 6666 oil pressure relief valve nut. The oil pressure relief valve plunger has a flat spot on the head that permits a small volume of oil to flow past it during periods of low engine rpm. The later-model oil pump pressure relief valve is designed to open at 30 psi, which is suitable for a 1937–1940 Ford V8-60 engine.

OIL PAN AND PICKUP

The Ford 52-6675 stamped-steel oil pan, with a 4-quart capacity and an internal baffle, is a very sturdy item. The rear of the oil pan forms half of the bell housing and, as a result, supports part of the weight of the transmission. The starting motor mount is also incorporated into the right side at the back of the oil pan. There is a road-draft opening in the right front corner of the oil pan. Attach the flywheel to the crankshaft prior to installing the oil pan, as it will not fit through the rear of the engine block when the oil pan is bolted in place. It is also easier to attach the clutch disc and pressure plate to the flywheel prior to installing the oil pan.

The oil pan should be hot tanked and Redi-Stripped to ensure it is absolutely clean inside and out. Black polyurethane is the ideal paint to spray on an oil pan because it is extremely durable and will not show any road dirt. The oil pan should be secured in place with 16 pieces: stainless-steel 5/16-inch-NC by 3/4-inch-long hex-head

This is a 1939 Ford 52-6675 oil pan with a 4-quart capacity. The oil pump pickup is located directly over the disc in the bottom, and the road-draft opening is at the right front corner.

Here is a bottom view of the Ford 52-6675 oil pan for Ford V8-60 engines.

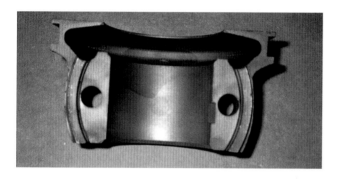

The flange at the back of this Ford V8-60 rear main bearing cap fits over the two crankshaft rear oil slingers and acts in lieu of the cord material oil seals.

bolts, lockwashers, and AN flat washers. The Best Gasket of California 24018 oil pan gasket set is available for Ford V8-60 engines. Immediately after purchasing the gasket set, remove the cord material front oil seals and place them in a can of motor oil. Let them soak in the oil for at least a week to be thoroughly saturated. These oil seals are extremely tough when they are new and dry, making installation a difficult proposition. The Ford 52-6750 dipstick and Ford 52-6754 dipstick tube were installed in the left side of Ford V8-60 oil pans. Refer to Chapter 24 for information about the dipstick tube boss.

The Ford V8-60 engines did not use the cord material rear oil seals; instead, the crankshaft incorporated two rear oil slingers in front of the flywheel flange. The crankshaft oil

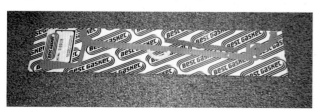

This is a Best Gasket of California 24018 oil pan gasket set for the Ford V8-60 engines.

slingers fit inside the Ford 52-6335 rear upper oil slinger retainer and the rear main bearing cap. Later-model Ford flathead V-8 engines used the cord material rear oil seals for a superior method of oil control. The Ford 52-6326 tube was attached to the rear main bearing cap and directed the return oil toward the center of the oil pan sump.

The Ford 52-6615 oil pump cover and inlet tube are attached to the rear of the 52-6603 oil pump with 6607 bolts and 34805-S lockwashers. The hex-head bolts have a hole through the heads in order to secure them with a safety wire. The Ford 52-6623 oil pump cover screen was held in position with the 52-6628 oil pump cover screen retainer clip.

FUEL PUMP PUSHROD BUSHING AND PUSHROD

The fuel pump pushrod bushing used in Ford V8-60 engines is manufactured using thin wall brass without a lubrication hole for the pushrod, and it is 0.376 inch i.d. The bushing does not have to be removed when the engine block is hot tanked and Redi-Stripped. Installing a multi-carburetor fuel system dictates that you should use an electric fuel pump, which means the stock mechanical fuel pump with the fuel pump pushrod will not be used. If the fuel pump pushrod is removed from the engine, there will be a loss of oil pressure. To prevent this, fabricate a slightly tapered 0.380-inch-diameter aluminum plug, and hammer it into the fuel pump pushrod bushing using Permatex aviation form-a-gasket. The Ford 52-9400 fuel pump pushrod installed in Ford V8-60 engines is 0.375 inch o.d. by 6.375 inches long.

VALVE LIFTER GALLERY BAFFLE

The Ford 52-6524 valve lifter gallery oil return hole baffle snaps into place with two clips and prevents unwanted debris from ending up in the oil pan. The baffle should be glass beaded and painted with Glyptal G-1228A medium-gray gloss enamel.

OIL FILLER TUBE

An oil filler/crankcase breather tube is located at the rear of the Ford V8-60 engine blocks on the left side of the bell housing, which is an impractical location considering it will most likely interfere with the firewall of a vehicle. Fabricate a 1 ¼-inch-diameter aluminum plug, and install it using Permatex aviation form-a-gasket. An aftermarket

A 1939 Ford 52-9400 fuel pump pushrod is pictured here. It is 0.375 inch o.d. by 6.375 inches long.

The Ford 52-6615 oil pump cover and inlet tube with the 6623 oil pump cover screen and 52-6628 oil pump cover screen retainer clip are shown here. They have all been sprayed with graphite.

Here are two Ford 52-6524 valve lifter gallery oil return hole baffles for Ford V8-60 engines.

intake manifold was installed in the engine described here, and most of these had a provision at the rear for the oil filler/crankcase breather tube.

B. LUBRICATION SYSTEM TOTAL

- Ford 52-9400 fuel pump pushrod, 0.375 inch o.d. by 6.375 inches long, installed. Ford 52-6524 valve lifter gallery oil return hole baffle painted with Glyptal G-1228A medium-gray gloss enamel and installed. Ford 6663 oil pressure relief valve plunger, Ford 6654 oil pressure relief valve spring, and Ford 6666 oil pressure relief valve nut installed using Permatex aviation form-a-gasket. Ford 52-6335 rear upper oil slinger installed using silicone sealant. **$79.16**

- The 1939 Ford 52-6603 oil pump, 6615 oil pump cover and inlet tube, 52-6623 screen, and 52-6628 screen retainer clip installed with Ford 6607 bolts and 34805-S lockwashers torqued to 15 ft-lbs using Loctite. Oil pump cover and inlet tube gasket installed using silicone sealant. **$91.67**

- The 1939 Ford 52-6675 stamped-steel oil pan, with internal baffle and 4-quart capacity, installed with new stainless-steel hex-head bolts, lockwashers, and AN flat washers using Loctite and torqued to 15 ft-lbs. Oil pan gaskets installed using silicone sealant. Ford 52-6751 dipstick tube boss installed using new stainless-steel pan-head screws, star washers, and nuts with Loctite. Dipstick tube boss gasket installed using silicone sealant. Ford 52-6700 cord material front oil seals soaked in SAE 30-weight motor oil and installed. Ford 52-6750 dipstick and 52-6754 dipstick tube installed using silicone sealant. Engine lubricated with 4 quarts of Pennzoil HD-30 weight motor oil. Oil pan, dipstick tube boss, dipstick tube, and dipstick painted with PPG 74000 red high-gloss polyurethane. **$254.17**

- Lubrication System Total: $425

CHAPTER 35
CAMSHAFT AND CYLINDER HEADS

A. CAMSHAFT AND CYLINDER HEADS
CAMSHAFT BEARINGS

Clevite 77 (Dana Corporation) and Federal-Mogul do not currently list camshaft bearings for the Ford V8-60 engine. Ford Motor Company and Federal-Mogul used to offer Ford V8-60 camshaft bearings in standard size, 0.005 inch oversize, and 0.010 inch oversize. The Egge Parts House F-2 camshaft bearings, standard size, are available for the current retail price of $47. The Ford Motor Company specified the

camshaft bearing clearance to be 0.001 to 0.002 inch and the camshaft end play to be 0.002 to 0.004 inch. The camshaft journal diameter is 1.490 inches. A NOS set of Michigan Engine Bearings 84CS, standard size, will be installed in the engine described in this section.

CAMSHAFT

A stock 1937–1940 Ford 52-6250 solid flat-tappet camshaft is not the ideal candidate for a street performance Ford V8-60 engine. Refer to Chapter 1 for information about camshaft terminology. Edward A. "Big Ed" Winfield (Glendale, California) was a brilliant automotive engineer considered by many to be the original hot rod camshaft

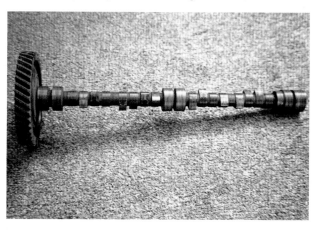

Here is a stock Ford 52-6250 camshaft for a 1939 Ford V8-60 engine. The 52-6256 fiber camshaft gear is pressed on the camshaft snout.

grinder. He produced some of the best camshafts for Ford flathead V-8 engines, including the Ford V8-60, and he personally ground every camshaft he sold. There were many aftermarket camshafts available for Ford V8-60 engines in the 1940s and 1950s, although most of them were ground for competition applications.

An example of a Big Ed product is the Winfield R-11-S solid flat-tappet camshaft that has an advertised duration of 256 degrees intake and 252 degrees exhaust. The lobe separation angle is 111 degrees, the net valve lift is 0.253 inch intake and 0.251 inch exhaust, and the valve lash (hot) is 0.012 inch intake and 0.014 inch exhaust. This is a racing camshaft.

This is a NOS set of Michigan Engine Bearings 84CS camshaft bearings, standard size, for a Ford V8-60 engine.

This is a NOS set of Federal-Mogul 1007M camshaft bearings, 0.010 inch oversize, for the Ford V8-60 engines.

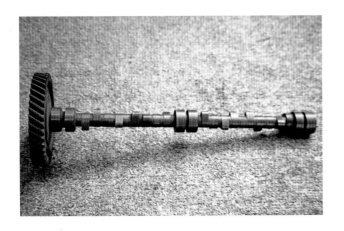

This is a Winfield R-11-S solid lifter racing camshaft for a Ford V8-60 engine. Advertised duration is 256 degrees intake and 252 degrees exhaust; lobe separation angle is 111 degrees; net valve lift is 0.253 inch intake and 0.251 inch exhaust; and valve lash (hot) is 0.012 inch intake and 0.014 inch exhaust.

In the 1950s, (Kenny) Harman & (Cliff) Collins (Los Angeles, California) was an established camshaft grinding company that also manufactured excellent magnetos. A Harman & Collins 6412 Full Race solid lifter camshaft was installed in the engine described here. The advertised duration is 250 degrees intake and exhaust, and the lobe separation angle is 112 degrees. The net valve lift is 0.272 inch intake and exhaust, and the valve lash (hot) is 0.010 inch intake and exhaust. This camshaft is quite radical for street performance use.

Camshafts manufactured from the 1940s to the 1960s did not have information about the duration at 0.050-inch lift, as this standard of measurement was not in use during that period. Timing events are listed as advertised duration, but the amount of lift the timing events were taken at was not given, thus making the comparison of vintage camshafts a very difficult task. Many of the better-known Ford V8-60 aftermar-

ket camshafts were ground in the 1940s and 1950s by some real hot rod legends. (Ed) Iskenderian Racing Cams was founded in the late 1940s and is still in business today. (Clay) Smith and (Dan) Jones (Long Beach, California) was founded in the 1940s and later became Clay Smith Engineering. (Harry) Weber Cam Grinding Company was located in Los Angles, California, in the early 1950s. Refer to the Appendix for vintage camshaft information.

The camshaft technology today far exceeds what was available in the 1940s and 1950s, which is one good reason to have a camshaft ground for a specific engine. Crower Cams & Equipment can regrind a stock Ford V8-60 camshaft and turn it into a suitable candidate for a street performance or competition engine. It will cost approximately $100 for this service.

DEGREE CAMSHAFT
The net valve lift in a Ford flathead V-8 engine is calculated by subtracting the valve lash from the camshaft lobe lift. Refer to Chapter 5 for information on how to degree a camshaft.

VALVE LIFTERS
The early-design Ford 52-6500 solid lifters installed in Ford V8-60 engines have a hollow body with oval slots in the side, and each one weighs 31 grams. The later-design Ford 52-6500 solid lifters have a solid body, and each one weighs 39 grams. All of them are 0.830 inches in diameter by 1.330 inches long and are nonadjustable.

The fact the Ford 52-6500 solid lifters are nonadjustable made a nightmare out of valve lash adjustment in Ford V8-60 engines. The installation of an aftermarket camshaft with a larger valve lift usually meant the valve stems had to be built up by welding, and then ground to obtain the proper valve lash. This tedious operation could take a day or more to per-

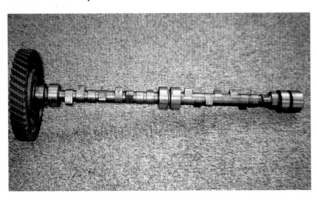

Here is a Harman & Collins 6412 Full Race solid lifter camshaft with an advertised duration of 250 degrees intake and exhaust, and lobe separation angle of 112 degrees. The net valve lift is 0.272 inch intake and exhaust, and the valve lash (hot) is 0.010 inch intake and exhaust. This camshaft was installed in the engine described here.

There should be no discussion as to what the weight of this early-design Ford 52-6500 hollow-body solid lifter for the Ford V8-60 engines is.

This is a set of the later-design Ford 52-6500 solid lifters for Ford V8-60 engines. Each lifter weighs 39 grams.

Here is a complete set of Ford 52-6500 intake and exhaust valves for Ford V8-60 engines. These valves have a mushroom tip.

form. It should be mandatory to install adjustable valve lifters in all Ford flathead V-8 engines.

Johnson solid adjustable lifters and Witteman Company (Alhambra, California) solid adjustable lifters were some of the first offered for Ford V8-60 engines. Occasionally, used sets of these solid adjustable lifters appear at swap meets and on eBay. Provided the adjustable valve lifter bodies are not badly pitted or scored and the adjusting screws are not damaged, the valve lifters can be refaced by any reputable camshaft grinding company for approximately $85. Red's Headers (see Resources) sells solid adjustable lifters for Ford V8-60 engines for the current retail price of $295 for a set of 16. Each of these lifters weighs 67.5 grams

Always install new valve lifters with a new camshaft. If installing new valve lifters with a used camshaft or vice versa, camshaft failure is almost certainly guaranteed. The valve lifters are referred to as "flat tappet", although the face of the valve lifter is actually convex. This permits the valve lifter to rotate, thereby encouraging even wear on the valve lifter face and camshaft lobe.

VALVES

The Ford 52-6505 intake and exhaust valves for Ford V8-60 engines were manufactured using chrome-nickel alloy steel, and they have mushroom tips. The intake valves have a 1.277-inch head diameter, 0.2795-inch stem diameter, are 4.355 inches long overall, and each weigh 58 grams. The exhaust valves have a 1.275-inch head diameter, 0.2795-inch stem diameter, are 4.355 inches long, and each weigh 61 grams. As far as I know, none of the major manufacturers of valves are reproducing valves for Ford V8-60 engines. Jitney Auto Parts is a good source for all the camshaft components in most Ford flathead V-8 engines. Refer to Chapter 5 for information about valve grinding. A NOS set of Ford V8-60 intake and exhaust valves was installed in the engine described here.

Ford 52-6505 intake and exhaust valves have a lip at the top of the valve stem near the underside of the valve head. The top of the valve guide bushing rests against this lip when

the valve is in the closed position. Remove this lip in a lathe. This will create a smooth radius from the top of the valve stem to the underside of the valve head, as well as result in a less obstructive path for the incoming air/fuel mixture and outgoing exhaust gases. Removing the lip will also simplify the assembly of the valves with the valve guide bushings, valve springs, and valve spring retainers.

VALVE GUIDE BUSHINGS

The Ford 52-6510 valve guide bushings for Ford V8-60 engines are a two-piece split design, which was necessary for the mushroom-tip valves to be installed. The valve guides are 0.850 inch in diameter, 1.810 inches long overall, and have no oil control O-rings installed on the intake valve guide bushings. The Egge Parts House G975 intake and exhaust valve guide bushings are available for the current retail price of $204 for a set of 16.

The Ford Motor Company specified the intake and exhaust valve-stem-to-valve-guide-bushing clearance to be 0.0015 to 0.0035 inch. A set of NOS Ford 52-6510-C valve guide bushings was installed in the engine described in this section.

Pictured here is a set of NOS Ford 52-6510-C two-piece split-design valve guide bushings for the Ford V8-60 engines.

This NOS set of Ford 52-6513 single helical coil valve springs for Ford V8-60 engines has been sprayed with graphite.

Here is a set of custom valve spring shims for a Ford V8-60 engine when a camshaft with a radical net valve lift is installed. They are 0.810 inch o.d., 0.590 inch i.d., and 0.190 inches thick.

VALVE SPRINGS

The NOS Ford 52-6513 single helical coil valve springs are suitable for a Ford V8-60 engine equipped with a street performance camshaft. The Ford 52-6513 valve springs are 0.830 inch o.d. and 2.370 inches long overall. The installed height is 26–30 pounds at 2 inches valves closed and 48–52 pounds at 1.761 inches valves open (0.239-inch net valve lift).

I am not aware of any company currently manufacturing aftermarket high-tension valve springs for Ford V8-60 engines. Egge Parts House VS404 replacement valve springs are available for the current retail price of $89 for a set of 16. You can increase the valve spring tension of the Ford 52-6513 valve springs by installing valve spring shims, which may be necessary if installing an aftermarket camshaft with a radical net valve lift.

VALVE SPRING RETAINERS

The Ford 52-6514 valve spring retainers for Ford V8-60 engines are a combination of valve spring retainer and valve stem lock. If they are damaged or some are missing, Jitney Auto Parts is a good source for replacements. To assemble the

Ford V8-60 valve components, slide the valve spring over the valve stem, and place the valve spring retainer in position. Then slide the two halves of the valve guide bushing into the top of the valve spring, and force them down until they lock into position on the lip at the top of the valve stem.

Ford 52-6512 crow's-foot valve guide bushing retainers secure the valve guide bushings in position. Egge Parts House G975K replacement valve guide bushings are available for the current retail price of $210 for a set of 16.

CAMSHAFT GEAR AND TIMING COVER

The Ford 52-6256 fiber camshaft gear has 42 teeth and is pressed on the snout of the Ford V8-60 camshaft. The fiber camshaft gear is acceptable for a street performance Ford V8-60 engine due to the low tension of the Ford 52-6513 single helical coil valve springs. Years ago, the Perfection Gear Company N-2709 fiber camshaft gear was a replacement model. The Egge Parts House TG2709 replacement fiber camshaft gear is available for the current retail price of $30.

The cast-iron timing gear cover is unique to the Ford V8-60 engine because it is a combination of timing gear cover, water pump mounting plate, and motor mounting plate. The water pump openings in the 1937 Ford 52-6019-A timing gear cover are tapered, while the openings in the late 1937–1940 Ford 52-6019-B timing gear covers are straight. Glass bead the timing gear cover, and spray the area on the back, which is in front of the camshaft gear, with Glyptal G-1228A medium-gray gloss enamel. You can paint the rest of the timing gear cover the same color as the engine block. Install the timing gear cover using eight pieces: 5/16-inch-NC by 3/4-inch-long stainless-steel hex-head bolts and lockwashers.

In the 1940s and 1950s, Ford V8-60 race motor owners commonly eliminated the stock Ford 52-6019 cast-iron timing gear cover and used aftermarket aluminum models, such as those produced by Eddie Meyer Engineering and Offenhauser. The aftermarket models have no provision for water pumps and do not have motor mount flanges. The Offenhauser 15957 cast-aluminum timing gear cover is still manufactured today, and the current retail price is $300, unpolished.

CYLINDER HEADS

The 1937 and 1938 Ford V8-60 cylinder heads were manufactured using aluminum, the 1939 cylinder heads were

The Ford 52-6514 valve spring retainers for Ford V8-60 engines are pictured here. This part also acts as the valve stem lock.

either aluminum or cast iron, and the 1940 cylinder heads were cast iron. The 1939 Ford 52-6050-C cast-iron cylinder heads have a 39-cc combustion chamber volume. The combination of stock Ford V8-60 cylinder heads and stock pistons resulted in a 6.6:1 compression ratio. Most hot rodders prefer the look of aftermarket finned-aluminum cylinder heads to the stock heads, although the stock aluminum cylinder heads can be buffed.

In the 1940s and 1950s, many aftermarket aluminum cylinder heads were manufactured for the Ford V8-60 engine. (Frank) Baron, Cyclone (Cooks Machine Shop), (Eddie) Edmunds, (Vic Sr.) Edelbrock, (Eddie) Meyer, (Fred) Offenhauser, and (Phil) Weiand (just to name a few) all produced some of the best aluminum cylinder heads. (Robert) Roof was one of the earliest speed-equipment manufacturers. He produced twin dual spark plug aluminum cylinder heads for the Ford V8-60 engine, and they were probably the most novel for their day.

A pair of original Edelbrock 1130 polished finned-aluminum cylinder heads, with a 9.0:1 compression ratio, 34-cc combustion chamber volume, and polished aluminum water outlet elbows was installed on the engine described here. These cylinder heads are rare, for they have the Edelbrock name in bold letters and not the usual script style. The Edelbrock 1130 aluminum cylinder heads were available with an 8.5:1, 9.0:1, 9.5:1, or 10.0:1 compression ratio. These cylinder heads are no longer being produced.

The Offenhauser 1070 finned-aluminum cylinder heads for Ford V8-60 engines are still manufactured today; they have a 9.5:1 compression when used with the stock bore and stroke. These cylinder heads are complete with aluminum water outlet manifolds, and the current retail price for an unpolished pair is $551.

When purchasing used aluminum cylinder heads, be cautious because they could have been planed sometime in the past. Also, they might be warped, the spark plug threads could be stripped, or some of the cylinder head stud (or bolt) holes could have been enlarged or drilled off-center. The

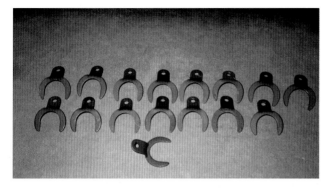

This set of Ford 52-6512 crow's-foot valve guide bushings for Ford V8-60 engines has been sprayed with graphite.

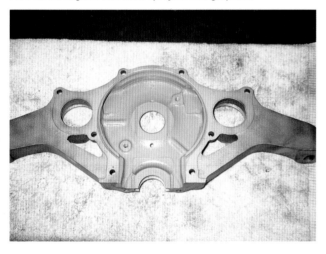

This Ford 52-6019-B timing gear cover, for late 1937–1940 Ford V8-60 engines, also mounts the water pumps and is the motor mounting plate. The inside has been painted with Glyptal G-1228A medium-gray gloss enamel.

This is an original Eddie Meyer Engineering cast-aluminum timing gear cover for Ford V8-60 engines. The ears block off the water pump openings in the engine block.

This is a pair of 1939 Ford 52-6050-C cast-iron cylinder heads for Ford V8-60 engines. They have a 39-cc combustion chamber volume.

This is a pair of original Edelbrock 1130 polished finned-aluminum cylinder heads for Ford V8-60 engines. The combustion chamber volume is 34 cc, and the compression ratio is 9.0:1. The polished-aluminum water outlet elbow is in place.

This is a Roy Nacewicz Enterprises R-96-04 cylinder head stud kit for Ford V8-60 engines. It includes the R-9604 studs, R-260 hardened-steel flat washers, and R-619 stud nuts.

worst situation is when an older aluminum cylinder head is cracked. The quality of the aluminum used today is far superior to older aluminum, which is usually porous. When attempting a welding repair, the cracks tend to spread due to the residue that bubbles out when the aluminum is heated. A used set of aluminum cylinder heads should be cold tanked, Magnafluxed, pressure tested, and surfaced.

Ford 52-6065 short cylinder head studs, 2 1/4 inches long, and Ford 52-6066 medium cylinder head studs, 2 3/4 inches long, were installed in the Ford V8-60 engines, along with Ford 351385-S flat washers and 33800-S stud nuts. The original studs, flat washers, and nuts can be reused provided they are not badly corroded or have stripped threads. They should be glass beaded and painted. The cylinder head studs have 3/8-inch-NC threads on the engine block end and 3/8-inch-NF threads on the cylinder head end. There are 11 medium-length cylinder head studs and six short-length cylinder head studs for each side of the engine block. Install the cylinder head studs in the engine block using Permatex aviation form-a-gasket, coat the shanks with anti-seize compound, and install the stud nuts using Molykote. NOS Ford V8-60 cylinder head stud kits are available from Jitney Auto Parts. Ford Motor Company specified the Ford

V8-60 cast-iron cylinder heads be torqued to 50 ft-lbs and the aluminum cylinder heads to 30 ft-lbs.

Some aftermarket aluminum cylinder heads, such as the Offenhauser 1070, require all medium-length (2 3/4-inch) cylinder head studs. The Roy Nacewicz Enterprises (www.fordbolts.com) R-96-04 cylinder head stud kit (with all medium-length studs) is available for the current retail price of $55, complete with R-9604 studs, R-260 hardened-steel flat washers, and R-619 stud nuts. You should always use hardened-steel flat washers when installing cast-iron or aluminum cylinder heads on a street performance engine. It is especially important to do this when using aluminum cylinder heads to prevent the aluminum from galling. Adding a set of J. C. Whitney & Company 38SZ2776R chrome acorn nut covers, for a 5/8-inch head size, will provide some luster to the old flathead engine, and a set costs about $20.

Do not have cylinder heads planed if they are going to be used on a street performance Ford flathead V-8 engine. Years ago, this common practice was thought to raise the compression ratio. If the cylinder heads are planed, in all likelihood the upper combustion chamber area of the cylinder heads will have to be milled to provide adequate valve-to-cylinder-head clearance. Milling the combustion chambers will increase the volume, thereby defeating any benefit that might have been gained when the cylinder heads were planed. The engine described here has a compression ratio of 9.0:1; this is close to the maximum compression ratio at which a street performance engine can properly function when using today's highest octane, unleaded gasoline.

CYLINDER HEAD GASKETS

Ford 52-6051 composite cylinder head gaskets were installed in all Ford V8-60 engines. Victor 1005K composite cylinder head gaskets are stock replacements. Edelbrock recommends using copper sandwiched cylinder head gaskets with its aluminum cylinder heads. Victor 1005C large-bore copper sandwiched cylinder head gaskets are available for Ford V8-60 engines with a cylinder bore up to 2.725 inches (0.125 inch oversize). Install the copper sandwiched cylinder head gaskets using Permatex copper spray-a-gasket with the stud nuts torqued to 30 ft-lbs when using aluminum cylinder heads.

WATER OUTLET ELBOWS

The water outlet elbows are cast into the top of the stock Ford V8-60 cylinder heads. The water outlet elbows are bolted on the top center of the Edelbrock 1130 finned-alu-

This is a pair of Victor 1005C large-bore copper sandwiched cylinder head gaskets for Ford V8-60 engines.

Here is a pair of Victor 1005K composite cylinder head gaskets for Ford V8-60 engines. These are stock replacement gaskets.

minum cylinder heads, and the water outlet manifolds are bolted on the top of the Offenhauser 1070 finned-aluminum cylinder heads. Thermostats should be installed in the engine of any vehicle that will be driven on the street. Removing the thermostats will cause the coolant in the engine to move too fast for the heat to be dissipated. The thermostats in Ford V8-60 engines were placed in the top of the water outlet elbow on the cylinder heads prior to installing the top radiator hose. Dole Valve Company used to manufacture the correct butterfly-type thermostats for Ford V8-60 engines.

EXHAUST BAFFLES

You should install exhaust port baffles in a street performance Ford V8-60 engine block. There is a common exhaust port for the two center cylinders in each side of the engine block, thus the exhaust gases from the two center ports will collide with each other. The exhaust baffles will assist with correcting this situation.

The Speedway Motors 916-15201 exhaust baffle kit is available for the current retail price of $35 for a pair. These exhaust baffles will have to be trimmed in order to fit the Ford V8-60 exhaust ports properly.

Replace the stock cylinder head stud with an extended stud, which will hold the exhaust baffle in place. Drill a small hole through the exhaust runner into the exhaust baffle, and install an irontite plug using Loctite. This plug will ensure the exhaust baffle does not come free, as well as obstruct the exhaust runner if the extended stud securing the exhaust baffle ever loosens. The extended studs included with the Speedway Motors 916-15201 kit have 7/16-inch-NC threads and will not fit the Ford V8-60 engine block. Two studs will have to be fabricated using 3/8-inch-NC threaded rod.

B. CAMSHAFT
AND CYLINDER HEADS SUMMARY

- NOS Michigan Engine Bearings 84CS camshaft bearings installed allowing for 0.002-inch camshaft clearance and 0.003-inch end play. Nos. 1 and 2 bearings: SH-32, housing bore 1.6095 to 1.6105 inches. No. 3 bearing: SH-33, housing bore 1.6095 to 1.6105 inches. Camshaft journal diameter: 1.490 inches. **$47**
- Harman & Collins 6412 Full Race cast-iron alloy solid

lifter camshaft with advertised duration of 250 degrees intake and 250 degrees exhaust. Lobe separation angle, 112 degrees; net valve lift, 0.272 inch intake and exhaust; valve lash (hot), 0.010 inch intake and exhaust. Camshaft degreed. **$325**
- New Red's Headers hardenable iron, solid adjustable valve lifters, 0.830 inches in diameter and 1.330 inches long, installed. Hollow body valve lifter weight: 67.5 grams each. **$295**
- NOS Ford 52-6513 single helical coil valve springs with installed height: 30 pounds at 2.00 inches valves closed and 55 pounds at 1.750 inches valves open; 0.830 inch o.d., 2.370 inches long overall. The 1939 Ford 52-6514 valve spring retainers installed. NOS Ford 52-6510-C two-piece valve guide bushings, 0.850 inch in diameter, 1.810 inches long overall, installed allowing for 0.0015-inch valve guide boss clearance. The 1939 Ford 52-6512 crow's-foot valve guide bushing retainers installed. **$336**
- NOS Ford 52-6505 chrome-nickel alloy steel intake valves, 1.277-inch head diameter, 0.2795-inch stem diameter, and 4.355 inches long overall, installed. Intake valve weight: 58 grams. NOS Ford 52-6505 chrome-nickel alloy steel exhaust valves, 1.275-inch head diameter, 0.2795-inch stem diameter, and 4.355 inches long overall, installed. Exhaust valve weight: 61 grams. Valves installed with Serdi-machined multi-angle blueprint valve grind and allowing for 0.0015-inch valve guide bushing clearance. **$216**
- NOS Ford 52-6256 fiber camshaft timing gear, 42 teeth, installed. The 1939 Ford 52-6019-B cast-iron timing gear cover installed with new polished stainless-steel hex-head bolts and lockwashers using Loctite and torqued to 15 ft-lbs. Timing gear cover gasket installed using silicone sealant. Inside of timing gear cover painted with Glyptal G-1228A medium-gray gloss enamel, and exterior surface painted with PPG 74000 red high-gloss polyurethane. **$180**
- New Victor 1005C large-bore copper sandwiched cylinder head gaskets installed using Permatex copper spray-a-gasket. Edelbrock 1130 polished finned-aluminum cylinder heads—9.0:1 compression ratio, 34-cc combustion chamber volume—installed with new Roy Nacewicz Enterprises R-96-04 cylinder head stud kit (R-9604 studs, R-260 hardened-steel flat washers, and R-619 stud nuts) using Permatex aviation form-a-gasket and torqued to 30 ft-lbs. New J. C. Whitney & Company 38SZ2776R chrome acorn nut covers, 5/8-inch head size, installed. NOS Dole Valve Company butterfly-type thermostats, 180 degrees (Fahrenheit), installed. Valve-to-cylinder-head clearance: 0.105 inch intake and 0.148 inch exhaust (without cylinder head gasket). **$750.85**

- **Camshaft and Cylinder Heads Total: $2,149.85**

CHAPTER 36
INTAKE SYSTEM

A. INTAKE SYSTEM
INTAKE MANIFOLD

The Ford 52-6520 cast-aluminum high-rise intake manifold was installed on Ford V8-60 engines. Its design is great with well-laid-out runners. Honest Charley installs the Ford 52-6250 intake manifold on the Ford V8-60 engines in its motorcycles.

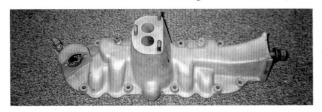

The factory installed this Ford 52-6250 cast-aluminum high-rise intake manifold on Ford V8-60 engines. It has a very good runner design. The oil pressure line fitting is seen behind the fuel pump boss.

In the 1940s and early 1950s, literally dozens of companies manufactured cast-aluminum dual-carburetor intake manifolds for Ford V8-60 engines. The intake manifolds manufactured on the West Coast of the United States appeared to receive far more publicity than those produced elsewhere, such as the (Robert) Roof cast-aluminum two-piece intake manifold. The upper section of the intake manifold mounted the dual carburetors and was bolted to the lower section. Although it was a very advanced design for the 1940s, very few people today have ever heard of this intake manifold. R & R Manufacturing Company of Anderson, Indiana, cast all of the aluminum cylinder heads and intake manifolds for Robert Roof.

Original Eddie Meyer Engineering cast-aluminum cylinder heads and cast-aluminum super dual intake manifold with two Holley 94 carburetors are installed on this 1940 Ford V8-60 engine. This engine is from a boat, which explains why the carburetors are mounted backward.

Pictured here is a vintage Edelbrock 1035 polished cast-aluminum super dual-carburetor intake manifold for Ford V8-60 engines.

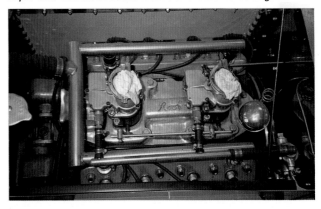

Here is the rarest of the rare. This Ford V8-60 midget race car engine is equipped with Robert Roof polished-aluminum cylinder heads and a super dual-carburetor intake manifold. The carburetors are Stromberg 81s.

Edelbrock, Evans, Meyer, Offenhauser, and Weiand sold some of the more popular cast-aluminum dual-carburetor intake manifolds for Ford V8-60 engines. The Offenhauser 11006 cast-aluminum super dual-carburetor intake manifold is still manufactured today and is available for the current retail price of $351 unpolished. The carburetors on the super dual-carburetor intake manifolds are better situated over the intake ports for more equal fuel distribution. The generator must be mounted on one of the cylinder heads if installing a super dual-carburetor intake manifold. A vintage Edelbrock 1035 polished cast-aluminum super dual-carburetor intake manifold was installed on the engine described here.

CARBURETORS

The 1937 and 1938 Ford V8-60 engines were all equipped with a Stromberg 81 carburetor, which was the smallest two-barrel carburetor Stromberg produced. The venturi is 81/100 (13/16) inch, and each carburetor flows approximately 125

This is a pair of very rare Stromberg 81 two-barrel carburetors with 81/100-inch (13/16-inch) venturi. They each flow approximately 125 cfm.

This is the famous polished (Stu) Hilborn 239-F-8A mechanical fuel injection with 10-inch-high F142 ram tubes for Ford flathead V-8 engines.

Although this brand-new Austin cast-aluminum blower intake manifold is for a Ford flathead V-8 and not a Ford V8-60 engine, I wanted to include it. This is a Balstin model named after the designers, Luke Balogh and Ken Austin.

cfm. Only a limited amount of Stromberg 81 carburetors were manufactured, making them hard to find today. In the early 1950s, Stromberg carburetors were reportedly notorious for fuel leaks between the air horns and main body. The emulsion tubes are very delicate and can be easily damaged. The float is side-hung, which has a tendency to cut off the fuel supply when a vehicle is making a sharp, fast turn. Expect to pay a large amount of money for a Stromberg 81 carburetor today. The rebuilding of the Stromberg 81 should be left to an expert, such as Charley Price at Vintage Speed. A pair of Stromberg 81 carburetors was installed on the engine described here.

The 1939 and 1940 Ford V8-60 engines were all equipped with a Holley 94 91-99 carburetor. Refer to Chapter 26 for information about the Holley 94 carburetor. The Ford V8-60 engines installed in motorcycles by Honest Charley are all equipped with a Holley 94 carburetor. In the 1940s and 1950s, many Ford V8-60 engines installed in midget race cars were equipped with a pair of the famous Big Ed Winfield SR one-barrel carburetors.

FUEL PRESSURE REGULATOR AND FUEL BLOCK
The factory installed the Ford 52-9350 mechanical fuel pump on Ford V8-60 engines. Many Ford V8-60 engine

owners have successfully run dual Stromberg 81 carburetors on their engines with a stock Ford 52-9350 mechanical fuel pump. An electric fuel pump should be installed to ensure a reliable fuel supply when using more than one two-barrel carburetor on a Ford flathead V-8 engine. Refer to Chapter 26 for information about the fuel pressure regulator.

There are a few companies manufacturing fuel blocks for dual carburetor setups, which are inexpensive. The Mooneyes USA MO1010 cast-aluminum finned fuel block and the Speedway Motors 550-6150 chrome T-style fuel block are available today.

FUEL LINES AND LINKAGE
Refer to Chapter 26 for information regarding fuel lines and fuel line fittings. The Offenhauser 2864 standard inline dual-carburetor linkage, the Offenhauser 2865 super dual-carburetor inline linkage, the Vintage Speed CL-2B ball-end standard inline carburetor linkage, and the Vintage Speed CL-1006 ball-socket universal inline dual-carburetor linkage are all available today for around $25–$40.

AIR CLEANERS
> Refer to Chapter 26.

BOLTS
The Ford 20406-S intake manifold bolts can be reused if they are glass beaded and painted, provided they are not badly corroded and the threads are not stripped. Alternatively, use new Grade 8 or stainless-steel 5/16-inch-NC by 1-inch-long hex-head bolts and AN flat washers. The Edelbrock 1035 aluminum super dual-carburetor intake manifold requires 11 pieces of each, and they should be covered with J. C. Whitney & Company 38SZ2774U chrome acorn nut covers (for 1/2-inch head size).

PCV VALVE
A positive crankcase ventilation (PCV) valve should be installed in a Ford V8-60 engine to be driven on the street.

This rebuilt Ford 52-9350 mechanical fuel pump for Ford V8-60 engines has been in storage for such a long time that the grease on the fuel pump pushrod rocker arm has hardened.

This is an obsolete Fenton dual-carburetor chrome fuel block.

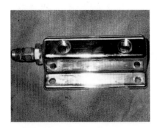

Here is a Speedway Motors 550-6150 chrome T-style dual-carburetor fuel block.

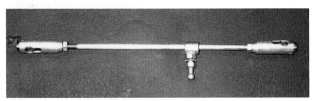

This is a Vintage Speed CL-1006 ball-end universal inline dual carburetor linkage kit.

Here is a pair of original Moon Equipment Company 1250 (now Mooneyes USA JE9600) chrome air scoops.

Drill and tap a 1/8-inch-NPT hole in the center front of the intake manifold (approximately 2 inches from the front), and install a new Weatherhead 3400-2 polished-brass 90-degree

This is a vintage Tattersfield carburetor block-off plate for intake manifolds utilizing two-barrel Holley 94 or Stromberg 97 carburetors.

elbow, 1/8 inch NPT. Install a Mopar Performance Parts (Chrysler Corporation) BU-1412 PCV valve (one end is threaded for 1/8 inch NPT) in the 90-degree elbow. Drill and tap a 1/8-inch-NPT hole on the right side of the intake manifold approximately 1 1/2 inches below the carburetor mounting flange (the front one, if dual), and install a new Weatherhead 3400-2 polished-brass 90-degree elbow, 1/8 inch NPT. Install a new Weatherhead 1068-4 polished-brass male connector, 1/4-inch-i.d. hose to 1/8 inch NPT, in the 90-degree elbow. Connect the PCV valve and hose fitting using a piece of 1/4-inch-i.d. PCV hose with stainless-steel line clamps. Block off the road-draft opening in the oil pan. Fresh air will be drawn through the crankcase breather/oil filler tube, and the crankcase will be vented through the PCV valve.

B. INTAKE SYSTEM SUMMARY

- Edelbrock 1035 polished cast-aluminum super dual-carburetor intake manifold installed with new stainless-steel hex-head bolts and AN flat washers using Loctite and torqued to 25 ft-lbs. Intake manifold gasket installed using silicone sealant. New J. C. Whitney & Company 38SZ2774R chrome acorn nut covers installed. **$450**
- Rebuilt two x two-barrel Stromberg 81 carburetors, 81/100-inch (13/16-inch) venturi, 250 cfm (approximate total) installed with new Papco 264-016 engine studs, 5/16 by 1 3/4 inches long (reduced to 1 1/2 inches long), and new polished stainless-steel acorn nuts and lockwashers using anti-seize compound. New Vintage Speed CL-1006 ball-socket universal inline dual-carburetor linkage installed. NOS Moon Equipment Company 1250 chrome air scoops installed. **$879**
- Rebuilt Ford 52-9350 mechanical fuel pump installed with new polished stainless-steel hex-head bolts and lockwashers using Loctite. Fuel pump gasket installed using silicone sealant. New Mr. Gasket 6151 chrome fuel block with new Weatherhead 1068-4-4 polished male connectors, 5/16-inch-i.d. hose to 1/4 inch NPT, installed with new Mooneyes USA AF4215 red vinyl fuel lines, 5/16 inch i.d., using new stainless-steel line clamps. **$97.80**

- Intake System Total: **$1,426.80**

CHAPTER 37
IGNITION SYSTEM

A. IGNITION SYSTEM
DISTRIBUTOR

The Ford 12130 dome-type distributor that the factory installed on 1937–1940 Ford V8-60 engines was described as a three-bolt model, although there are four mounting bolts. This distributor was also used on 1937–1941 Ford flathead V-8 engines, which have a slightly different three-bolt pattern, thus the reason for the four mounting bolt holes. Since this distributor utilizes dual breaker points and operates on 6 volts, it was not installed on the engine described here. The Ford 12036 ignition coil is part of the Ford 12130 dome-type distributors. The distributor is secured to the front of the timing gear cover with three pieces: 5/16-inch-NC by 1-inch-long hex-head bolts and lockwashers.

This Ford 12130 dome-type polished distributor was used on Ford V8-60 engines. The Ford 12036 ignition coil mounted on top is 6 volts.

This Mallory 5072001 magnetic breakerless distributor is for 1942–1948 Ford flathead V-8 engines. Aside from the bolt pattern, it is the same as the Mallory 5072101 model for the pre-1942 flathead and Ford V8-60 engines.

A number of aftermarket three-bolt distributors were produced for Ford flathead V-8 engines in the 1940s and 1950s. The Joe Hunt magneto, Harman & Collins dual-point/dual-coil distributor, Kong dual-point/dual-coil distributor, Mallory dual-point distributors, Spaulding Brothers dual-point/dual-coil distributor, and the Wico (Witherbee Ignitor Company of Springfield, Massachusetts) magneto were some of the more popular types.

A good electronic ignition is mandatory today for any street performance Ford V8-60 engine. The Mallory (Mr. Gasket) 5072101 magnetic breakerless distributor and Mallory 3772101 Unilite model, which is triggered by a self-contained photo-optic infrared LED system, are excellent crab-style centrifugal (mechanical) advance distributors for Ford V8-60 and pre-1942 Ford flathead V-8 engines. The current retail price for either model is $320, and they are available from any Mr. Gasket dealer.

Installing the Mallory 611 power cell is highly recommended when using a Mallory magnetic breakerless or Unilite distributor. It will protect the distributor module from power surges, especially when used in conjunction with a generator.

The MSD 8353 Pro-Billet distributor is the three-bolt model for pre-1942 Ford flathead V-8 engines. This quality distributor is available from most speed-equipment dealers for the current retail price of $340. The MSD 8353 distributor must be used with the MSD 6A or 6AL multiple-spark discharge ignition control, or similar magnetic triggered controls. Note: The Mallory and MSD distributors just described are all 12 volts, negative ground.

COIL AND IGNITION CONTROL
> *Refer to Chapter 7.*

SPARK PLUG WIRES AND SPARK PLUGS
The Ford 52-12280 and 52-12281 spark plug wire tubes were installed on each side of the Ford V8-60 intake manifold. The tubes do not look bad, although they do nothing to keep the spark plug wires separated. Refer to Chapter 27 for information pertaining to spark plug wires and spark plugs.

GENERATOR
The Ford 81A-10000-D generator was installed on 1937–1940 Ford V8-60 engines. This generator was the two-brush design and operated on 6 volts. As a result, it was not used on the engine described here; instead, a 1956 Ford B6A-10002-A generator was installed. Refer to Chapter 27 for information about the Ford B6A-10002-A generator.

STARTING MOTOR
If the starting motor is not being constantly used, a 12-volt electrical system will not damage the 6-volt Ford 18-11002 starting motor used on Ford V8-60 engines. If it is, the 6-volt start-

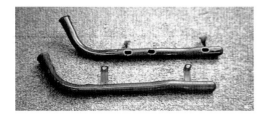

This Ford 81A-10000-D generator was installed on Ford V8-60 engines. It is a two-brush design and operates on 6 volts. The reverse current cut-out switch is mounted on the top.

These are the Ford 52-12280 and 52-12281 spark plug wire tubes for Ford V8-60 engines. They certainly do not keep the spark plug wires separated.

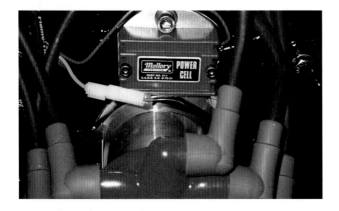

This is a NOS Ford 52-11375 starter drive spring for Ford V8-60 starting motors.

This Mallory 611 power cell should be installed when a generator is used with the Mallory 5072101 or 3772101 distributors.

ing motor will not last. It was used on both the Ford flathead V-8 engines and the Ford V8-60 engines, but the starter drive is smaller in the Ford V8-60 starting motors. Ford V8-60 starter drives are becoming harder to locate, and at the present time, no aftermarket company is manufacturing a replacement starting motor.

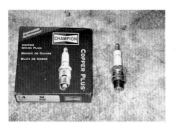

Here is a set of Champion H10C Copper Plus resistor-type 18-millimeter spark plugs, which are suitable for any Ford flathead V-8 engine.

B. IGNITION SYSTEM SUMMARY

- New Mallory 5072101 magnetic breakerless crab-style distributor (for 1932–1941 Ford) full centrifugal (mechanical) advance, installed with new polished stainless-steel hex-head bolts and lockwashers using anti-seize compound. New MSD 6A 6200 multiple-spark discharge ignition control and new MSD 8200 Blaster 2 chrome ignition coil, 45,000 volts, installed. New Mr. Gasket 6777 chrome ignition coil bracket installed. **$513.76**
- New Pertronix Performance Products 808290 Flame Thrower high-performance 8-millimeter spark plug wires, black 90-degree boots, installed with new Spectre 4245 chrome/plastic professional wire separators. New Champion H10C Copper Plus resistor-type 18-millimeter spark plugs installed with 0.050-inch gap using anti-seize compound and torqued to 15 ft-lbs. **$64.55**
- Rebuilt 1956 Ford B6A-10002-A chrome generator, rated at 30 amps and 15 volts, installed with polished stainless-steel custom mounting brackets. New Koyo K62002RS03 front bearing and 62032RSC3 rear bearing installed. New Super Sunny S8867 polished-aluminum generator fan installed with new polished-aluminum custom generator pulley. **$326.40**
- Rebuilt 1939 Ford V8-60 starting motor, 6 volts, installed. Starting motor painted with PPG DGHS 9000 black high-gloss polyurethane. **$179.17**

- Ignition System Summary: **$1,083.88**

The Ford 18-11002 starting motor operates on 6 volts. The starter drive assembly is smaller than those on Ford flathead V-8 starting motors.

CHAPTER 38
COOLING SYSTEM AND MISCELLANEOUS

A. COOLING SYSTEM AND MISCELLANEOUS
WATER PUMPS

The two holes for the water pumps in the timing gear cover installed on the 1937 Ford V8-60 engine are tapered. These water pump bodies are tapered to fit the holes. The two holes for the water pumps in the timing gear cover for the late 1937–1940 Ford V8-60 engines are straight. The late 1937–1940 Ford V8-60 water pump bodies are straight to fit the holes. There were reportedly four different water pumps for Ford V8-60 engines. Aside from the two types of water pumps just mentioned, any other differences are most likely cosmetic in nature, such as rubber cones over the shafts at the front of the pulleys.

Locating repair kits for Ford V8-60 water pumps is very difficult nowadays. Jitney Auto Parts has recently been able to find enough individual parts to assemble complete water pump repair kits. It is the only source for repair kits that I am aware of, other than the occasional repair kit or water pump appearing on eBay.

A common practice for Ford V8-60 racing engines is to eliminate the Ford 52-6109 timing gear cover and Ford 52-8505 water pumps. The cast-iron timing gear cover was replaced with an aftermarket aluminum model, such as those manufactured by Eddie Meyer and Offenhauser, which blocked off the water pump openings in the engine block. The baffles inside the engine block behind the water pumps were ground away, and the water elbows on the sides at the front (behind the water pumps) of the engine block were blocked off. Both sides of the engine block were drilled and tapped for the installation of water manifolds, which were connected to a crankshaft-driven water pump. The Offenhauser 10701 cast-aluminum water manifolds are still manufactured today, and the retail price is $180 for an unpolished pair. The Offenhauser 15958 crankshaft-driven water pump is also available for the current retail price of $300. This system is designed for race use and should not be applied to a street performance Ford V8-60 engine.

LABOR

The labor costs for checking clearances, gapping piston rings, degreeing the camshaft, painting and detailing, trial assembly of the engine, final assembly of the engine, and the initial startup of the engine have not been included in Section B of the previous chapters on the Ford flathead V8-60 engine. I will include that cost at the end of this chapter.

Here is a pair of rebuilt Ford 52-8505 water pumps for late 1937–1940 Ford V8-60 engines. The bodies are straight and not tapered like those used on the early 1937 Ford V8-60 engines.

B. COOLING
SYSTEM AND MISCELLANEOUS SUMMARY

- Rebuilt 1939 Ford 52-8505 water pumps installed. Water pump gaskets installed using silicone sealant. Water pumps painted with PPG 74000 red high-gloss polyurethane. **$208.33**
- Labor for checking clearances, gapping piston rings, degreeing the camshaft, painting and detailing, trial engine assembly, final engine assembly, and initial engine startup. **$1,200**

- Cooling System and Miscellaneous Total: **$1,408.33**

Note: The estimated output of this engine is: 145 horsepower at 5,500 rpm and 152 ft-lbs. Torque at 4,000 rpm (See Dyno Printouts).

Ford Flathead V8-60 Engine Total:
$1,536.66 Engine block total
$707 Crankshaft total
$1,394.67 Connecting rods and pistons total
$425 Lubrication system total
$2,149.85 Camshaft and cylinder heads total
$1,426.80 Intake system total
$1,083.88 Ignition system total
$1,408.33 Cooling system and miscellaneous total
$10,132.19 Total

CHAPTER 39
MISSING PARTS

EXHAUST MANIFOLDS

The Ford 52-9430 cast-iron exhaust manifolds were mounted on Ford V8-60 engine blocks using Ford 352675-S exhaust manifold studs, which have 5/16-inch-NC threads on both ends. If the exhaust manifold studs are damaged or missing,

The Ford 52-9430 cast-iron exhaust manifolds for Ford V8-60 engines are pictured here.

install new Papco 264-016 engine studs, 5/16 inch by 1 3/4 inches long. These engine studs have 5/16-inch-NC threads on the engine block end and 5/16-inch-NF threads on the exhaust manifold end. Install the exhaust manifold studs in the engine block using Permatex aviation form-a-gasket, and apply anti-seize compound to the threads on the exhaust manifold end. Install the exhaust manifold gaskets using Permatex ultra copper high-temperature silicone sealant, and torque the exhaust manifold stud nuts to 25 ft-lbs.

Red's Headers manufactures high-quality headers and exhaust systems for most Ford flathead V-8–powered hot rods and custom vehicles. The exhaust headers are fabricated with 3/8-inch-thick flanges and 16-gauge steel tubing. They are available with a straight nickel finish, chrome plating, or metallic-ceramic coating. Red's Headers should also be able to supply exhaust headers for a Ford V8-60 engine.

This is a Ford 52-6384 flywheel, a Ford 52-7563 Borg & Beck pressure plate, and a Ford 52-7550 clutch disc, 8.750 inches o.d. for Ford V8-60 engines.

FLYWHEEL AND CLUTCH ASSEMBLY

The Ford 52-6384 heat-treated steel flywheel is 12.250 inches o.d., the ring gear has 120 teeth, and the flywheel weighs 33 pounds. The Ford 52-7563 Borg & Beck pressure plate is used with the Ford 52-7550 clutch disc, 8.750 inches o.d. Ford V8-60 engines were equipped with a three-speed standard (manual) transmission designed specifically for that engine. To adapt a later-model transmission to Ford V8-60 engines, a custom bell housing adapter will have to be fabricated.

The Ford 52-6384 flywheel is installed with 52-6387 dowels (two), the 52-7609 flywheel bolt washer plate, and 350645-S flywheel bolts (four). The flywheel bolts are torqued to 65 ft-lbs using Loctite. The Ford 52-7563 pressure plate is installed with 350433-S pressure plate bolts (six) and 34846-S lock washers (six). The pressure plate should be torqued to 35 ft-lbs using Loctite. If the pressure plate bolts are damaged or missing, install ARP 150-2201 high-performance series hex-head pressure plate bolts, 170,000 psi.

CHAPTER 40
ASSEMBLY

ASSEMBLY

Note: The engine described in this section was not assembled and completed. However, the following information will explain how to properly assemble a Ford V8-60 engine. The pictures at the end of this chapter and in Dyno Printouts are of vehicles in the collection of the appropriately named Ron Ford, owner of Ocean Park Ford (a dealership in Surrey, BC, Canada) and a lifelong hot rodder. These photographs will give the reader an idea of what types of vehicles ran Ford V8-60 engines.

ENGINE BLOCK

1. Clean the camshaft bearings with clean solvent using a clean, lint-free cloth. Install the camshaft bearings dry in the engine block using a camshaft bearing installation tool (this is a must!). Take special care to line up the oil holes in the camshaft bearings with the oil holes in the engine block. Do not lubricate the camshaft bearing bosses.

2. Install a new stainless-steel 1/8-inch-NPT plug in the oil gallery line at the front of the engine block (behind the camshaft gear) using pipe thread sealant. Install a new stainless-steel 1/8-inch-NPT plug in the oil gallery line at the rear of the engine block (above the camshaft rear boss plug) using pipe thread sealant. Install the camshaft rear boss plug using Permatex aviation form-a-gasket, and tap it into position using a similar-size socket with a rubber mallet. Install the fuel pump pushrod bushing plug using Permatex aviation form-a-gasket, and tap it into place with a rubber mallet. Install the two freeze plugs in the bottom center of the oil pan rails (one on each side) using Permatex aviation form-a-gasket, and tap them into place using a similar-sized socket with a rubber mallet. Install two new stainless-steel 1/4-inch-NPT water jacket drain plugs in the front of the engine block (one on each side behind the water pumps) using pipe thread sealant.

3. Install the camshaft gear on the snout of the camshaft using a hydraulic press. The line on the camshaft gear must line up with a line on the camshaft snout to guarantee accurate timing. Lubricate the camshaft bearings using Clevite 77 Bearing Guard, and generously apply camshaft assembly lubricant (provided by the camshaft manufacturer) to the lobes of the camshaft. Gently slide the camshaft into the engine block, taking care not to nick the camshaft bearings.

CRANKSHAFT

1. Install the rear upper oil seal retainer in the rear of the engine block using silicone sealant, and tap it into position with a rubber mallet.

2. Clean the main bearings with clean solvent using a clean, lint-free cloth. Line up the locking tang on the main bearings with the notch in the main bearing saddles, and install the main bearings in the engine block dry. Do not lubricate the main bearing saddles in the engine block. Use Clevite 77 Bearing Guard to lubricate the face of the main bearings after installing them in the engine block. Line up the locking tang on the main bearings with the notch in the main bearing caps, and install the main bearings in the main bearing caps dry. Do not lubricate the main bearing caps. Use Clevite 77 Bearing Guard to lubricate the face of the main bearings after installing them in the main bearing caps.

3. Place the crankshaft gear woodruff key in the crankshaft using anti-seize compound, and gently tap the woodruff key into position with a hammer. Apply anti-seize compound to the snout of the crankshaft, and slide the crankshaft gear onto the snout as far as it will go by hand. The side with the dot or line on the crankshaft gear faces outward. Line up the crankshaft gear with the crankshaft gear woodruff key, and gently tap the crankshaft gear into position using a piece of pipe a little larger than the diameter of the crankshaft snout.

4. Install the main bearing cap studs in the engine block using Molykote, and tighten them snugly in position by hand.

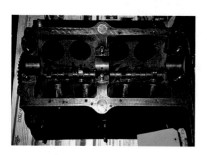
The camshaft has been installed to check the end play. It will be removed and the lobes coated with camshaft assembly lubricant prior to the final installation.

The pistons have been installed on the connecting rods, and the assemblies are now ready for the installation of the piston rings.

The crankshaft has been installed, and the main bearing cap stud nuts have been torqued to 80 ft-lbs. Notice the oil pump on the No. 1 main bearing cap and the two frost plugs in the bottom center of the oil pan rails.

Gently lower the crankshaft into the main bearing saddles, taking special care not to nick the crankshaft bearings. Make certain to line up the timing marks on the crankshaft and camshaft gears. The crankshaft gear has a dot or line, as does the camshaft gear. Vertically line up these marks with each other. Place the main bearing caps in their correct order in the engine block, with the locking tang in the engine block and the locking tang in the main bearing caps on the same side. Lubricate the main bearing cap studs with Molykote, install the stud nuts, and torque them to 80 ft-lbs. Weave a piece of stainless-steel wire through the holes in the main bearing cap studs for each of the main bearing caps. This procedure is not mandatory, but it is a good safety practice. The crankshaft should now turn freely in the engine block. Slide the oil slinger onto the crankshaft snout.

CONNECTING RODS AND PISTONS

1. Remove the wrist pin from the pistons. Coat the wrist pin bushings in the connecting rods and the wrist pins with motor oil. Some cast pistons have an arrow marking on the piston head, or an "F" cast into the side, to indicate which side faces the front of the engine block. The cylinder numbers stamped in the bottom of the connecting rods always face outward from the crankshaft.

2. Assemble the connecting rods and pistons, and install the wrist pin retainers. Gap all the piston rings for all the cylinders. Install the piston rings on the pistons using a piston ring expander tool, and rotate each of the piston rings on the pistons so they are within the manufacturer's recommended arc, also known as "preferred ring gap location".

3. Clean the connecting rod bearings with clean solvent using a clean, lint-free cloth. Apply Clevite 77 Bearing Guard to both sides of all the connecting rod bearings. Place plastic connecting rod bolt protectors on the connecting rod studs. Apply motor oil to the inside of the piston ring compressor, and place the piston ring compressor around the piston. Tighten the piston ring compressor, and insert the connecting rod into the cylinder with the cylinder number on the bottom of the connecting rod facing outward from

the crankshaft. Gently tap the piston down into the cylinder using the handle of a rubber mallet or a piece of wood. Guide the connecting rod studs around the crankshaft journal while pushing the piston downward. Just before the connecting rod is on the crankshaft journal, install one of the connecting rod bearings on the crankshaft journal and tap the connecting rod into position. After the connecting rod is in place on the crankshaft journal, install the other half of the connecting rod bearing on the crankshaft journal. Install the connecting rod cap with the locking tang on the same side as the locking tang in the connecting rod. Install the connecting rod nuts using Loctite, and torque them to 40 ft-lbs. Repeat this procedure for the rest of the connecting rod and piston assemblies. Weave a piece of stainless-steel wire through the holes in the connecting rod studs for each of the connecting rods. This procedure is not mandatory, but it is a good safety practice.

4. Install the crankshaft bolt in the crankshaft, and turn the crankshaft. The rotating assembly should turn over smoothly. Use a feeler gauge to check the side clearance for each pair of connecting rods.

LUBRICATION SYSTEM

1. Install the oil pump cover and inlet tube gasket using silicone sealant. Lubricate the oil pump gears with motor oil, and install the oil pump cover and inlet tube using Loctite on the bolts, and torque them to 15 ft-lbs. Weave a piece of stainless-steel wire through the head of the oil pump cover and inlet tube bolts. Make certain the oil return tube is in position in the rear main bearing cap.

2. Apply some anti-seize compound to the crankshaft snout, slide the crankshaft pulley on the crankshaft snout, and line it up with the crankshaft gear woodruff key. Tap the crankshaft pulley into position using a piece of wood and a hammer. Install the crankshaft pulley bolt and flat washer using Loctite, and torque the bolt to 50 ft-lbs.

3. Install the cord material front oil seal in the timing gear cover by rolling it in place with a large socket, or use the

The white paint on the camshaft and crankshaft gears indicates the timing marks. The oil pan is in place to check the oil pump pickup screen clearance. Notice the oil slinger.

head of a large ball peen hammer and tap the head with another hammer. Install the timing gear cover gasket using silicone sealant. Install the timing gear cover using Loctite on the bolts and lockwashers, and torque them to 15 ft-lbs.

4. The flywheel must be installed prior to installing the oil pan. Place the flywheel on the end of the crankshaft, and install the flywheel bolt washer plate and flywheel bolts using Loctite and torque them to 65 ft-lbs. Install the pilot bearing in the crankshaft using anti-seize compound. It is easier to install the clutch disc and pressure plate before installing the oil pan. Install the pressure plate bolts and lockwashers (or flat washers) using Loctite, and torque them to 35 ft-lbs.

5. Place some putty on the oil pump pickup screen, and position the oil pan. Push down firmly on the oil pan, and then remove it. Measure the compressed thickness of the putty. The proper oil-pan-to-oil-pump-pickup-screen

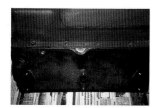

The oil pan is ready to be bolted in place. The exhaust manifold studs have been installed. Notice the water outlet elbow cast into the front of the engine block.

clearance should be 3/4 to 1 inch. If the clearance is correct, carry on. If the clearance is not correct, adjust the oil pump pickup arm until the correct clearance is obtained. Install the cord material front oil seal in the oil pan by rolling it in place with a large socket, or use the head of a large ball peen hammer and tap the head with another hammer. Install the cork material rear oil pan seal on the rear main bearing cap using silicone sealant. Install the oil pan gaskets using silicone sealant. Place the oil pan in position, and install the oil pan bolts, lockwashers, and AN flat washers using Loctite and torque them to 15 ft-lbs. Screw the dipstick tube into the dipstick tube boss using silicone sealant, and install the dipstick.

CAMSHAFT AND CYLINDER HEADS

Refer to Chapter 10 for information on how to degree the camshaft.

1. Lubricate the body of the valve lifters with motor oil, and apply camshaft assembly lubricant (provided by the camshaft manufacturer) to the face of the valve lifters. Install all the valve lifters in the engine block.

2. Lubricate the valve stems with motor oil, slide the valve springs over the valve stems, and install the valve spring retainers. Lubricate the valve guide bushings with motor oil, and slide them down the top of the valve springs until the two pieces are locked together. Insert the valve assembly in the valve guide boss, and pull the valve guide bushing down using a valve spring compressor. Then install the crow's-foot valve guide bushing retainer. Repeat this procedure for the rest of the valve assemblies.

The Ford 52-6513 valve springs, 52-6514 valve spring retainers, and 52-6512 crow's-foot valve guide bushing retainers are laid out for assembly.

3. Refer to Chapter 10 for information on how to adjust the valves. Place some putty on any intake and exhaust valves for the same cylinder, and then place the cylinder head in position on the engine block. Lightly tighten the cylinder head down using two cylinder head studs and nuts (at each end). Do not use a cylinder head gasket. Turn the crankshaft through 360 degrees at least twice. Remove the cylinder head and measure the thickness of the compressed putty. The absolute minimum valve-to-cylinder-head clearance is 0.040 inch.

4. Install the valve lifter gallery oil pressure relief valve using Permatex aviation form-a-gasket. Snap the valve lifter gallery baffle into position.

5. Install the cylinder head studs in the engine block using Permatex aviation form-a-gasket, and tighten them snugly. Coat the shank of the cylinder head studs with anti-seize compound. Spray the copper sandwiched cylinder head gaskets with Permatex copper spray-a-gasket, and then install them. Place the cylinder heads over the cylinder head studs, and install the hardened flat washers and cylinder head stud nuts using Molykote. Torque the cylinder head stud nuts to 30 ft-lbs (for aluminum cylinder heads) using the factory-approved torque pattern. Do not install the chrome acorn nut covers until the engine has been initially started and the cylinder heads have been retorqued.

INTAKE SYSTEM

1. Install the carburetor studs in the intake manifold using anti-seize compound. Place the carburetor gaskets in position on the intake manifold. Install the carburetors on the intake manifold using anti-seize compound on the studs, and tighten the acorn nuts and lockwashers snugly. Do not over-

The Ford 52-6524 valve lifter gallery baffle and 52-6310 oil slinger for the Ford V8-60 engine have been painted with Glyptal G-1228A medium-gray gloss enamel.

tighten these nuts. Install and adjust the carburetor linkage using anti-seize compound on the linkage arm screws. Install the fuel pump gasket using silicone sealant. Place the fuel

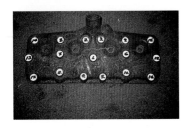
The factory-recommended torque pattern for the Ford V8-60 cylinder heads is shown here.

pump in position on the rear of the intake manifold, and torque the bolts to 15 ft-lbs using anti-seize compound.

2. Trace the outline of the intake manifold on the intake manifold gasket, and trim the gasket accordingly. Install the intake manifold gasket using silicone sealant. Place the intake manifold in position on the engine block, install the bolts and AN flat washers using Loctite, and torque them to 25 ft-lbs. Install the chrome acorn nut covers on the intake manifold bolts. Install the air cleaners and the crankcase breather/oil filler tube cap.

3. Install the fuel fittings in the carburetors and the fuel block using pipe thread sealant. Cut the fuel line to length, install it from the fuel block to the carburetors, and tighten the fuel line clamps.

IGNITION SYSTEM

1. Rotate the crankshaft until the engine is set with the No. 1 piston at 10 degrees before top dead center (TDC), and insert the distributor in the timing gear cover with the distributor rotor at the No. 1 spark plug lead position. The distributor will only fit in one position because the distributor drive slot in the camshaft nose is offset. Install the three distributor housing bolts and lockwash-

The Edelbrock 1035 polished-aluminum super dual intake manifold with Stromberg 81 carburetors is pictured here. The Ford 52-9350 mechanical fuel pump, Vintage Speed CL-2B carburetor linkage, and Moon Equipment Company 1250 chrome air scoops have been installed.

ers using anti-seize compound, and tighten them snugly.

2. Gap the spark plugs at 0.050 inch (for use with an ignition control box), and install them in the cylinder heads using anti-seize compound and torque them to 15 ft-lbs (for aluminum cylinder heads). Lay out the spark plug wires, and cut them to length for each cylinder. The cylinders on the right side are numbered 1, 2, 3, and 4 from the front of the engine block. The cylinders on the left side are numbered 5, 6, 7, and 8 from the front of the engine block. The firing order is 1, 5, 4, 8, 6,

3, 7, and 2. Install the spark plug wires on the spark plugs and in the distributor cap. Install the ignition coil with the ignition coil bracket. Connect the ignition coil wire to the distributor.

3. Install the generator mounting brackets on the cylinder head on the left side, and install the generator in the generator mounting brackets using anti-seize compound on the bolts. Install the starting motor in the oil pan using anti-seize compound on the bolts.

4. Install the water pump gaskets using silicone sealant. Screw the water pumps into the timing gear cover, and tighten them snugly. Install the crankshaft pulley/water pump pulleys/generator pulley V-belt, allowing for 3/4 inch to 1 inch slack.

5. Install the exhaust manifold studs in the engine block using Permatex aviation form-a-gasket. Install the exhaust manifold gaskets using Permatex ultra copper high-temperature silicone sealant. Place the exhaust manifolds over the studs, and install the stud nuts and lockwashers using anti-seize compound and torque them to 25 ft-lbs.

6. Mount a radiator with some water in it, connect the ignition system with a starter switch, and hook up a battery. Start the engine, and adjust the timing and carburetors. Allow the engine to run at approximately 2,000 rpm for 30 minutes to break in the camshaft. After the engine is at full operating temperature, shut it off and allow the engine to cool. Retorque the cylinder heads using the factory-approved torque pattern, and install the chrome acorn nut covers on the cylinder head stud nuts.

A 1939 Ford 52-6019-B cast-iron timing gear cover and a pair of rebuilt Ford 52-8505 water pumps are shown here.

This 1939 midget race car is powered by a Ford flathead V8-60 engine equipped with Robert Roof cylinder heads and intake manifold (shown in Chapter 36). Ron Ford purchased the car from a collector in San Diego, California, in 1987.

APPENDIX A
DYNO PRINTOUTS

CHEVROLET 348-CI TURBO-THRUST V-8 ENGINE

Note: The estimated output of this engine is 251 horsepower at 4,000 rpm and 375 ft-lbs torque at 3,000 rpm.

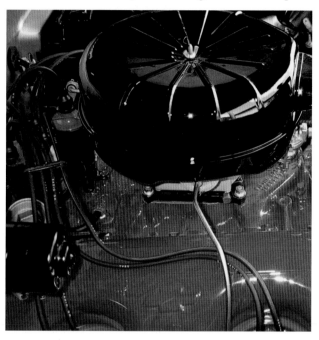

This is the Chevrolet 348-ci V-8 engine described in Section I. It was built by High Performance Engines for installation in a daily-driven 1958 Chevrolet Bel Air Impala sports coupe, two-door hardtop.

SHORT BLOCK

Block: CHEVROLET.	Bore: 4.155 in	Stroke: 3.250 in
Cylinders: 8	Cyl Vol: 722.1 cc	Total Vol: 352.5 ci

CYLINDER HEADS

Cylinder Heads:	Wedge/Stock Ports And Valves		
Air Flow File:	***		
Intake Valves:	1	Exhaust Valves:	1
Intake Valve:	1.938 in	Exhaust Valve:	1.656 in

COMPRESSION

Compression Ratio:	9.50	Combustion Space:	85.0 cc

INDUCTION

Induction Flow:	486.0 cfm	@ 1.5 inHg	Fuel: Gasoline
Manifold Type:	Dual-Plane Manifold		N20: 0.0 lbs/min

Blower: None		Intercooler: *** %
Flow: *** cfm	Pressure Ratio: ***	Boost Limit: *** psi
Speed: *** rpm	Belt Gear Ratio: ***	Surge Flow: *** cfm
Eff: *** %	Internal Gear Ratio: ***	

EXHAUST

Exhaust System:	H.P. Manifolds And Mufflers

CAMSHAFT

Camshaft Type:	S.P. #CS-171.	Cam File: ***
Lifter:	Hyd.	Lobe Center: 112.0
Cam Specs @:	0.050-Lift	Valve Overlap: -30.0
Int Lift@Valve:	0.400 in	Int Duration: 190.0
Exh Lift@Valve:	0.412 in	Exh Duration: 198.0
Nominal Timing		Timing@ Adv(+)/Ret(-): 0.0

IVO (BTDC): -13.0	IVC (ABDC): 23.0	IVO: -13.0	IVC: 23.0
EVO (BBDC): 35.0	EVC (ATDC): -17.0	EVO: 35.0	EVC: -17.0
ICA (ATDC): 108.0	ECA (BTDC): 116.0	ICA: 108.0	ECA: 116.0

CALCULATED POWER AND ENGINE PRESSURES

Engine RPM	Power (Fly)	Torque (Fly)	Int Man Pressure	Vol Eff %	IMEP Pressure	FMEP Pressure	BMEP Pressure
2000	141	369	14.63	76.0	206.0	17.0	160.2
2500	178	373	14.58	77.7	199.7	18.3	162.0
3000	214	375	14.52	79.7	197.6	19.6	162.6
3500	238	357	14.44	79.6	187.0	21.1	155.1
4000	251	329	14.36	77.7	173.9	22.6	142.7
4500	249	290	14.29	73.8	157.9	24.3	126.0
5000	230	242	14.25	68.2	137.2	26.0	104.9
5500	204	194	14.23	62.6	117.2	27.9	84.3
6000	164	144	14.23	56.3	95.9	29.8	62.4
6500	122	98	14.25	50.7	77.0	31.8	42.6
7000	72	54	14.28	45.4	58.6	33.9	23.3
7500	23	16	14.31	40.7	43.6	36.2	7.0
8000	0	0	14.35	36.1	28.1	38.5	-9.8
8500	0	0	14.39	32.2	16.2	40.9	-23.3
9000	0	0	14.42	28.5	4.8	43.4	-36.4
9500	0	0	14.46	25.0	-5.3	46.0	-48.4
10000	0	0	14.49	22.2	-12.8	48.7	-58.0
10500	0	0	14.52	19.4	-19.9	51.5	-67.3
11000	0	0	14.55	17.2	-25.2	54.4	-75.1

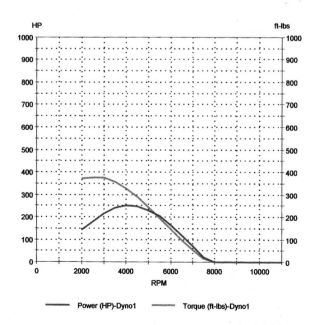

Power (HP)-Dyno1   Torque (ft-lbs)-Dyno1

Dyno Printouts

CHEVROLET 409-CI V-8 ENGINE

Note: The estimated output of this engine is 485 horsepower at 5,500 rpm and 551 ft-lbs torque at 3,500 rpm.

This is the Chevrolet 409-ci V-8 engine described in Section II. It was built by High Performance Engines and completed by the owner for installation in a 1964 Chevy II Nova two-door coupe.

SHORT BLOCK

Block: CHEVROLET.		Bore: 4.353 in	Stroke: 4.000 in
Cylinders: 8		Cyl Vol: 975.5 cc	Total Vol: 476.2 ci

CYLINDER HEADS

Cylinder Heads:	Wedge/Pocket Porting, Large Valves		
Air Flow File:	***		
Intake Valves:	1	Exhaust Valves:	1
Intake Valve:	2.200 in	Exhaust Valve:	1.735 in

COMPRESSION

Compression Ratio:	8.00	Combustion Space: 139.4 cc

INDUCTION

Induction Flow:	1200.0 cfm @ 1.5 inHg		Fuel: Gasoline
Manifold Type:	Forced Induction		N20: 0.0 lbs/min

Blower:	Roots- BDS 671 (Street)			Intercooler:	*** %
Flow:	390.0 cfm	Pressure Ratio:	***	Boost Limit:	4.5 psi
Speed:	*** rpm	Belt Gear Ratio:	1.10	Surge Flow:	*** cfm
Eff:	55.0 %	Internal Gear Ratio:	***		

EXHAUST

Exhaust System:	Forced Induction Exhaust

CAMSHAFT

Camshaft Type:	ISKY #296HYD.	Cam File:	***
Lifter:	Hyd.	Lobe Center:	110.0
Cam Specs @:	0.050-Lift	Valve Overlap:	14.0
Int Lift@Valve:	0.509 in	Int Duration:	234.0
Exh Lift@Valve:	0.509 in	Exh Duration:	234.0
Nominal Timing		Timing@ Adv(+)/Ret(-):	0.0

IVO (BTDC): 7.0	IVC (ABDC): 47.0	IVO: 7.0	IVC: 47.0
EVO (BBDC): 47.0	EVC (ATDC): 7.0	EVO: 47.0	EVC: 7.0
ICA (ATDC): 110.0	ECA (BTDC): 110.0	ICA: 110.0	ECA: 110.0

CALCULATED POWER AND ENGINE PRESSURES

Engine RPM	Power (Fly)	Torque (Fly)	Int Man Pressure	Vol Eff %	IMEP Pressure	FMEP Pressure	BMEP Pressure
2000	178	466	16.02	76.8	194.9	18.2	149.8
2500	245	515	17.06	85.0	205.1	19.9	165.4
3000	307	537	18.09	91.0	210.4	21.7	172.4
3500	368	551	19.10	97.1	213.1	23.6	177.1
4000	412	541	19.05	99.3	210.0	25.7	173.8
4500	455	531	19.00	100.9	208.6	28.0	170.4
5000	479	503	18.95	100.9	201.6	30.4	161.5
5500	485	463	18.89	99.5	190.6	32.9	148.7
6000	470	411	18.84	96.3	175.7	35.6	132.1
6500	443	358	18.81	92.1	160.2	38.5	114.8
7000	404	303	18.78	87.7	144.6	41.4	97.3
7500	356	249	18.77	82.4	129.5	44.6	80.1
8000	312	204	18.77	78.0	117.4	47.8	65.7
8500	247	153	18.76	72.7	103.2	51.3	49.0
9000	206	120	18.77	69.2	95.7	54.8	38.6
9500	134	74	18.77	64.7	83.7	58.5	23.8
10000	83	44	18.78	61.4	77.2	62.4	14.0
10500	14	7	18.78	57.9	68.8	66.4	2.3
11000	0	0	18.80	54.1	59.8	70.5	-10.1

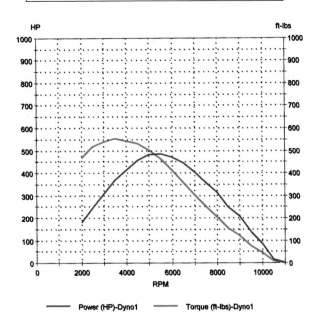

Power (HP)-Dyno1 ——— Torque (ft-lbs)-Dyno1

LINCOLN 337-CI FLATHEAD V-8 ENGINE

Note: The estimated output of this engine is 223 horsepower at 3,500 rpm and 373 ft-lbs torque at 2,000 rpm.

This is the Lincoln 337-ci flathead V-8 engine described in Section III. Luke's Custom Machine & Design built this engine for installation in a 1931 Ford Model A two-door sedan.

SHORT BLOCK

Block: LINCOLN "FLATHEAD".	Bore: 3.560 in	Stroke:	4.375 in
Cylinders: 8	Cyl Vol: 713.6 cc	Total Vol:	348.4 ci

CYLINDER HEADS

Cylinder Heads:	Low Performance/Stock Ports And Valves	
Air Flow File:	***	
Intake Valves:	1	Exhaust Valves: 1
Intake Valve:	1.795 in	Exhaust Valve: 1.505 in

COMPRESSION

Compression Ratio: 9.50	Combustion Space: 84.0 cc

INDUCTION

Induction Flow: 480.0 cfm @ 1.5 inHg		Fuel: Gasoline
Manifold Type: Dual-Plane Manifold		N20: 0.0 lbs/min

Blower: None			Intercooler:	*** %
Flow: *** cfm	Pressure Ratio:	***	Boost Limit:	*** psi
Speed: *** rpm	Belt Gear Ratio:	***	Surge Flow:	*** cfm
Eff: *** %	Internal Gear Ratio:	***		

EXHAUST

Exhaust System: H.P. Manifolds And Mufflers

CAMSHAFT

Camshaft Type:	CROWER "STREET"	Cam File: ***	
Lifter:	Solid	Lobe Center:	112.0
Cam Specs @:	0.050-Lift	Valve Overlap:	-12.0
Int Lift@Valve:	0.340 in	Int Duration:	212.0
Exh Lift@Valve:	0.340 in	Exh Duration:	212.0
Nominal Timing		Timing@ Adv(+)/Ret(-):	0.0

IVO (BTDC):	-2.0	IVC (ABDC):	34.0	IVO: -2.0	IVC:	34.0
EVO (BBDC):	42.0	EVC (ATDC):	-10.0	EVO: 42.0	EVC:	-10.0
ICA (ATDC):	108.0	ECA (BTDC):	116.0	ICA: 108.0	ECA:	116.0

CALCULATED POWER AND ENGINE PRESSURES

Engine RPM	Power (Fly)	Torque (Fly)	Int Man Pressure	Vol Eff %	IMEP Pressure	FMEP Pressure	BMEP Pressure
2000	142	373	14.63	74.3	212.1	18.8	163.8
2500	177	371	14.58	75.6	203.0	20.7	162.7
3000	208	364	14.53	77.1	197.7	22.8	159.8
3500	223	335	14.46	75.9	182.2	25.0	146.9
4000	221	290	14.39	72.2	162.2	27.4	127.1
4500	201	235	14.35	66.3	139.4	30.0	103.2
5000	170	179	14.33	60.0	116.0	32.8	78.5
5500	129	123	14.34	53.5	92.8	35.7	53.9
6000	80	70	14.36	47.3	71.4	38.8	30.7
6500	25	20	14.38	41.7	51.6	42.1	9.0
7000	0	0	14.41	36.5	33.3	45.6	-11.6
7500	0	0	14.45	31.8	17.8	49.2	-29.6
8000	0	0	14.48	27.9	4.9	53.0	-45.4
8500	0	0	14.51	23.9	-7.0	57.0	-60.4
9000	0	0	14.55	21.0	-15.6	61.2	-72.4
9500	0	0	14.57	18.3	-22.7	65.5	-83.2
10000	0	0	14.59	15.8	-28.6	70.0	-93.0
10500	0	0	14.61	13.8	-33.3	74.7	-101.8
11000	0	0	14.62	11.8	-37.5	79.5	-110.4

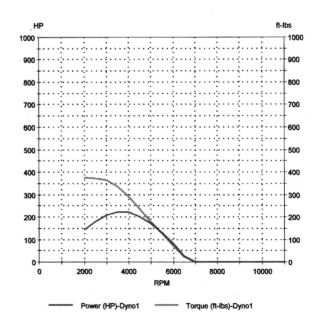

Power (HP)-Dyno1   Torque (ft-lbs)-Dyno1

FORD FLATHEAD V8-60 ENGINE

Note: The estimated output of this engine should be viewed with some caution. I had to fudge the bore and stroke numbers to achieve the displacement. My computer program for the dynometer simulation will not calculate with a bore of less than 2.800 inches. The estimated output of this engine is 145 horsepower at 5,500 rpm and 152 ft-lbs torque at 4,000 rpm.

Ron Ford owns this beautiful 1915 Ford Model T roadster. The Ford flathead V8-60 engine is featured on the front cover of this book.

SHORT BLOCK

Block: FORD V8-60.	Bore: 2.800 in	Stroke: 2.850 in
Cylinders: 8	Cyl Vol: 287.6 cc	Total Vol: 140.4 ci

CYLINDER HEADS

Cylinder Heads:	Low Performance/Stock Ports And Valves
Air Flow File:	***
Intake Valves: 1	Exhaust Valves: 1
Intake Valve: 1.277 in	Exhaust Valve: 1.275 in

COMPRESSION

Compression Ratio: 9.00	Combustion Space: 35.9 cc

INDUCTION

Induction Flow: 250.0 cfm @ 1.5 inHg	Fuel: Gasoline
Manifold Type: Dual-Plane Manifold	N20: 0.0 lbs/min
Blower: None	Intercooler: *** %
Flow: *** cfm Pressure Ratio: ***	Boost Limit: *** psi
Speed: *** rpm Belt Gear Ratio: ***	Surge Flow: *** cfm
Eff: *** % Internal Gear Ratio: ***	

EXHAUST

Exhaust System: H.P. Manifolds And Mufflers

CAMSHAFT

Camshaft Type: H & C #6412.	Cam File: ***
Lifter: Solid	Lobe Center: 112.0
Cam Specs @: Seat-To-Seat	Valve Overlap: 26.0
Int Lift@Valve: 0.272 in	Int Duration: 250.0
Exh Lift@Valve: 0.272 in	Exh Duration: 250.0
Nominal Timing	Timing@ Adv(+)/Ret(-): 0.0

IVO (BTDC): 14.0	IVC (ABDC): 56.0	IVO: 14.0	IVC: 56.0
EVO (BBDC): 58.0	EVC (ATDC): 12.0	EVO: 58.0	EVC: 12.0
ICA (ATDC): 111.0	ECA (BTDC): 113.0	ICA: 111.0	ECA: 113.0

CALCULATED POWER AND ENGINE PRESSURES

Engine RPM	Power (Fly)	Torque (Fly)	Int Man Pressure	Vol Eff %	IMEP Pressure	FMEP Pressure	BMEP Pressure
2000	50	131	14.66	67.5	184.5	16.5	142.4
2500	64	135	14.64	69.8	182.4	17.5	147.3
3000	83	146	14.61	74.8	192.7	18.6	159.0
3500	101	151	14.56	78.4	195.8	19.8	164.5
4000	116	152	14.50	80.4	196.6	21.1	165.5
4500	129	151	14.44	81.3	196.6	22.5	164.2
5000	139	146	14.37	81.4	193.0	23.9	159.6
5500	145	138	14.30	80.2	184.9	25.4	150.4
6000	143	125	14.24	76.8	171.2	27.0	136.0
6500	137	111	14.20	73.0	156.4	28.6	120.5
7000	128	96	14.18	69.1	141.2	30.3	104.6
7500	117	82	14.16	65.0	127.0	32.1	89.5
8000	104	68	14.16	61.2	112.5	34.0	74.1
8500	91	56	14.16	57.7	100.5	35.9	60.9
9000	73	42	14.16	53.8	87.0	38.0	46.2
9500	54	30	14.18	50.3	74.8	40.0	32.8
10000	36	19	14.19	47.0	63.9	42.2	20.4
10500	15	8	14.21	44.2	53.4	44.5	8.4
11000	0	0	14.23	40.9	42.7	46.8	-3.9

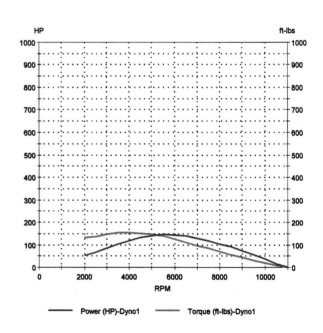

Power (HP)-Dyno1   Torque (ft-lbs)-Dyno1

APPENDIX B
RESOURCES

Listed in alphabetical order are the parties and parts sources I believe are important to know for anybody who wants to build an engine. I have given a brief explanation about these companies, which I am currently dealing with on a regular basis. I have had positive dealings with all of them. I have not received any promotional or financial considerations from any of these companies in order to mention them. This is most unfortunate, because I do not believe a container load of Beck's beer from these companies would be inappropriate!

Many excellent speed-equipment manufacturers and engine building shops are located across North America. I have not mentioned all of them in this book; for the companies that I have not used their services, I am (understandably) hesitant to recommend. It is definitely not intended as a snub of anyone or any business.

There are hundreds of manufacturers and parts outlets across North America, and it would be impossible to list them all in this book. I have mentioned a few of those companies. Most readers will have their own source for parts.

BLOWER DRIVE SERVICE
12140 East Washington Boulevard
Whittier, California 90606
Phone: 562-693-4302
Fax: 562-696-7091
Website: www.blowerdriveservice.com

CRANE CAMS
530 Fentress Boulevard
Daytona Beach, Florida 32114
Phone: 386-252-1151
Tech line: 386-258-6174
Fax: 386-258-6167
Website: www.cranecams.com

CROWER CAMS & EQUIPMENT
6180 Business Center Court
San Diego, California 92154
Phone: 619-661-6477
Fax: 619-661-6466
Website: www.crower.com
I have been buying camshafts and valvetrain components from Crower Cams & Equipment over the past number of years. Its products are of the highest quality at an affordable price.
Jerry MacLaughlin, of its technical department, has been extremely helpful and courteous with any questions I have had over the years relating to camshafts for specific applications. Every camshaft Jerry has recommended has performed exceptionally. Jerry had the nerve to retire recently; however, the technical department will continue to look after its customers.

CUNNINGHAM RODS
550 West 172 Street
Gardena, California 90248
Phone: 310-538-0605
Fax: 310-538-0695
Website: www.cunninghamrods.com
E-mail: staff@cunninghamrods.com

EDELBROCK CORPORATION
2700 California Street
Torrance, California 90503
Phone: 310-781-2222
Fax: 310-320-1187
Website: www.edelbrock.com

EGGE PARTS HOUSE
11707 Slauson Avenue
Santa Fe Springs, California 90670
Toll Free: 1-800-886-3443
Phone: 562-945-3419
Fax: 562-693-1635
Website: www.egge.com
E-mail: info@egge.com

HEDMAN STREET HEDDERS
16410 Manning Way
Cerritos, California 90703
Phone: 562-921-0404
Fax: 562-921-7515
Website: www.hedman.com
E-mail: techsupport@hedman.com

HIGH PERFORMANCE ENGINES

4329 Buchanan Street
Burnaby, British Columbia V5C 3X7
Canada
Phone: 604-299-6131
Fax: 604-299-6017

Bud Child founded High Performance Engines about 40 years ago, and his son, Dave, now owns and operates the company. Bud still turns up at the shop for limited work detail, in the hopes of receiving a handout from Dave to supplement his meager government pension!

High Performance Engines builds engines for customers from all over the Pacific Northwest, and many of these engines have produced drag racing and drag boat winners.

HONEST CHARLEY

1309 Chestnut Street
Chattanooga, Tennessee 37402
Toll free: 1-888-795-7077
Phone: 423-326-0505
Fax: 423-648-8572
Website: www.honestcharley.com
E-mail: parts@honestcharley.com

ISKENDERIAN RACING CAMS

16020 South Broadway, PO Box 30
Gardena, California 90247
Phone: 323-770-0930
Fax: 310-515-5730
Website: www.iskycams.com

JITNEY AUTO PARTS

Mr. Keith Lee
PO Box 23048, Sub 31
Saskatoon, Saskatchewan S7J 5H3
Canada
Phone: 306-668-3673
Fax: 306-668-3658

Keith Lee, the owner of Jitney Auto Parts, is one of the most knowledgeable persons about Ford flathead V-8 engines. Keith stocks most aftermarket flathead speed equipment, as well as a huge inventory of new old stock (NOS) flathead parts. He also has transmissions, rear ends, and suspension parts for early Fords. Keith is well known for his polite, prompt, and professional service, as well as his amazing packaging.

LECTRIC LIMITED

6750 West 74th Street, Suite A
Bedford Park, Illinois 60638
Phone: 708-563-0400
Fax: 708-563-0416
Website: www.lectriclimited.com

LUKE'S CUSTOM MACHINE & DESIGN

Mr. Luke Balogh
1457 Charlotte Road
North Vancouver, British Columbia V7V 1H1 Canada
Phone: 604-980-8617
Fax: 604-980-8656

Luke Balogh is an automotive machinist by trade and renowned for his aluminum designs, fabrication, and welding. He produces complete blower setups for just about any type of engine. Luke has built a variety of engines over the years, although his preferences are the Ford flathead V-8, the Ardun, and early Chrysler hemispherical engines.

MANLEY PERFORMANCE PRODUCTS

1960 Swarthmore Avenue
Lakewood, New Jersey 08701
Phone: 732-905-3366
Fax: 732-905-3010
Website: www.manleyperformance.com

MOONEYES USA

10820 South Norwalk Boulevard
Santa Fe Springs, California 90670
Phone: 562-944-6311
Fax: 562-946-2961
Website: www.mooneyes.com

OFFENHAUSER SALES CORPORATION

5300 Alhambra Avenue
PO Box 32218
Los Angeles, California 90032
Phone: 323-225-1307

PACIFIC FASTENERS (US)

18866 72nd Avenue South
Kent, Washington 98032
Phone: 425-251-3587
Fax: 425-251-1491
Website: www.pacificfasteners.com
E-mail: pacfast-us@pacificfasteners.com

PACIFIC FASTENERS

3934 East 1st Avenue
Burnaby, British Columbia V5C 5S3
Canada
Phone: 604-294-9411
Fax: 604-294-4730
E-mail: pacfast@pacificfasteners.com

Pacific Fasteners is one of the best sources for any type of high-quality stainless-steel fastener. This company appears to stock everything that is required for an engine or an automobile. You can buy fasteners individually or in bulk quantities; however, there is usually a $5 minimum purchase. Pacific Fasteners will ship via Federal Express or United Parcel Service (UPS) to just about anywhere in the world.

REDI-STRIP METAL CLEANING CANADA
7961 Vantage Way
Delta, British Columbia V4G 1A6
Canada
Phone: 604-946-7761
Fax: 604-946-5936

Redi-Strip Metal Cleaning Canada has been in business for over 20 years and specializes in metal cleaning, from engine blocks to entire automobile body shells. It does excellent work, and its prices are affordable.

RED'S HEADERS
Mr. Red Hamilton
22950 Bednar Lane
Fort Bragg, California 95437
Phone: 707-964-7733
Website: www.reds-headers.com
E-mail: info@reds-headers.com

THE ROD SHOP
Mr. Ken Austin
PO Box 111
2601 Crestview Drive
Newburg, Oregon 97132
Phone: 503-349-1360
Fax: 503-537-2760

ROSS RACING PISTONS
625 South Douglas Street
El Segundo, California 90245
Toll Free: 1-800-392-7677
Tech Line: 310-536-0100
Fax: 310-536-0333
Website: www.rosspistons.com

The only pistons I have bought for my own engines over the past few years are manufactured by Ross Racing Pistons. It produces top-quality forged-aluminum pistons using state-of-the-art CNC machining technology. Ross Racing Pistons can produce pistons in various sizes, from lawnmower to aircraft, at an affordable price.

SANDERSON HEADERS
517 Railroad Avenue
South San Francisco, California 94080
Phone: 650-583-6617
Fax: 650-583-8475
Website: www.sandersonheaders.com
E-mail: sales@sandersonheaders.com

SHOW CARS AUTOMOTIVE (DR. 409)
58375 Country Road 21
New Ulm, Minnesota 56073
Phone: 507-354-1958 or 507-233-1958
Fax: 1-800-647-7329 or 507-354-1959
Website: www.dr409.com
E-mail: showcars@newulmtel.net

STEF'S FABRICATION SPECIALTIES
693 Cross Street
Lakewood, New Jersey 08701
Phone: 732-367-8700
Fax: 732-367-8793
Website: www.stefs.com
E-mail: joestef99@aol.com

SPEEDWAY MOTORS
PO Box 81906
Lincoln, Nebraska 68501
Phone: 402-323-3200
Fax: 402-323-3211
Website: www.speedwaymotors.com

I have been buying Ford flathead V-8 engine and hot rod parts from Speedway Motors since 1983, and it has always been polite and efficient when filling my orders. This is one of the best sources for flathead speed equipment.

SUMMIT RACING EQUIPMENT
PO Box 909
Akron, Ohio 44398
Toll Free: 1-800-230-3030
Fax: 330-630-5333
Website: www.summitracing.com

VINTAGE SPEED
Mr. Charles Price
1916 63rd Court
Vero Beach, Florida 32966
Phone: 772-778-0809
Fax: 772-569-7028
Website: www.vintagespeed.com

WILKINSON'S AUTOMOBILIA
2531 Ontario Street
Vancouver, British Columbia V5T 2X7
Canada
Phone: 604-873-6242
Fax: 604-873-6259
Website: www.eautomobilia.com
E-mail: info@wilkinsonsauto.com

One of the finest sources for vintage and current automotive books, shop manuals, chassis manuals, and hot rod magazines is Wilkinson's Automobilia. Some of its publications in stock date back to the early part of the twentieth century, and it seems to have just about everything. The employees are extremely helpful and very friendly.

APPENDIX C
VINTAGE CAMSHAFT SPECS

In my previous book, *How to Build Ford Flathead V-8 Horsepower*, I listed a number of vintage camshafts for Ford flathead V-8 engines. Over the years, I have also managed to accumulate some information pertaining to vintage camshafts for Ford flathead V8-60-horsepower engines. The camshafts I will list are all solid flat tappet (with the exception of two). They are usually regrinds, and the majority of them are designed for midget track or boat racing. As previously mentioned, the duration at 0.050-inch lift will not be included with any of these camshafts because this standard of measurement was not in use during their period of manufacture. The timing events are listed as the advertised duration, because the amount of lift the timing events were taken at was not provided. Many of the camshafts lacked all the necessary information to produce an accurate picture for comparison purposes. Fortunately, there was enough information to enter into my computer dyno simulation program, which resulted in the following camshaft list.

In order to compare these camshafts, I have given the estimated output of the Ford flathead V8-60-horsepower engine described in Section IV when using each of the camshafts. Many of these camshafts are designed to operate continuously at high rpm. I have designated the camshafts "street" and/or "competition" based on the manufacturer's description and the computer dyno simulation results. Most of these vintage camshafts have a large overlap, which results in higher engine emissions. This could be a problem if the owner happens to reside in a jurisdiction where there is mandatory vehicle emissions testing.

A note of caution: I have done my absolute best to provide accurate information for the camshafts listed. However, this information is over 50 years old and, therefore, it is provided without any guarantee. I have also encountered camshafts in the past from the same manufacturer with the same grind number, yet they had different timing events.

MANUFACTURER: HARMAN & COLLINS, INC.
1. CAMSHAFT NUMBER: 6412; GRIND: FULL RACE
Application: Street and competition
Type: Solid flat tappet
Advertised Duration: 250 degrees intake and exhaust
Lobe Separation Angle: 112 degrees
Net Valve Lift: 0.272 inch intake and exhaust
Valve Lash (hot): 0.010 inch intake and exhaust
Overlap (with advertised duration): 26 degrees
IVO: 14; **IVC:** 56 degrees; **EVO:** 58 degrees; **EVC:** 12 degrees
Estimated Output: 145 horsepower at 5,500 rpm and 152 ft-lbs torque at 4,000 rpm
2. CAMSHAFT NUMBER: N/A; GRIND: MIDGET
Application: Competition
Type: Solid flat tappet
Advertised Duration: 270 degrees intake and exhaust
Lobe Separation Angle: 114 degrees
Net Valve Lift: 0.246 inch intake and 0.244 inch exhaust
Valve Lash (hot): 0.010 inch intake and 0.012 inch exhaust
Overlap (with advertised duration): 42 degrees
IVO: 22 degrees; **IVC:** 68 degrees; **EVO:** 70 degrees; **EVC:** 20 degrees
Estimated Output: 144 horsepower at 6,000 rpm and 139 ft-lbs torque at 4,500 rpm

3. CAMSHAFT NUMBER: N/A; GRIND: SUPER
Application: Street and competition
Type: Solid flat tappet
Advertised Duration: 262 degrees intake and 264 degrees exhaust
Lobe Separation Angle: 111.5 degrees
Net Valve Lift: 0.247 inch intake and 0.246 inch exhaust
Valve Lash (hot): 0.009 inch intake and 0.010 inch exhaust
Overlap (with advertised duration): 40 degrees
IVO: 24 degrees; **IVC:** 58 degrees; **EVO:** 68 degrees; **EVC:** 16 degrees
Estimated Output: 144 horsepower at 5,500 rpm and 147 ft-lbs torque at 4,000 rpm

MANUFACTURER: ISKENDERIAN RACING CAMS
1. CAMSHAFT NUMBER: 606; GRIND: 3/4 RACE
Application: Street and competition
Type: Solid flat tappet
Advertised Duration: 250 degrees intake and exhaust
Lobe Separation Angle: 114 degrees
Net Valve Lift: 0.246 inch intake and exhaust
Valve Lash (hot): 0.014 inch intake and exhaust
Overlap (with advertised duration): 22 degrees
IVO: 12 degrees; **IVC:** 58 degrees; **EVO:** 60 degrees; **EVC:** 10 degrees
Estimated Output: 139 horsepower at 5,500 rpm and 149 ft-lbs torque at 4,000 rpm

2. CAMSHAFT NUMBER: 603; GRIND: TRACK

Application: Street and competition
Type: Solid flat tappet
Advertised Duration: 254 degrees intake and exhaust
Lobe Separation Angle: 114 degrees
Net Valve Lift: 0.256 inch intake and exhaust
Valve Lash (hot): 0.014 inch intake and exhaust
Overlap (with advertised duration): 26 degrees
IVO: 14 degrees; **IVC:** 60 degrees; **EVO:** 62 degrees; **EVC:** 12 degrees
Estimated Output: 142 horsepower at 5,500 rpm and 148 ft-lbs torque at 4,000 rpm

3. CAMSHAFT NUMBER: 604; GRIND: TRACK

Application: Competition
Type: Solid flat tappet
Advertised Duration: 272 degrees intake and exhaust
Lobe Separation Angle: 114 degrees
Net Valve Lift: 0.309 inch intake and 0.307 inch exhaust
Valve Lash (hot): 0.012 inch intake and 0.014 inch exhaust
Overlap (with advertised duration): 44 degrees
IVO: 23 degrees; **IVC:** 69 degrees; **EVO:** 71 degrees; **EVC:** 21 degrees
Estimated Output: 151 horsepower at 6,000 rpm and 141 ft-lbs torque at 5,000 rpm

4. CAMSHAFT NUMBER: 620-03; GRIND: TRACK

Application: Competition
Type: Solid flat-tappet mushroom lifter
Advertised Duration: 255 degrees intake and 254 degrees exhaust
Lobe Separation Angle: 113 degrees
Net Valve Lift: 0.300 inch intake and 0.256 inch exhaust
Valve Lash (hot): 0.012 inch intake and 0.014 inch exhaust
Overlap (with advertised duration): 28 degrees
IVO: 14 degrees; **IVC:** 61 degrees; **EVO:** 60 degrees; **EVC:** 14 degrees
Estimated Output: 148 horsepower at 6,000 rpm and 150 ft-lbs torque at 4,500 rpm

5. CAMSHAFT NUMBER: 404 JR; GRIND: TRACK

Application: Competition
Type: Radius lifter
Advertised Duration: 250 degrees intake and exhaust
Lobe Separation Angle: 114 degrees
Net Valve Lift: 0.331 inch intake and exhaust
Valve Lash (hot): 0.014 inch intake and exhaust
Overlap (with advertised duration): 22 degrees
IVO: 12 degrees; **IVC:** 58 degrees; **EVO:** 60 degrees; **EVC:** 10 degrees
Estimated Output: 155 horsepower at 6,000 rpm and 160 ft-lbs torque at 4,500 rpm

MANUFACTURER: SMITH & JONES

1. CAMSHAFT NUMBER: N/A; GRIND: BOAT

Application: Competition
Type: Solid flat tappet
Advertised Duration: 266 degrees intake and exhaust
Lobe Separation Angle: 110.5 degrees
Net Valve Lift: 0.242 inch intake and 0.241 inch exhaust
Valve Lash (hot): 0.012 inch intake and 0.013 inch exhaust
Overlap (with advertised duration): 45 degrees
IVO: 22.5 degrees; **IVC:** 63.5 degrees; **EVO:** 63.5 degrees; **EVC:** 22.5 degrees
Estimated Output: 102 horsepower at 6,000 rpm and 92 ft-lbs torque at 5,000 rpm

2. CAMSHAFT NUMBER: N/A; TYPE: MIDGET

Application: Competition
Type: Solid flat tappet
Advertised Duration: 254 degrees intake and 252 degrees exhaust
Lobe Separation Angle: 112 degrees
Net Valve Lift: 0.242 inch intake and 0.241 inch exhaust
Valve Lash (hot): 0.012 inch intake and 0.013 inch exhaust
Overlap (with advertised duration): 29 degrees
IVO: 15 degrees; **IVC:** 59 degrees; **VO:** 58 degrees; **EVC:** 14 degrees
Estimated Output: 122 horsepower at 6,000 rpm and 112 ft-lbs torque at 5,000 rpm

MANUFACTURER: CLAY SMITH ENGINEERING

1. CAMSHAFT NUMBER: B-3; GRIND: BOAT

Application: Competition
Type: Solid flat tappet
Advertised Duration: 270 degrees intake and 268 degrees exhaust
Lobe Separation Angle: 112.5 degrees
Net Valve Lift: 0.248 inch intake and 0.247 inch exhaust
Valve Lash (hot): 0.012 inch intake and 0.013 inch exhaust
Overlap (with advertised duration): 44 degrees
IVO: 22 degrees; **IVC:** 68 degrees; **EVO:** 66 degrees; **EVC:** 22 degrees
Estimated Output: 98 horsepower at 6,000 rpm and 89 ft-lbs torque at 5,500 rpm

2. CAMSHAFT NUMBER: M-3. GRIND: MIDGET

Application: Competition
Type: Solid flat tappet
Advertised Duration: 254 degrees intake and 253 degrees exhaust
Lobe Separation Angle: 113 degrees
Net Valve Lift: 0.248 inch intake and 0.247 inch exhaust
Valve Lash (hot): 0.012 inch intake and 0.013 inch exhaust
Overlap (with advertised duration): 27 degrees
IVO: 14 degrees; **IVC:** 60 degrees; **EVO:** 59 degrees; **EVC:** 13 degrees
Estimated Output: 123 horsepower at 6,000 rpm and 113 ft-lbs torque at 5,000 rpm

MANUFACTURER: WEBER CAM GRINDING COMPANY

1. CAMSHAFT NUMBER: S-2; GRIND: BOAT

Application: Competition
Type: Solid flat tappet
Advertised Duration: 281 degrees intake and 282 degrees exhaust
Lobe Separation Angle: 114 degrees
Net Valve Lift: 0.255 inch intake and exhaust
Valve Lash (hot): 0.010 inch intake and exhaust
Overlap (with advertised duration): 53 degrees
IVO: 23 degrees; **IVC:** 78 degrees; **EVO:** 72 degrees; **EVC:** 30 degrees
Estimated Output: 85 horsepower at 6,000 rpm and 77 ft-lbs torque at 5,500 rpm

2. CAMSHAFT NUMBER: S-1; GRIND: MIDGET

Application: Competition
Type: Solid flat tappet
Advertised Duration: 272 degrees intake and exhaust
Lobe Separation Angle: 115 degrees
Net Valve Lift: 0.255 inch intake and exhaust
Valve Lash (hot): 0.010 inch intake and exhaust
Overlap (with advertised duration): 42 degrees
IVO: 22 degrees; **IVC:** 70 degrees; **EVO:** 72 degrees; **EVC:** 20 degrees
Estimated Output: 98 horsepower at 6,000 rpm and 88 ft-lbs torque at 5,500 rpm

MANUFACTURER: EDWARD A. "BIG ED" WINFIELD

1. CAMSHAFT NUMBER: SUPER. GRIND: TRACK

Application: Competition
Type: Solid flat tappet
Advertised Duration: 272 degrees intake and exhaust
Lobe Separation Angle: 112 degrees
Net Valve Lift: 0.238 inch intake and 0.236 inch exhaust
Valve Lash (hot): 0.012 inch intake and 0.014 inch exhaust
Overlap (with advertised duration): 48 degrees
IVO: 24 degrees; **IVC:** 68 degrees; **EVO:** 68 degrees; **EVC:** 24 degrees
Estimated Output: 93 horsepower at 6,000 rpm and 85 ft-lbs torque at 5,500 rpm

2. CAMSHAFT NUMBER: R-11-S; GRIND: TRACK

Application: Competition
Type: Solid flat tappet
Advertised Duration: 256 degrees intake and 252 degrees exhaust
Lobe Separation Angle: 111 degrees
Net Valve Lift: 0.253 inch intake and 0.251 inch exhaust
Valve Lash (hot): 0.012 inch intake and 0.014 inch exhaust
Overlap (with advertised duration): 32 degrees
IVO: 16 degrees; **IVC:** 60 degrees; **EVO:** 56 degrees; **EVC:** 16 degrees
Estimated Output: 120 horsepower at 6,000 rpm and 109 ft-lbs torque at 5,000 rpm

INDEX

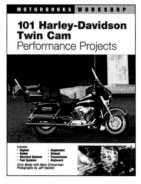